T0306531

Traditionalism

Traditionalism
The Radical Project for Restoring Sacred Order

MARK SEDGWICK

OXFORD
UNIVERSITY PRESS

OXFORD
UNIVERSITY PRESS

Oxford University Press is a department of the University of Oxford. It furthers the University's objective of excellence in research, scholarship, and education by publishing worldwide. Oxford is a registered trade mark of Oxford University Press in the UK and certain other countries.

Published in the United States of America by Oxford University Press
198 Madison Avenue, New York, NY 10016, United States of America.

Library of Congress Cataloging-in-Publication Data

Names: Sedgwick, Mark J., author.
Title: Traditionalism : the radical project for restoring sacred order / Mark Sedgwick.
Description: New York, NY, United States of America : Oxford University Press, [2023] |
Includes bibliographical references and index.
Identifiers: LCCN 2023008585 (print) | LCCN 2023008586 (ebook) |
ISBN 9780197683767 | ISBN 9780197683781 (pdf) | ISBN 9780197683774 (epub)
Subjects: LCSH: Guénon, René. | Tradition (Philosophy) Classification: LCC B2430.
G84 S395 2023 (print) | LCC B2430.G84 (ebook) | DDC 148—dc23/eng/20230320
LC record available at https://lccn.loc.gov/2023008585
LC ebook record available at https://lccn.loc.gov/2023008586

Printed by Sheridan Books, Inc., United States of America

Contents

ACKNOWLEDGEMENTS   ix

INTRODUCTORY

CHAPTER 1
Traditionalism and the Traditionalists   3

CHAPTER 2
Historical perennialism   21

PART I: FOUNDATIONS

CHAPTER 3
Traditionalist perennialism   43

CHAPTER 4
Traditionalist history   67

CHAPTER 5
The Traditionalist critique of modernity   93

CHAPTER 6
Traditionalism, thought, and society   119

PART II: CORE PROJECTS

CHAPTER 7
Self-realization   139

CHAPTER 8
Religion   179

CHAPTER 9
Politics   199

PART III: FURTHER PROJECTS

CHAPTER 10
Art   229

CHAPTER 11
Gender   259

CHAPTER 12
Nature   289

CHAPTER 13
Dialogue   309

PART IV: POST-TRADITIONALISM

CHAPTER 14
The radical right   331

PART V: CONCLUDING

CHAPTER 15
Conclusion   359

SELECT BIBLIOGRAPHY OF TRADITIONALIST WORKS   371

NOTES   377

INDEX   399

Acknowledgements

I would like to thank my editor at Pelican, Maria Bedford, for her careful and constructive reading of the draft of this book. I would also like to thank Boaz Huss for his help with Kabbalah, David R. M. Irving for his help with music, Dorthe Jørgensen for her help with philosophy, Jafe Arnold for his help with Aleksander Dugin, Joscelyn Godwin for his help with Julius Evola, Manni Crone for general comments, Marianne Qvortrup Fibiger for her help with Hinduism, Patrick Laude for his comments on Frithjof Schuon, Patrick Ringgenberg and Ricarda Stegmann for general comments, and Shankar Nair for help with connections between Greece and India. I have not always followed their advice, however, and the book is my responsibility, not theirs.

Introductory

Traditionalism and the Traditionalists

Traditionalism is today's least-known major philosophy, and my aim in this book is to make it and its radical project for restoring sacred order more widely known and better understood. It is not my aim to convert people to Traditionalism. This is partly because I am by training and trade a historian of ideas, and thus professionally neutral. It is also because the outcomes of the Traditionalist project are, as we will see in later chapters, mixed.

Traditionalism has been used to encourage respect for the environment, compose great music, and reduce hostility between followers of different religions. It has also been used to support very different causes, from the election of Donald Trump as president of the United States of America to what many would call fascism and racism, not to mention terrorism. Some have blamed a Russian Traditionalist, Aleksandr Dugin, for Vladimir Putin's invasion of Ukraine. The Traditionalist philosophy, then, needs to be handled with care. It is not always a good thing for someone to become a Traditionalist. It would be good, however, if those who oppose fascism, racism, and terrorism could more easily recognize Traditionalism when they see it.

To be able to recognize Traditionalism and make sense

of its project, we need to understand the ideas on which it is built, and its somewhat specialized terminology. The 'tradition' in 'Traditionalism', for example, is not what is generally meant by the word, but rather a group of sacred teachings that are understood to have been handed down since time immemorial and are the basis for the proper order of things, a sacred order. These traditional teachings have something of the philosophical and something of the religious about them, so Traditionalism is both philosophical and religious, although some Traditionalists prefer the term 'metaphysical', which combines those two aspects.

The sacred order that once derived from tradition is often contrasted with modern disorder, and Traditionalism is anti-modern as well as metaphysical. This anti-modernism has important political implications, as liberalism and democracy are both modern, and anti-modernism is thus hardly compatible with liberal democracy, and may imply its rejection. Traditionalism is thus political as well as metaphysical. It is a radical political ideology as well as a religious philosophy. But if a single term is needed, 'philosophy' usually works best, with that word used in its oldest and widest sense, denoting not the contents of contemporary university courses but rather a coherent body of theory concerning fundamental questions of existence. The Traditionalist project is a philosophical or intellectual project, not an organized or institutional undertaking.

Traditionalists understand the traditional teachings that their philosophy is based on as ancient and timeless – and some of them really are very ancient. The way that they are understood and interpreted by Traditionalists, however, is much more recent. The Traditionalist philosophy that this book examines originated in the 1920s and 1930s, and has since then been developed in various directions. Many philosophies that were important in the 1920s and 1930s have now vanished, but Traditionalism has not. It remains little known partly because it has never sought a mass audience, and partly because it can be difficult to follow. This book aims to make it (relatively) easy to understand.

Traditionalism

I myself first encountered Traditionalism during the 1990s, when I was living in Cairo and studying the history of Sufism. Sufism is a sort of lay monasticism within Islam. Just as Catholic and Orthodox Christians who are drawn to the spiritual life can join monastic orders, Sunni and Shia Muslims who are drawn to the spiritual life can join Sufi orders. One major difference is that Christian monasticism is a full-time, lifelong commitment, while Sufism is part-time, and need not be lifelong. Another difference is that some Sufi theology is further from mainstream Islam than most monastic theology is from mainstream Christianity. Mainstream Islamic theology is generally fairly down-to-earth, while Sufi theology stretches into realms of imagination beyond time and space.

In the 1990s, I was especially interested in understanding how Sufi orders change over time, and how they adapt as they spread from one part of the world to another. I collected oral histories and documents from the descendants of great Sufi shaykhs, as Sufi masters are called, in isolated villages in Sudan, travelling across the empty desert in the trucks that are the main form of transport in rural areas. I attended Sufi festivals in villages in Upper Egypt, and visited Sufis in towns and villages across Malaysia, parts of Thailand, and Singapore. Finally, I ended up in Italy, where a charismatic gentleman called Abd al-Wahid Pallavicini, who had once worked in Singapore, now lived in a large house in Milan where his Sufi followers met. They were all well-educated young people who, like their shaykh, had Muslim first names and Italian surnames. During their meetings they often discussed questions that seemed to me to have more to do with Western philosophy than with the Sufism I had found in Sudan, Egypt, and Southeast Asia. They were, in fact, Traditionalists as well as Sufis.

It was Shaykh Pallavicini who first told me about Traditionalism and gave me a copy of a biography of Traditionalism's founder, René Guénon.[1] I read the biography, and realized that Shaykh Pallavicini was not the first Traditionalist I had met. Some American and European converts to Islam I knew in Cairo, it became clear, were also Traditionalists. After I got home from Milan, the more I looked, the more I found. I even found Traditionalists in Moscow, newly open to Western scholars after the collapse of the Soviet Union. When I first met Dugin, then still relatively unknown, he told me that he thought that Guénon was the undiscovered Marx.

After writing up my research on Sufism between Sudan and Malaysia, I started to work on Traditionalism. I published a book on the history of Traditionalism, *Against the Modern World*, in 2003.[2] In that book I traced the origins, development, and spread of the movement that Guénon had started, which turned out to be a far larger phenomenon than I or anyone else had suspected. One reason that nobody had heard of Traditionalism, I discovered, was that Traditionalist writers almost never identified themselves as such. Unlike

Marxists, they never tried to reach the masses, whom they considered no longer capable of understanding traditional teachings. Traditionalists sought to change the world and restore sacred order more quietly, in other ways.

In the conclusion to *Against the Modern World*, written in 2002, I suggested that the Traditionalist project had run its course, and was even in decline. That turned out to be quite wrong. In 2002, there were indeed fewer Traditionalists writing about Sufism, Islam, and art than there had been twenty or thirty years before, but there were already more politically active Traditionalists. I did not see this at the time, but the key reference was fast becoming not Guénon but Julius Evola, an Italian Traditionalist writer who had died in 1974 and had once advised Mussolini on race before moving to Germany as a guest of the Nazis.

Politically active Traditionalists who referred more to Evola than to Guénon were becoming more and more visible. In Russia, Dugin's 1997 book *The Foundations of Geopolitics: The Geopolitical Future of Russia*, discussed in a later chapter, became a bestseller.[3] When Russia invaded Ukraine in February 2022, some turned to Dugin's views on geopolitics for an explanation, and, in August 2022, a car bomb probably aimed at Dugin instead killed his 29-year-old daughter, Darya, who was driving home from a literary festival entitled 'Tradition', where her father had spoken on 'Tradition and History'. It seems likely that the bomb was planted by Ukrainians.

After 1997, Dugin became the best-known politically active Traditionalist, but there were others. A Hungarian Traditionalist, Gábor Vona, founded a right-wing political party called Jobbik that did surprisingly well in the 2010

Hungarian elections, winning 47 seats in parliament and coming third overall. Something similar happened in Greece. And then, in early 2017, as the world was trying to come to terms with the unexpected election of Donald Trump, the *New York Times* reported that Trump's campaign manager and counsellor, Steve Bannon, had been citing Evola. As the *New York Times* contacted me to try to find out who on earth Evola was, I began to wonder whether Dugin had been right, and whether Guénon really was the new Marx. Traditionalism certainly seemed to be thriving as a political ideology.

The popularity of ideologies and philosophies always has a lot to do with circumstances. Traditionalism has been doing well in the new world created by the slow collapse of the centre-left and centre-right political parties that dominated Western politics after the end of the Second World War. The centre-left historically depended on the votes of industrial workers and the support of the union movement, and inevitably suffered from the shift in Western economies from industry to services. As industrial workers became fewer and fewer, and union membership declined, the centre-left was bound to be in trouble. The centre-right suffered from the decline of the centre-left, against which it had always defined itself, and from the rise of new issues that it had never really thought through, notably immigration, which worried more and more Western voters. The collapse of centre-left and centre-right parties made room for new parties like the Greens and, especially, for nationalist parties that would once have been beyond the pale, like Vona's Jobbik in Hungary and Trump's version of Republicanism in America. Even when they do not win power, such parties pull the larger parties towards those of their policies that voters seem to like. The collapse of centre-left and centre-right parties made room for new ideologies as well as new parties. Traditionalism is one of these new, or newly important, ideologies.

Even if Guénon is the new Marx, Traditionalism will never be the new Marxism. It is not suitable as the basis for a mass ideology like communism, and the days of mass ideologies have passed, anyhow. Marxism, like Nazism, needed industrial workers, and industrial workers are now in short supply in advanced economies. Nor are politicians like Trump ever going to read Guénon's or Evola's books; they are far too difficult, and politicians need to be flexible and pragmatic. Politicians are well advised not to get too ideological, or even too consistent. But politicians need advisers and activists, who may be both ideological and consistent, and Bannon is not the only activist adviser to be inspired and motivated by Traditionalism. Shortly after Bannon's appreciation of Evola was revealed in the *New York Times*, for example, a parliamentary aide from the AfD, the German nationalist party that had come third in the federal German elections in 2017 (but fifth in 2021), approached me at a conference and said that he had read the German translation of my *Against the Modern World*. He lamented that most AfD activists knew nothing of Traditionalism. But even if most AfD activists know nothing of Traditionalism, some do, as my conversation with the aide made clear. So do activists in less famous parties and in groups that have never won any parliamentary seats at all, but still matter in other ways. This is why those who support liberalism and oppose nationalism need to be able to recognize Traditionalism and its project when they see it.

This book

Many introductions to Traditionalism have been published over the years, but all of them have been written by Traditionalists aiming to recruit people to their cause. Some readers of these books have become Sufis, and some have joined the far right, but most stopped reading after a few pages, bemused by how bizarre some Traditionalist ideas can seem. This book is different from those other introductions in two ways. Firstly, as I have already said, it does not seek to recruit new Traditionalists, but rather to explain Traditionalism and its project as neutrally and as comprehensibly as possible. Secondly, it introduces Traditionalist ideas not as timeless wisdom, which is how Traditionalists tend to see and present them, but as contributions to ongoing intellectual debates. Almost nothing about Traditionalism is entirely new. Most elements of the Traditionalist philosophy connect to discussions with which readers will already be familiar. What is new and powerful about Traditionalism is what these different ideas and elements all add up to.

This book will examine Traditionalism in four parts. First come its foundations, the ideas and perspectives that are fundamental for all varieties of Traditionalism, for Sufis and presidential campaign managers alike. Most fundamental of these is perennialism, the idea that beneath all the different forms of tradition, from Catholicism to Buddhism, there lies one single, timeless and esoteric sacred tradition – 'the' tradition. This is the basis of sacred order. The second fundamental idea is a view of history that replaces the general assumption that things get better over time with the conviction that things are actually getting worse, giving rise to the Traditionalist critique of modernity, seen as the opposite of sacred order. The final foundation of Traditionalism is its perspective on how and when thought can change society.

We then look at the core projects of Traditionalism in three central areas of human life: self-realization, religion, and politics. These projects have interested all Traditionalists, and the applications of Traditionalism to them are at the core of Traditionalism's significance today. Different Traditionalists have understood self-realization in different ways, but all have seen it as the fulfilment of one's true nature through some form of consciousness of the transcendent. Non-Traditionalist understandings of self-realization, in contrast, often omit the sacred. Traditionalist understandings of self-realization and of religion give us the Traditionalist Sufi project, and Traditionalist understandings of self-realization and of politics give us the Traditionalist political project. There could also have been a chapter on symbolism, as nearly all Traditionalists have also been interested in the interpretation and use of non-verbal, usually visual, expressions of traditional teachings. Traditionalist understandings of symbolism, however, have not had any major impact, and so are of limited interest to non-Traditionalists.

Traditionalism has also been applied beyond these central areas. Traditionalist thought has been applied fruitfully to four further areas: art, gender, nature, and interfaith dialogue. These further projects are discussed in the book's third part, taken in chronological order. There are Traditionalist understandings of what art is and should be, and also Traditionalist artists. Similarly, there are Traditionalist understandings of gender, though these have never really been put into practice. Traditionalist understandings of nature as sacred and in need of protection have contributed to today's environmental movement. Finally, Traditionalist understandings of religion have been used as a basis for interfaith dialogue.

The book's final part contains only one chapter, and looks at today's radical right, and at what some call 'post-Traditionalism'.

First of all, however, this chapter will introduce the major thinkers who developed the foundations of the Traditionalist philosophy. Their names will come up time and time again in later chapters, so it is good to know who they were.

The Traditionalists

The first of the three major thinkers who developed the foundations of the Traditionalist philosophy was René Guénon, a French Orientalist and philosopher. Traditionalism might, in fact, almost be called 'Guénonism', rather as communism is often called 'Marxism'. It was Guénon whose works began the development of Traditionalist thought during the 1910s and 1920s and continued that development until his death in 1951, and it was he who established Traditionalism's most important foundations and who was responsible for Traditionalist philosophy's early application. The application of Traditionalism to self-realization is primarily his work. Then comes Julius Evola, an Italian painter and journalist who developed the political project of Traditionalism on bases laid by Guénon, first under Fascism and then during the immediate post-war period. The third name that will be encountered very often is that of Frithjof Schuon, a Swiss Sufi who was younger than

Guénon and Evola, and who was responsible for Traditionalism's most important religious applications.

Today, some Traditionalists read both Evola and Guénon and focus on politics, while some read both Schuon and Guénon, or just Guénon, and focus on religion and self-realization. Those who do not read Evola commonly regard him with the horror with which fascists are generally regarded in the post-war world. 'Schuon and Guénon' or 'Guénon only' versus 'Evola and Guénon' is the most important division in the contemporary Traditionalist movement.

RENÉ GUÉNON

All three of these foundational Traditionalist thinkers led interesting lives. Guénon's was the quietest. He was born in 1886 to a respectable middle-class family in provincial France and moved to Paris as a student. He became involved in the occultist circles that flourished there during the Belle Époque, and in 1909, at the age of 23, founded a small and short-lived journal, *La Gnose* (Gnosis), subtitled 'A Monthly Review Dedicated to the Study of the Esoteric Sciences'. It ceased publication in 1911, but not before it had published the articles from which the Traditionalist philosophy would later develop. Some were written by Guénon, and some were written by Abdul-Hadi, a Sufi who had made a deep study of the philosophical and theological works of the leading mystical theorist of Islam, Muhyi al-Din Ibn Arabi, while living in Cairo. Abdul-Hadi was not an Egyptian, but a Parisian painter and art critic of Swedish origin, also known as Ivan Aguéli. He died in 1917, before the foundations of Traditionalism were fully developed. He was more a precursor of Traditionalism than an actual Traditionalist.

After the First World War, Guénon moved on from those occultist circles to Catholic ones. He studied philosophy and Hinduism at the University of the Sorbonne and then independently. His perspectives were incompatible with those of the Orientalist scholars of his day, as he was more interested in recovering and restoring sacred order than in philological analysis or intellectual history. His early attempts at an academic career thus failed. He supported himself with a variety of teaching jobs while writing the books that later became the main Traditionalist canon, and also writing articles for a longer-lasting journal, *Études traditionnelles* (Traditional Studies), that a collaborator of his edited. Twelve books were published in French during the 1920s and early 1930s. Some were translated into English and other languages, mostly in the 1940s and 1950s. Since 2000, all have been translated.

In 1930, Guénon moved to Cairo, where he lived the rest of his life, supported by gifts from admirers. This move was the most dramatic event in what was otherwise a quiet life. It involved a change not just of residence, but also of religion – Guénon in Cairo was a Muslim and a Sufi – and of nationality. When it became clear that he was never going to return to France, Guénon, who had married an Egyptian woman with whom he had had several children, took Egyptian nationality so that his children could be citizens of the country in which they had been born. (Egyptian nationality then passed solely through the father, not the mother.)

Guénon's Cairo period was not an important one for his writing, with only one major new book being published, in 1945. Instead, he focused on *Études traditionnelles*, on compiling and editing collections of his earlier articles, and on conducting an extensive correspondence with readers around the world. His following was a loose network rather than a formal group, but Guénon himself thought it was an important project and that it might lead to intellectual, social, and political changes that would strengthen tradition against anti-traditional modernity.

Guénon died in Cairo in 1951. His importance lies, above all, in his writings, which are discussed in the remainder of this book, as are their applications and implications. The network that he had established did not survive his death.

JULIUS EVOLA

Julius Evola's life was more dramatic than Guénon's. He was born in Rome in 1898 and christened Giulio. He served in the Italian army during the First World War. He then became an avant-garde painter, and the somewhat prosaic name Giulio was replaced by its more classical version, Julius. It was around this period that the title of 'Baron' somehow became attached to his name. Evola's Dadaist paintings are good, if not first rate. His first two books, published in the 1920s, were on art. He was also interested in philosophy, which he studied privately, and he published four books in the late 1920s that dealt with philosophical topics. Like many other painters of the time, he was involved in the occultist milieu, and it was in this milieu that he encountered the work of Guénon.

Evola was an early supporter of the Fascist leader Benito Mussolini, as were some others in Italian artistic and occultist milieus, and after Mussolini came to power he worked as a journalist on a Fascist newspaper, while writing eleven Traditionalist books, mostly on political topics; these later became a canon in their own right. The first, *Pagan Imperialism*, was published in 1928.[4] In 1936, Evola started writing on race, and these writings attracted Mussolini's attention. They also interested some Nazis, and German translations of Evola's major works were published in the 1930s and 1940s. Evola was never a major figure in the Fascist regime, however, and was at first kept at arm's length by the Nazis. His views were too unusual and too controversial.

After the fall of Mussolini, Evola took refuge in the German Reich, where he was briefly involved in high politics and attempts to restore Fascism in Italy, once even visiting the Wolf's Lair, Hitler's headquarters in Rastenburg, East Prussia (now Kętrzyn, Poland). He spent the last period of the war studying and writing in Vienna, where he was badly injured in an air raid in 1945. After the defeat of Germany, confined to a wheelchair by his injuries, he returned to Italy, and lived the rest of his life in a small flat in Rome, writing books and articles that, together with some translations and occasional donations, allowed him to live simply but comfortably. Seven books published between 1949 and 1963 form a second Evolian canon. During this period, Evola was arrested and tried for attempting to re-establish Fascism, but was acquitted. This was probably the right verdict, as by then what Evola wanted to establish was very different from Mussolini's Fascism. He was turning instead to heroic political action as a means to self-realization. After publishing five books of lesser importance in the later 1960s and early 1970s, he died in 1974.

Evola never led any group (at least after his early occultist days), and none of his multiple political initiatives ever succeeded, so his significance today derives purely from his writings. These writings were important in three very different periods. First, they played a very minor part in the development of Italian Fascist race laws and acquired a small readership in Nazi Germany. Second, rather different writings inspired post-war Italian neofascism, which was an important political force in the 1970s, involved in both parliamentary and extra-parliamentary politics, including terrorism. There was some interest in Evola outside Italy in this period, but not much. Third, starting in the 1990s, Evola's books began to be translated into more and more languages, and his readership grew and grew, until he became one of the key intellectual references of the radical right, the position he occupies today.

FRITHJOF SCHUON

Frithjof Schuon was born in Switzerland in 1907 to a German musician father and a French mother. He grew up in Switzerland and then, after the death of his father when he was thirteen, in France. He worked in France as a textile designer, reading Guénon, whose works inspired him to convert to Islam and visit Algeria in search of a Sufi shaykh. He joined the Alawiyya, a major Algerian Sufi order, in 1932, and then established a branch of the Alawiyya in Switzerland, together with some Swiss friends who were also readers of Guénon.

During the Second World War, Schuon moved from occupied France back to neutral Switzerland and devoted himself to leading his Sufi order and to writing, supported financially by his followers. His first full-length book, *The Transcendent Unity of Religions*, was his major work, published in French in 1948.[5] Five more books, all in French, followed during the

1950s, and a further six during the 1960s and 1970s. These were generally translated into English fairly soon after their publication, and in some cases into other languages. During these years, membership of his Sufi order, which became independent of the Algerian Alawiyya, grew, mostly among intellectuals and academics in Europe, the Americas, and elsewhere. The order was renamed the Maryamiyya in honour of the Virgin Mary, known as Maryam in Arabic, following a series of visions in which Schuon saw the Virgin.

In 1980, at the age of 73, Schuon moved from Switzerland to America, where he had many followers, and where he had been spending time since becoming interested in Native American religion during the 1950s. Schuon and some of his followers began attending Native American rites as sympathetic observers, as well as practising Sufi and Islamic rituals. Several more books were published with the help of his followers during the 1980s and 1990s. He died in Indiana in 1998.

Schuon's importance lies not only in his own writings but also in his Sufi order and in the writings of other members of that order. His own books were never bestsellers, but the total sales of all the books written by all the members of his order were significant. These books exercised only a limited influence on the general public but had a real impact on scholars and intellectuals studying Islam, religious studies, art, and some other subjects. The peak of their influence was between the 1970s and the 1990s.

These, then, are the major thinkers who developed the foundations of the Traditionalist philosophy: a French scholar who led a retired life in Paris and then Cairo, an Italian activist who played a small part on the margins of great and terrible events, and a Swiss religious leader who saw the Virgin Mary in visions. There are others, who further developed and applied Traditionalism, like, for example, Dugin. They will be introduced in later chapters.

Conclusion

Traditionalism is a radical project for restoring sacred order. It finds that order in metaphysical tradition, and sees modernity as its opposite. It is a metaphysical religious philosophy that has inspired Sufis, and a radical political ideology that has expanded into the gap created by the decline of the centre-left and the centre-right. It is ultimately based on the foundations laid between the 1910s and 1950s by Guénon, Evola, and Schuon: perennialism; a view of history in which things are seen to be getting worse not better; a critique of modernity; and certain perspectives on how thought can change society. After surveying historical perennialism, we will proceed to look at these foundations, and then at their application to Traditionalism's various projects.

CHAPTER 2

Historical Perennialism

Traditionalists see tradition and myth as a body of understandings, handed down through the ages, that is the key to making sense of the sacred order, and of the modern disorder that has replaced it. It is also fundamental that one single, timeless tradition is understood to underlie all the different forms of tradition, myth, and religion that exist and have existed. Belief in such a single, timeless tradition is known as 'perennialism', from the adjective 'perennial', meaning everlasting or timeless. Perennialism is so central to Traditionalism that some Traditionalists refer to themselves as 'perennialists'. But, while all Traditionalists are perennialists, not all perennialists are Traditionalists. There are also non-Traditionalist perennialists who do not share Traditionalism's other fundamental ideas, and perennialism has a long history in Western thought.

Traditionalist perennialism builds on a discussion that goes back to the Renaissance. That discussion is now mostly forgotten, but it was once important, and survives in certain contemporary academic debates. This chapter therefore looks at the history of perennialism and of two related concepts, tradition and myth. In line with my approach elsewhere in the book, it seeks to introduce ongoing intellectual debates rather than to provide a comprehensive account of them. Certain non-Traditionalist philosophers and thinkers will be referred to from time to time, but not all non-Traditionalists who contributed to every debate will be mentioned. The following chapter will then move on to the Traditionalist understanding of perennialism.

Tradition

Tradition is an important part of human culture. For progressives, certain traditions may be an obstacle to reform, but even progressives usually follow family traditions when it comes to birthdays and holidays. Festivals like Christmas and Thanksgiving are built out of tradition quite as much as they are built out of community. For conservatives, it is important to maintain traditions, which may offer protection against hasty or unwise reform. Conservatives who have lost a fight against reform may still attempt to recover particular traditions, and the label 'traditionalist' is thus often applied to those who are attempting to defend what are, actually, already lost causes. Traditionalist Catholics, for example, reject the liberalizing reforms introduced into doctrine and liturgy by the Second Vatican Council of 1962–5. They have become more and more marginal over the decades. This more general sense of the word 'tradition' is quite distinct from the Traditionalism that this book is discussing.

A tradition is, literally, something which is handed down. The English word is a form of the Latin *traditio*, which is derived from the verb *tradere*, which means to hand over or hand down. One of the traditions which may be handed down is a way of doing things, from conducting elections to celebrating Christmas or Thanksgiving. Another thing that may be handed down is a teaching, and this is the primary meaning of 'tradition' for the Traditionalist philosophy: a teaching that has been handed down since time immemorial.

A historian might distinguish three overlapping categories of this sort of teaching. The oldest teachings that are handed down take the form of myth, the stories which the earliest human cultures developed that explain creation and account for the invisible forces thought to be behind events, often identified as spirits or gods. Then there is philosophy, initially developed when some thinkers in Ancient Greece moved beyond myth and sought to understand the structures of creation and human consciousness. Finally, there is religion. For those living at the western end of the Eurasian landmass and in the Americas, the most historically important religion is Judaism, which established the monotheistic model that is sometimes called 'Abrahamic' and that, in its Christian and then its Islamic versions, became dominant first around the Mediterranean, then across northern Eurasia, and finally also in Africa and the Americas.

Myth, philosophy, and religion are all in some sense tradition, as they are all handed down, though philosophy also develops over time in a way that religion and myth do not. All three also overlap, as religion contains myth, and theology contains philosophy. All three forms of tradition have lost much of their authority in the West since the Enlightenment, which stressed reason against myth and religion, drew philosophy away from religion, and led ultimately to the triumph of the scientific method. With the Enlightenment, reason and science replaced myth and religion as the standard bases of a reliable explanation of reality, making space for non-sacred conceptions of 'natural' order, and secularized philosophy receded from the centre of the public sphere. Neither myth nor religion vanished, however, and we will now see what happened to them.

Myth

The triumph of Enlightenment rationalism was never complete. The poets of the Romantic movement were quick to challenge a purely material understanding of existence, as the great British philosopher Isaiah Berlin showed in 1979 in a famous essay, 'The Counter-Enlightenment'.[1] Philosophers and artists like William Blake, Johann Gottfried Herder, and Friedrich Schiller objected, Berlin thought, to 'cold political dehumanization, to the straitjacket of lifeless . . . rules in which the living body of [the] passionate and poetical . . . is to be held fast'.[2] For these early agents of the Counter-Enlightenment, the great Enlightenment thinkers 'tell us that men seek only to obtain pleasure and avoid pain, but this is absurd. Men seek to live, create, love, hate, eat, drink, worship, sacrifice, understand, and they seek this because they cannot help it. Life is action.'[3] Berlin never looked at Traditionalism, but if he had, he would certainly have placed it in the Counter-Enlightenment.

During the nineteenth century, myth took on new significance for those who were interested in the passionate and poetical, in life as action. Jacob and Wilhelm Grimm collected and published Germanic legends and tales to general acclaim,[4] John Keats and Percy Bysshe Shelley drew on Greek myth for the 'Ode on a Grecian Urn' and *Prometheus*

Unbound, respectively, and Richard Wagner drew on Norse myth for his *Ring* cycle. Myth was of great importance for the nineteenth-century Romantic imagination.

Myth was also studied in the universities, notably at Cambridge University by James Frazer, whose study of 'primitive superstition', first published in 1890 as *The Golden Bough*, had grown to twelve volumes by 1915. Frazer traced similarities between different myths from different civilizations, finding a universal common ground in which the most prominent features were magic, the sacrifice of a divine king, and the mirroring of the rhythms of the agricultural year – the death and resurrection of vegetation. He saw his work as a contribution to intellectual and institutional history, and also as something that would help 'to follow the long march, the slow and toilsome ascent, of humanity from savagery to civilisation'. The study of myth had practical value for Frazer, as it might 'expedite progress if it lays bare certain weak spots in the foundations on which modern society is built – if it shews that much which we are wont to regard as solid rests on the sands of superstition rather than on the rock of nature'.[5] In understanding progress in terms of the triumph of 'the rock of nature' over 'the sands of superstition', and in taking positions that were generally hostile to religion, which he saw as a development of magic, Frazer was placing himself squarely within the Enlightenment project. His emphasis on the sacrifice of the divine king as a central feature of universal myth in fact stood on shaky foundations and was soon forgotten, but the idea of myth as a treasury of meaning persisted.

Myth was also used by Sigmund Freud, in whose hands it formed part of an argument against the exclusive dominance of reason in human affairs, if not an attack on the Enlightenment as such. Freud's reading of the myth of Oedipus was central to his psychoanalytical theory. Myth was understood slightly differently by Freud's one-time Swiss pupil Carl Gustav Jung, who proposed that just as instincts intervened in human consciousness, so did the 'primordial images' that he called 'archetypes'. These inhabited the collective unconscious. He thought that these images could be found most easily in the myths of 'primitive peoples', where he found ideas 'of magic power or magic substance, of spirits and their behaviour, of demons and gods and their legends'[6] that were very similar across cultures. Jung agreed with Frazer that a universal common ground could be found in primordial myths, and that these provided a key to understanding modern society: 'We see the perfection of those images, and at the same time their envelopment by rational forms, in the great religions of the world,' Jung concluded.[7]

The idea of myth as a source of truth, then, survived the Enlightenment rather better than one might have thought. There was disagreement about quite what sort of truth myth contained – the living body of the passionate and poetical for the Romantics, the shaky foundations of modern society for Frazer, the functioning of the unconscious for Freud, or archetypical ideas and images for Jung. But all agreed that myth mattered. The Traditionalists, as we will see, thought the same.

Religion

Religion, or at least the Christian Churches, attempted to fight back against Enlightenment rationalism. Even so, rationalism and the discoveries of natural science helped push the

Churches in Europe and much of America down a long road from dominance to marginality. It was not just rationalism and natural science that pushed Christianity down this road, however. Another issue was the problem of religious variety. This issue is especially important for Traditionalism.

One classic understanding of the problem of religious variety was advanced in 1979 by the American sociologist Peter Berger. When all that anyone knew was Christian doctrine, thought Berger, that doctrine was automatically believable. Nothing else was plausible. Once other, contradictory doctrines became known, however, as they did in Europe from the seventeenth century onwards, Christianity lost its apparent monopoly of truth, and its plausibility suffered. This resulted in what Berger called the 'heretical imperative', a play on words, as 'heretical' is derived from the Greek *hairesis*, a choice. Faced with religious variety, people had to choose, and what they chose, implied Berger, was something other than the old orthodoxy: a sort of heresy. He modified these views later, but his 1979 understanding remains classic.

Perennialism

In fact, the pre-modern human religious landscape was never quite as flat as Berger thought in 1979. One of the first Europeans to confront the problem of religious variety was a Catholic priest in fifteenth-century Florence, Marsilio Ficino. The development of perennialism starts with Ficino and ends with Aldous Huxley, the English novelist best known for his dystopian *Brave New World*, who published *The Perennial Philosophy* in 1945 – and, of course, with the Traditionalists.

RENAISSANCE PERENNIALISTS

Unusually for his time, Ficino learned Ancient Greek, and read and translated rare pre-Christian manuscripts, notably Greek texts by Plato, the late-antique philosopher Plotinus, and Hermes Trismegistus, then also considered a great philosopher, and now known to have been a mythical figure to whom the authorship of a variety of texts was assigned. Ficino's problem was that, as a Catholic priest, he necessarily regarded the Christian revelation as the ultimate and authoritative source of truth, but the pre-Christian texts he was reading and translating seemed to him also to be repositories of truth. What they were saying appeared to fit neatly enough with what the Christian revelation was saying. His solution to this problem, which others later developed further, and which Traditionalism still relies on, was to propose that these pre-Christian philosophers were not pagans but ancient theologians (*prisci theologi*) whose teaching was compatible with Christian teachings. This argument was assisted by giving the ancient theologians a Jewish origin, as the Hebrew Bible was already understood to be compatible with Christian teachings (hence its adoption into Christian doctrine as the Old Testament). Ficino thus proposed a transmission of ancient theology from Moses and Zoroaster, to Hermes Trismegistus, Orpheus, Iamblichus (a follower of Plotinus), Pythagoras, and finally Plato. This chain of transmission makes no historical sense in terms of current knowledge, but seemed plausible in the fifteenth century.

Ficino's solution was further developed by the Renaissance philosopher Giovanni Pico della Mirandola and then by the sixteenth-century Italian scholar Agostino Steuco, who named the teachings of Ficino's ancient theologians the 'perennial philosophy' (*philosophia perennis*), perennial because they had endured over the years and were in a sense timeless. For Steuco, the word 'philosophy' had a somewhat different meaning from that which it has today. Today, philosophy is generally placed by most non-philosophers in opposition to religion, as the repository of reason, not of revelation. In Steuco's time, as in the ancient world, philosophy was a description of truth, just as was religion, and might well derive ultimately from revelation. Philosophy was not then seen as being in opposition to religion, a position that some philosophers still take today.

Steuco expanded Ficino's chain of transmission, starting with Noah, and proceeding to the Chaldeans (Zoroaster), the Jews (Moses), the Egyptians (Hermes Trismegistus), and then the Greeks. Other, later perennialists embellished their chains of transmission even further, sometimes starting with Adam and Abraham, and occasionally introducing the Druids and the Knights Templar. These chains of transmission were, however, a weak part of early perennialist theory, and soon fell victim to advances in historical knowledge. One immediate problem was that the Ancient Egyptian civilization clearly preceded Moses, even in the biblical account, so one could hardly base Egyptian wisdom on a supposed transmission from the Jews.

EARLY MODERN PERENNIALISM

The ahistoricity of these chains of transmission was not the only problem confronting early perennialism, however. A second problem was that, even if some writings of the ancients were compatible with Christian understanding, others were clearly not. It was obvious that the Ancient Egyptians, Greeks, and Romans had, in their worship, all been polytheists. The solution to this second problem, which Traditionalism also still relies on, was found by the seventeenth-century Cambridge University theologian Ralph Cudworth, who explained away the apparent polytheism of the Ancient Egyptians in terms of the distinction between a secret theology, 'arcane and recondite . . . – that was concealed from the vulgar' and was monotheistic, and a 'vulgar and fabulous theology' that was not concealed and was polytheistic. Cudworth compared this distinction to the 'exoterics' and 'acroamatics' of Aristotle – the exoterics being his public teaching, and the acroamatics (from the Greek *akroaomai*, 'to listen') being his supposed secret and oral teachings.[8] This argument was repeated a century later by the Bishop of Gloucester, William Warburton, who replaced the little-used term 'acroamatic' with the easier term 'esoteric'. This pairing of exoteric and esoteric was an old one, going back to the Ancient Greeks, who had distinguished between the *exoterikos* (external) and the *esoterikos* (internal), and had also speculated about the esoteric teachings of the Ancient Egyptians.

With Cudworth and Bishop Warburton, then, the perennial becomes esoteric and what is taught to the vulgar becomes exoteric. This satisfied Cudworth and Warburton, but those who were losing faith in Christian doctrine as the Enlightenment progressed were less accepting of this identification of the esoteric with the teachings of Christianity. Among those who had lost faith in Christian doctrine was John Toland, a controversial Irish writer who had proposed in 1720 the existence of

a two-fold doctrine: the one *popular*, accommodated to
the prejudices of the vulgar, and to the received customs
or religions; the other *philosophical*, conformable to the
nature of things, and consequently to truth, which . . .
they [ancient philosophers] communicated only to friends
of known probity, prudence, and capacity. These they
generally called the *exoteric* and *esoteric*, or the *external* and
internal doctrines.[9]

Toland then went on to explain exoteric doctrine as serving the interests of the powerful, a variation on the well-
established view, also expressed by Bishop Warburton, that
exoteric religion served the cause of public order. Toland
identified the esoteric philosophy not with Christianity but
with Deism, a then-popular response to the decline of Christianity that rejected the details of Christian theology, including sometimes even the idea that Jesus was divine, and
focused instead on a set of clear and reasonable propositions
that they held to be universally true.

Thus, the idea of an esoteric perennial philosophy that,
as we will see, is so important for Traditionalism, started in
fifteenth-century Florence with Ficino, was developed over
the following centuries by scholars in Italy and England, and
reached a mature form with Toland, who identified the perennial philosophy with Deism and exoteric religion with the
self-interest of the powerful.

UNIVERSALIST AND THEOSOPHICAL PERENNIALISM

A second response to the decline of Christianity and the
problem of religious variety was universalism. This resembles

perennialism, but differs in one important respect. Perennialism proposes one single truth found in different places, while universalism finds multiple truths of comparable value, or even regards all religious claims as equally true. One of the first great universalist events was the World's Parliament of Religions, held in Chicago in 1893, a massive public event during which representatives of America's various Christian Churches were joined by representatives of Hinduism, Buddhism, and Islam. In their speeches, these representatives spoke in favour of religious universalism, and presented their own religions in universalist terms. Swami Vivekananda, representing Hinduism, quoted from a Hindu hymn:

> As the different streams having their sources in different
> places all mingle their water in the sea, so, O Lord,
> the different paths which men take, through different
> tendencies, various though they appear, crooked or
> straight, all lead to thee.[10]

Vivekananda did not mention the previous lines of the 'Hymn About the Greatness of Shiva' that he was quoting, which make clear that the 'different streams' in question are those of three specific *astika* schools of Veda Hinduism: Samkhya, the School of Shiva, and the Vaisheshika. Nobody else spotted this at the time, and Vivekananda's universalism was widely welcomed.

In practice, universalism is usually restricted or qualified in some way. No 'Indians', as Native Americans were then still called, were invited to the World's Parliament of Religions in Chicago. When, almost a century later, Pope John Paul II gathered the religions of the world to pray for peace in Assisi in 1986, the various Christian Churches and the Jews were put in one group, while other religions such as Muslims and Hindus were put in another group. On this occasion, Native Americans were invited, but Neopagans were not. Even the most dedicated universalists do not normally extend their universalism to Satanists.

Universalism remains widely popular, though the term is not now widely used. People who read poems by Rumi or Kahlil Gibran at Christian funerals are universalists, whether or not they realize it. Universalism is the default position of many contemporary Westerners, even if that position is not often named.

A further response to the decline of Christianity, one which became very popular and then declined precipitously, was the Theosophy of the Theosophical Society. Founded in New York in 1875, the Theosophical Society was so named because it proposed to investigate the divine in a scientific, philosophical fashion. It was perennialist and esotericist, identifying its esoteric philosophy – which it called the 'secret doctrine' – not with Christian monotheism like Bishop Warburton or with Deism like Toland but with Hinduism and Buddhism, two systems that were then becoming more widely known in the West. This was an important development in the history of the West.

The English Theosophist Alfred Sinnett explained in his *Esoteric Buddhism* in 1883 that the 'secret doctrine' was that of esoteric Buddhism and also of 'Brahminical philosophy' (that is, Hinduism).[11] Sinnett's esoteric doctrine was imaginative and in fact had little to do with what most Buddhists would see as Buddhism. Since his standard reference was secret teachings that had allegedly been communicated to him alone, there was little to constrain him. His esoteric Buddhism included many elements that would later be taken up in the New Age movement, including the astral sphere and Atlantis, and even the Illuminati. Sinnett's book was far from scientific. What had started with Ficino as serious thought was now passing into the absurd. This is the fate from which Traditionalism later rescued it, as did Huxley.

Huxley moved to America in 1937 and was subsequently in contact with the Vedanta Society, which derived from the Chicago World's Parliament of Religions and taught a universalist understanding of Hinduism, and with Jiddu Krishnamurti, who had for a long time been a central figure in the Theosophical Society. In 1945, Huxley published *The Perennial Philosophy*, which brought together accounts and writings by a wide variety of mystics.[12] This became the best-known non-Traditionalist expression of perennialism in the later twentieth century.

Sinnett had used the term 'occult knowledge' more or less interchangeably with 'esoteric science', and the general modern understandings of the terms 'occultism' and 'esotericism' owe much to him, as does the generally low reputation of both. In 1971, the American sociologist Marcello Truzzi argued for occultism as 'a residual category, a wastebasket, for knowledge claims that are deviant in some way, that do not fit the established claims of science or religion'.[13] This is how many people still regard the occult – as a wastebasket, the contents of which are best left unexamined. This, without doubt, is one of the reasons for the decline of Theosophy. In fact, Theosophy was not just a wastebasket. It was a treasure trove of ideas that was drawn on for more than a century. But that is another story.

Subsequent generations of scholars have objected to Truzzi's view, partly on the grounds that it is not useful to approach the study of a phenomenon that is visibly important to so many people in quite such a negative fashion; partly because 'residual categories' are never very useful; and partly because the definition is somewhat circular: if it is not religious it is occult, and if it is occult it is not religious. Recently, many scholars have come to see esotericism as a major strand in Western religious history, less immediately visible than Christianity, but also important. Christianity was a system that dominated Western religious life for centuries; esotericism was never hegemonic like Christianity, but it was still a fairly coherent system that, in a similar fashion, persisted over the centuries and was followed by many. These scholars generally adopt a somewhat narrow definition of esotericism, preferring its more intellectually sophisticated expressions (like Steuco and Ficino) to movements based around flying saucers or Atlantis. Even so, Truzzi's wastebasket continues, for many, to discredit the occult and the esoteric.

ACADEMIC PERENNIALISM

There is also a respectable academic perennialism, though it is no longer as much in fashion as it once was. The great American philosopher and psychologist William James argued in 1902, in his widely read *The Varieties of Religious Experience*, that what lay at the heart of religion was not creeds and institutions, as many had come to suppose, but the religious experience, especially the mystical experience, understood as a 'feeling of enlargement, union, and emancipation'.[14] The 'methodical cultivation' of this experience or consciousness was, for James, 'an element of the religious life. Hindus, Buddhists, Mohammedans, and Christians all have cultivated it methodically'.[15] 'The most diverse philosophies and theologies' could be combined with the mystical experience.[16] This view is, in effect, perennialist (though James did not use the term), since it envisages a single common core, of experience rather than teaching, that is common to various and multiple philosophical and theological expressions. If we think of James's 'diverse philosophies and theologies' as exoteric, and of his core of mystical experience as esoteric, then his implicit perennialism becomes visible.

A similar approach was arrived at on a slightly different basis by a German philosopher and theologian, Rudolf Otto, who published his *The Idea of the Holy: An Inquiry into the Non-Rational Factor in the Idea of the Divine and its Relation to the Rational* in 1917.[17] Like James's book, this too was very widely read. Part of 'the holy', Otto argued, was what he called 'the numinous', much what we now call 'the transcendent'. What James called the religious experience was, for Otto, the experience of the numinous. Once again, there is a single common core of experience, and multiple forms of understanding it. Indeed, one of Otto's more famous studies was his *Mysticism East and West*, in which he compares the Christian mystic Meister Eckhardt with the Hindu philosopher Shankara.[18]

Within academia, James and Otto are the two best-known non-Traditionalist exponents of perennialism, though the term 'perennialist' is only occasionally applied to them. They are still respected by academic scholars of religion, but sometimes criticized for their assumption that there is one single experience of the numinous, independent of culture. They are thought by some to have misrepresented the mystics whom they cite, focusing on the common elements that fitted their conceptions and ignoring the distinct elements that made each mystic who they were. For many contemporary scholars, Otto's comparison of Eckhardt and Shankara misrepresents both. James and Otto are also criticized for failing to recognize that they were not looking directly at mystical experiences but at descriptions of those experiences, descriptions in human languages that inevitably reflected the cultures in which they had developed. Despite this, many scholars of religion are still at least implicitly sympathetic to perennialism, especially in America.

Huxley was one of those who inspired a young American Methodist minister and academic, Huston Smith, to give a series of televised lectures on different religions in 1955. These lectures presented each religion with respect, as part of the universal human religious experience. 'Every religion is a blend of universal principles and local setting,' wrote Smith in 1958 in *The Religions of Man*, the book that grew out of the television series.[19] His aim was to bring out the universal in a way that would make sense to contemporary Americans, an aim in which he certainly succeeded; *The Religions of Man* has now sold some three million copies, mostly in America and many under the revised, gender-neutral title *The World's Religions*, making it one of the most successful books on religion of the later twentieth century.

Conclusion

Although Enlightenment rationalism replaced myth and religion with reason and science, both remained important. As part of the Counter-Enlightenment, the Romantic movement continued the importance of myth. Myth was also studied by scholars such as James Frazer in the service of progress, and by Carl Gustav Jung as 'primordial images' or 'archetypes' in the attempt to understand the unconscious. As we will see, the Traditionalists use myth in ways that are not entirely different.

Religion in some ways fared worse than myth. As well as facing the challenges of reason and science, it also faced the problem of religious variety. This was a problem that had already been faced in the Renaissance by Marsilio Ficino, and by others who developed the perennial philosophy: perennial because it was ancient, and philosophy not because it was opposed to religion, but because it was the source of truth. This went through various evolutions, most importantly the identification of the perennial philosophy as secret and esoteric, in contrast to exoteric religion, understood by John Toland not as true but as serving the interests of the powerful. As we will also see in the following chapter, the idea of an esoteric perennial philosophy is central to Traditionalism.

Toland died in poverty in 1722, but perennialism and its cousin universalism have remained important. Universalism and the perennialist Theosophical Society were both popular in the late nineteenth century, and universalism remains popular today. Theosophy identified its esoteric philosophy with Hinduism and Buddhism, but was unselective and ended up with a mixture of teachings that seemed to many to fit the sociological category of the wastebasket, a classification that many still associate with occultism.

Some celebrated twentieth-century academics were and are also perennialists, though the term is not always applied to them. Frazer and Jung were perennialists, with their universal common ground. So too were William James with his universal mystical experience and Rudolf Otto with the numinous. In the later twentieth century, Aldous Huxley and Huston Smith were both widely read perennialists.

All this non-Traditionalist perennialism, early modern and modern, universalist, Theosophical and academic, provides the context for Traditionalist perennialism, to which we will now turn.

PART I
Foundations

CHAPTER 3

Traditionalist Perennialism

The Traditionalist version of perennialism, the idea that beneath all the different forms of tradition from Catholicism to
Buddhism there lies one single, timeless and esoteric sacred
tradition, is the single most important of the foundations of
the Traditionalist philosophy. As this chapter shows, Traditionalist perennialism builds on historical perennialism in
ways that avoid many of the problems suffered by other versions of perennialism: for example the historical impossibility of the narrative of Marsilio Ficino's and Agostino Steuco's
Renaissance perennialism; the exposure of the Christian perennialism of Ralph Cudworth and Bishop Warburton to the
decline of faith in Christianity; and the unselective and often
dubious factual basis of much of the literature produced by the
once-popular Theosophical Society, including Alfred Sinnett's
Esoteric Buddhism. This helps explain why Traditionalism has
flourished while earlier and once more popular alternative
religious systems, from occultism to Theosophy, have not.

Traditionalism takes from historical perennialism the idea
that there is a perennial philosophy – or, in René Guénon's
own terminology, a 'primordial tradition' – that is found in
ancient teachings and is esoteric, distinct from the exoteric
religion that is taught openly to everyone – or to the 'vulgar',

in the terminology of the seventeenth and eighteenth centuries that we encountered in the previous chapter. This is a central part of what the Russian Traditionalist Aleksandr Dugin calls Traditionalism's 'paradigmatic matrix':[1] the Traditionalist conceptual model that can be used as a basis for a variety of analyses and purposes. One matrix can contain different values, of course, as when different classes can be fitted into the Marxist paradigm of class struggle: bourgeoisie against feudalism, proletariat against bourgeoisie.

The contents of the Traditionalist matrix differ from those of historical perennialism. They have almost nothing in common with the contents of the perennial philosophy of Christian perennialists like Bishop Warburton, Deistic perennialists like John Toland, or Theosophical perennialists like Alfred Sinnett. Guénon's primordial tradition is not Christian, Deist, or occultist. Traditionalism thus avoids Marcello Truzzi's wastebasket problem, the problem that, for many people, discredits works like Sinnett's *Esoteric Buddhism*, which can indeed appear as no more than collections of rejected and deviant knowledge. Traditionalism emphasizes its own seriousness by criticizing the lack of seriousness of Theosophy and similar currents. Sinnett's book, Guénon argued, 'merely presented quite imaginary conceptions, derived neither from authentic Buddhism nor from any real esoteric doctrine'.[2] Traditionalism claims that the contents of its primordial tradition are derived only from authentic sources, and that it – unlike Sinnett and his peers – has found real esoteric doctrine.

Although the Traditionalist understanding of the primordial tradition, the ancient, perennial, and esoteric teachings that are distinct from exoteric religion, is based on ancient teachings, it does not propose historically problematic chains of transmission (with one important exception, discussed below). The focus is more on what the primordial tradition is, not on how it got from place to place or time to time. This helps avoid the risk of the Traditionalist narrative being discredited by historians, as they cannot challenge what has never been proposed in the first place. For good measure, Guénon also explicitly rejected the authority of the 'historical method', a phrase that he always puts in scare quotes, on the basis that historians and Orientalists lack the metaphysical and esoteric understandings that are needed to make sense of the texts that they work with, when they are not actually prejudiced against such understandings in the first place. 'The habits which grow with the use of such [purely scholarly] methods narrow the intellectual horizon and cause irremediable harm to those who submit to them,' wrote Guénon.[3] The primordial tradition is not something that can be investigated, established, or understood in terms of historical development. And Westernized Easterners have no more authority than Western Orientalists. In Guénon's view, their understandings are also limited, and any criticism of Traditionalism that they may make can be ignored.

Although Traditionalism has one single, paradigmatic matrix for what the primordial tradition is, and although all Traditionalists seek only what they see as authentic sources, different Traditionalists have in practice drawn on different sources. Guénon emphasized Vedanta, a major body of Hindu texts that are now thought to have been composed between the fifth and eighth centuries AD, based on earlier texts and traditions. Julius Evola drew on ancient myth in general, after the manner of James Frazer at Cambridge and Carl Gustav Jung in Switzerland. Frithjof Schuon, unusually, also drew on exoteric religion. Rather as different people may mean much the same thing by 'poetry' while reading different poems, different Traditionalists share a common understanding of the primordial tradition, while reading its contents rather differently. We will now review these different approaches.

Guénon's perennialism

Guénon placed the primordial tradition, which he also called 'metaphysics', in opposition to religion, which he termed 'external', i.e. exoteric. He further distinguished the primordial tradition from modern philosophy, which he saw as rationalist (like natural science), and thus neither esoteric nor exoteric, but simply limited in scope and application.

Guénon then identified religion with social order, agreeing with Bishop Warburton and many others, stressing that religious rites bind together the community that participates in them. This might be understood by some as 'sacred order', but not by Guénon, who was interested in the more important order produced by the esoteric primordial tradition. For him, the social function of religion is a 'sentimental' function; the term 'sentimental', always used pejoratively, is one that Guénon often applied to religion. Belief and dogma are sentimental, as are morals. Theology, given its connection to religion, is also sentimental. The metaphysical, in contrast, is not sentimental but 'intellectual', a term that Guénon uses as the opposite of 'sentimental'. His usage is, unfortunately, confusing. For Guénon, 'intellectual' does not mean what it normally means, but almost the opposite. In normal usage, the intellect is much the same as the mind, and 'intellectual' therefore means much the same as 'rational'. For Guénon, however, the intellect is not the thinking mind but a separate faculty that can perceive the absolute. In Traditionalist usage, 'intellectual' refers to that separate faculty; it means spiritual (but not in a sentimental way). It almost means esoteric.

Most civilizations, thought Guénon, have both social and metaphysical systems. China, for example, has Confucianism as the basis of its social order, and Taoism as its metaphysical system. Islam has Sharia, the sacred rules derived from revelation, as its social basis, and Sufism as its metaphysical system. Something similar is true of Judaism, which also has both sacred rules and a metaphysical system. India, however, only has a metaphysical system that is not the source of sacred rules, and the modern West has neither a metaphysical nor a normal social system, as religion is only an element in its social system, not the basis for it. This is an abnormal situation, writes Guénon, the result of modernity; we will discuss this idea in a later chapter. The West may not have always been abnormal, however. Guénon thought that Scholasticism, the European philosophy of the thirteenth and fourteenth centuries, was partly esoteric, though too close to theology to be purely intellectual (i.e. spiritual). But Scholasticism might once have been the metaphysical counterpart of the West's exoteric religious system, so that the West of the thirteenth and fourteenth centuries came closer to what Guénon saw as the normal model.

Guénon was never very complimentary about religion, though he did recognize that a social order based on religion had its advantages. He was even less complimentary about the Christian religion, which he felt had lost contact with metaphysics, so that all that remained was the social and sentimental, in the form of morality and worship. Catholicism, he felt, was tending towards Protestantism, which was so purely sentimental and moralistic that it was actually 'no longer a religion at all'.[4]

Schuon, as we will see, took a different view of religion, but Guénon's view is the dominant one in Traditionalism as a whole. It means that those who have rejected Protestantism, Catholicism, or other exoteric religions can still embrace Traditionalism and the primordial tradition. In an age in which organized religion, especially organized Christianity, was becoming less and less attractive, this view of religion protected Traditionalism from the risk of collateral damage. Agnosticism with regard to religion does not stop someone from being a Traditionalist. In some ways, agnostics who hold Catholicism and Protestantism in low regard are already moving towards Guénon's position.

In his criticism of religion, and especially of contemporary Christianity, Guénon did not side with the Enlightenment but rather distanced himself from failed, Christian-based critiques of the Enlightenment. Equally, he distanced himself from Christian-based critiques of natural science that had also failed to make much impact. He did not attack reason and the natural sciences. He accepted that both had given rise to advances. He observed, however, that both also dealt only with the material, and could not address metaphysical questions. Natural science was all very well in its own terms, but those terms were necessarily limited to 'the study of sensible phenomena',[5] that is, such phenomena as can be sensed. Those who attempted to apply reason and science to metaphysical questions were making a mistake: for example, in supposing that, simply because one could observe evolution in biology, religion also evolved, as many academic historians of religion then thought. As Guénon's understanding of tradition did not seek to challenge natural science, it could less easily be challenged by it.

In Guénon's view, metaphysics is not for everyone. Metaphysics is often hard to understand (as is Guénon himself). Guénon made no apology for this. 'By attempting to bring down the [metaphysical] doctrine to the level of the common mentality under the pretext of making it accessible to all, it must inevitably be distorted and denatured in the process; it is not for the doctrine to abase itself or to conform to the limited powers of understanding of the many; it is for individuals to rise, if they can, to an appreciation of the doctrine in its integral purity.'[6] If, like most Westerners, a reader of Guénon failed to understand the primordial tradition, that was unfortunate, but only to be expected. The fault lay not in the primordial tradition but in the limited powers of understanding of the reader, who might give up, or try again. Paradoxically, difficulty has helped legitimize Traditionalism and its paradigmatic matrix. That which is not easy to understand is not easy to deny, and the difficulty of metaphysics, very much a minority pursuit, provides a convincing explanation of why something as true and important as Traditionalist metaphysics is so little known. This, too, is a reason why Traditionalism has flourished while other systems have not.

The sources that Guénon used to fill this matrix were

Vedanta and the East in general. We will now review these, before moving on to the alternative approaches of other Traditionalists. First, however, we must briefly consider the role of oral transmission.

GUÉNON AND ORAL TRANSMISSION

Although Guénon did not try to trace the transmission of the tradition through chains from Moses to Plato as some earlier perennialists had, he did understand the tradition as being transmitted orally, which implied a different sort of chain of transmission, 'the chain of a regular and unbroken "spiritual filiation"'.[7] This idea is also found in Sufism, which was one of Guénon's sources for it. In Sufism, a student studies with a teacher who has himself studied with a teacher who studied with a teacher who . . . in a chain that goes backwards for centuries, ending with the Prophet Muhammad, and then God Himself. Sufi chains of transmission have something in common with the Christian concept of the apostolic succession, and something in common with the professional certificates that are granted to qualified architects and accountants. Their historical accuracy is open to question, especially for the earlier centuries, but, even so, they serve as a guarantee of authenticity and quality. The idea of learning through transmission also means that there is no point in trying to discover truth by engaging in sceptical dialogue. While a modern seeker might question, a traditional seeker accepts. 'If there sometimes is occasion for discussion and controversy,' wrote Guénon, 'this only happens as a result of a defect in exposition or of an imperfect comprehension.'[8] Truth is not to be constructed by researchers; it has existed perennially. Sceptical dialogue is not a way to truth; truth is found by understanding the tradition that has been transmitted.

Guénon never published his own chain of transmission. This has resulted in much speculation over the years. No plausible Hindu teacher has ever been identified, which is a weakness in his claim to authority. A possible Taoist transmission has been identified, however, as has one certain Islamic transmission, passing through Abdul-Hadi, the Swedish student of the works of the great thirteenth-century Sufi Muhyi al-Din Ibn Arabi. To some extent, then, Guénon did benefit from a regular and unbroken spiritual filiation. This, however, was not the only source of his understanding of primordial tradition.

VEDANTA, AND THE EAST

All Traditionalists keep to the same basic structure in their paradigmatic matrix: the primordial tradition is found in ancient teachings and is placed in opposition to exoteric religion. As we have seen, where they look for these ancient teachings varies, although all their sources are in some way 'religious', using the general sense of that word that encompasses esoteric and exoteric, myth and religion, not the narrower, purely exoteric, Traditionalist sense.

Guénon's account of the primordial tradition rested on two main supports: Vedanta, and also the East in general. His study of Vedanta was sufficiently rigorous to be submitted as a PhD thesis to the Sorbonne – and sufficiently perennialist for the thesis to be rejected as ahistorical. The Sorbonne's Professor Sylvain Lévi adhered to the mainstream academic view that rejects perennialism as fanciful.

The classic expression of Guénon's perennialism is found in his first mature work, the *Introduction to the Study of the Hindu Doctrines*. This consists of four parts, only one of which – the third – actually deals with the Hindu doctrines. The first part deals with questions relating to East and West, and the second part with 'The General Character of Eastern Thought', and then (after 'The Hindu Doctrines') comes 'Western Interpretations'. An emphasis on the East as the source of the esoteric was implicit in Theosophy and became explicit in Guénon's Traditionalism. Some, but not all, later Traditionalists have followed him in this. He accepted that there was more than one Eastern civilization – the most important were Islamic, Indian, Chinese, and Indo-Chinese (Southeast Asian) – but maintained that all Eastern civilizations had certain things in common, especially when viewed in comparison to Western civilization.

Guénon proposed that slightly different understandings of the tradition that was found in Vedanta could also be found in other places in the East, notably in Taoism and Islam, and – to a lesser extent – in the West, in Scholasticism. Above all, he identified the tradition with Eastern thought, contrasted with Western thought, especially modern Western thought, which lacked any metaphysical element. In regard to Scholasticism, he noted – in a partial exception to the general rule of avoiding chains of transmission – that 'Arab influences . . . made themselves felt to an appreciable extent' in Scholasticism.[9] This is a proposition with which contemporary historians would agree. Although Guénon referred sometimes to Taoism, Islam, and the wider body of myth, however, he always based his writings solidly in Vedanta.

Guénon's binary opposition of East and West was not singled out for criticism by Professor Lévi in his rejection report on Guénon's PhD thesis, as such broad categories were then still widely used and not thought to be problematic. Modern scholars, however, would refer to the immensely influential book of the Palestinian-American scholar Edward Said, *Orientalism*, which shows how Western scholars constructed an imaginary East to bolster their own self-understanding as Westerners, and to legitimize Western imperialism. Said does not discuss Guénon, whose work he may not have known, but a Saidian approach would identify Guénon's work as a case of 'reverse Orientalism' – another construction of an imaginary East, this time bolstering a different Western self-understanding, and legitimizing an agenda that was not imperialist, but was still Western. Neither the actual critique of Professor Lévi nor the possible Saidian critique, however, has ever worried Traditionalists. Lévi's critique is disarmed by the Traditionalist understanding of Western Orientalists as unable to really understand the East, and Said's critique would be disarmed by the extension of that understanding to cover Westernized Easterners. Said was certainly Palestinian by origin, but he was Western by education, and lived most of his life in New York. What could he know of metaphysics? For non-Traditionalists, however, both Lévi and Said made important points that cannot be so easily dismissed.

Alternative approaches

Today's Traditionalist perennialism owes most of all to Guénon, but it also bears the influence of other Traditionalists, who shared Guénon's emphasis on Vedanta and the

East only to a limited extent. Evola rejected Guénon's binary opposition of East and West, and he and Schuon emphasized other sources more than Vedanta in their search for the contents of the primordial tradition, as did the Romanian-American scholar Mircea Eliade, who was a Traditionalist in his youth. What they agreed on was the conceptual model, the paradigmatic matrix. These variations on Guénon's understanding of Traditionalist perennialism will extend and complete our understanding of the most important of Traditionalism's foundations.

EVOLA AND MYTH

The first Traditionalist to advance an alternative to Guénon's understanding of the contents of the primordial tradition was Julius Evola, who much reduced the emphasis on Vedanta and on the pairing of East and West. For Evola, the tradition was not so much ancient truth as a *repository* of truths, and in this he resembles Jung. While Guénon refers constantly to the 'tradition', Evola usually refers to 'myth'. Myth is where we should look for truth. 'Materials having a "historical" and "scientific" value are the ones that matter the least; conversely, all the mythical, legendary, and epic elements denied historical truth and demonstrative value acquire here a superior validity and become the source for a more real and certain knowledge.'[10] Also: 'Every traditional mythology arises as a necessary process in the individual consciousness, the origin of which resides in real, though unconscious and obscure, relationships with a higher reality.'[11] Evola's understanding of myth is within touching distance of the idea of the archetype developed by Jung, but refers to 'a higher reality', which Jung did not. Evola does not insist that the many myths he draws on, including Guénon's favoured Vedanta, are actually or literally true, then; just that they are where truth can be found. Guénon believed in the authority and authenticity of Vedanta. Evola was more agnostic about the authority of myth.

Evola also advanced an alternative understanding of exoteric religion, combining with Guénon's criticism of Christianity an argument made by Nietzsche, who famously stated in 1887 that there were two types of morality, 'master morality' and 'slave morality'.[12] The first was identified with nobility, and the second with Christianity. Evola added Nietzsche's condemnation of Christianity to Guénon's.

Evola's perennialism, then, followed Guénon in some ways, but not all. As Evola's Traditionalism has become ever more prominent in recent decades, so has his myth-based understanding of the primordial tradition.

ELIADE AND THE ARCHAIC

A similar approach was taken by Mircea Eliade, a scholar and novelist of Romanian origin who in his youth had been close to Evola and to another Traditionalist who is discussed in a later chapter, Ananda Coomaraswamy. Eliade distanced himself from the Traditionalists in the post-war period, especially after he moved to America and was appointed Professor of the History of Religions at the University of Chicago, where he became one of the best-known scholars of religion in America. To what extent the mature Eliade should be considered a Traditionalist at all is disputed. But, although his version of perennialism is important primarily for its impact beyond Traditionalism, it is still part of the development of understandings of perennialism.

Eliade's stated objective was to contribute to intellectual and institutional history, as had been Frazer's. Unlike Frazer, however, Eliade did not want to expedite progress, but rather to convey an understanding of the sacred, of the spiritual world. An understanding of the sacred, he held, is part of being fully human, and is generally lacking in the modern world.

Like Guénon, Eliade sought the primordial tradition in ancient and non-Western teachings, and placed it in opposition to exoteric religion. He saw the sacred and the profane as 'two modes of being in the world', with the sacred mode being natural to traditional societies (which he generally termed 'archaic') and the profane mode being dominant among modern people. Eliade was ambivalent about the tradition, however, holding that 'for the man of the traditional and archaic societies, the models for his institutions and the norms for his various categories of behaviour are believed to have been "revealed" at the beginning of time'.[13] That 'are believed to' distances him from any supposition of transcendent origin, leaving him safely within the bounds of academic respectability. Just as Evola was somewhat agnostic about the authority and authenticity of myth, so was Eliade somewhat agnostic about the tradition he wrote about.

Eliade criticized Frazer for having made the mistake of supposing 'that the reaction of the human mind to natural phenomena is uniform'.[14] By 'natural phenomena' Eliade means the agricultural rhythms and processes that Frazer saw as fundamental to magic, myth, and then religion. In fact, writes Eliade, 'man's reactions to nature are often conditioned by his culture and hence, finally, by history',[15] a point made by many other modern scholars, who see the way that people understand any given phenomenon as revealing more about the people than about the phenomenon. This argument is now often made about people's understandings of the sacred, but was not applied in this way by Eliade: for him, there is one single 'religious experience', on which subject he refers to Rudolf Otto; Eliade's objective is 'to bring out the specific characteristics of the religious experience, rather than to show its numerous variations and the differences caused by history'.[16] Eliade, then, is a perennialist after the model of academic perennialists like Otto and William James, as well as after the model of Guénon and Evola.

As Guénon turned to Vedanta and Evola to myth, so Eliade turned to archaic symbol, myth, and rite as 'a complex system of coherent affirmations about the ultimate reality of things, a system that can be regarded as constituting a metaphysics'.[17] Myth is not historically true; that is not what it is for. What it does is reveal 'archetypes', a term that Eliade used often, meaning by it something different from what Jung meant, he said, as he was not investigating the collective unconscious. For Eliade, an archetype was an 'exemplary model' used to understand being and the universe; it was universal because it was primordial, originating in archaic man's original experience of the sacred. Eliade's archetypes have much in common with Guénon's metaphysics.

Eliade's method is closer to Evola's than to Guénon's. He refers somewhat indiscriminately to a variety of myths, and turns only occasionally to Vedanta. Instead, the archaic tradition on which he most often drew was shamanism, originally understood as the practice of pagan shamans in Siberia but expanded by Eliade to include North American (Native American) and Indonesian shamanism. Shamanism predates later, monotheistic religions and their theologies. While Guénon wrote of oral transmission but in practice sought the primordial mostly through surviving texts, Eliade sought it mostly through surviving persons. Both approaches are still used by scholars today, and both have advantages and disadvantages. Ancient texts offer apparently direct access to the time in which they were written, but there is no guarantee that we will understand them quite as they were originally understood. Living representatives of ancient cultures also appear to offer direct access to the past, but we may also misunderstand them, and – since no one lives in complete isolation – some of what appears ancient may actually be of more recent origin.

Eliade translated Traditionalism into terms that won widespread acceptance in and beyond academia for many years. His Traditionalist-inspired books were widely read, and not only in universities. He also came to conclusions of his own about the sacred that in some ways resembled Frazer's and have little to do with Traditionalism. Instead of the sacrifice of the divine king that James Frazer had earlier proposed as central to universal myth, Eliade identified patterns that he named the 'eternal return' and the '*axis mundi*'. The basic idea of the eternal return is that people seek to return to their mythical origins, often in cyclical fashion, and the basic idea of the *axis mundi* relates to sacred space: that people conceive of a sacred centre. These conclusions were more widely accepted among scholars of religion than Frazer's had been and lasted longer, though today they are increasingly ignored. They are the direct product not of Traditionalism, moreover, but of Eliade's investigation of archaic myth.

One later reader of Eliade, and also of Jung, was a Canadian psychologist, Jordan B. Peterson, who – alone among the Traditionalists discussed in this book – has never referred to Guénon, Evola, or Schuon, nor even used the terms 'esoteric' and 'exoteric'. In some ways, then, his Traditionalism is quite different from the Guénonian and post-Guénonian Traditionalism considered in this book. He has described himself as a Traditionalist, however, and the conclusions that he drew from Eliade's understanding of myth are comparable to those drawn by Traditionalists who did draw explicitly on Guénon, Evola, and Schuon. He will therefore be considered in subsequent chapters as a Traditionalist fellow-traveller.

Peterson's perennialism is as agnostic as Eliade's. He sees myth as a repository of human wisdom rather than as the product of any sort of revelation. Rather than investigating myth himself, he relies largely on Eliade's account. His importance lies not in his understanding of myth or perennialism, but in his application of this understanding, and especially in his political project.

SCHUON AND RELIGION

Schuon generally followed the Traditionalist matrix, but in a dramatic reversal of earlier positions he rehabilitated religion in general and Christianity in particular. His first major book, published in 1948, was entitled *The Transcendent Unity of Religions*, and this book was his major contribution to

Traditionalism. He refers not just to a primordial *tradition* but also to a primordial *religion*, often using the phrase '*religio perennis*'. His understanding of perennialism, like Evola's, became an important alternative within Traditionalism.

Schuon's views on religion are discussed at length in a later chapter. For the purposes of this chapter, it is enough to note that he never tried to identify the primordial tradition exclusively with Christianity. Although he did expose himself to the risk of collateral damage from the collapse of organized religion that other Traditionalists avoided, the rehabilitation of religion and Christianity allowed Schuon's Traditionalism to rejoin a major stream of discourse from which Guénon's and Evola's Traditionalism was excluded. To use Traditionalist terminology, Guénon and Evola abandoned the exoteric for the esoteric; Schuon brought the esoteric back into the exoteric. Because Schuon rehabilitated Christianity, his Traditionalism is much more acceptable and accessible than Guénon's to Western Christians, or Westerners who do not wish to reject Christianity, and, because he rehabilitated religion in general, it is also more accessible to people of other religions. While Guénon could only investigate the esoteric, Schuon could also investigate the exoteric.

Like Evola, Schuon saw the primordial tradition as a repository of truths, which might be in some ways multiple, more than as one single ancient truth, as Guénon saw it. Myth, for Schuon as for Evola, was a source of truth. 'A traditional narrative is always true,' he maintained, as 'there is no metaphysical or spiritual difference between a truth manifested by temporal facts and a truth expressed by other symbols, under a mythological form for example'.[18] The truth of Schuon's traditional narrative was established not only by assertion, but also by painstaking analysis of the commonalities between different religions, which Schuon saw as reflecting that narrative, each religion in its own way. Schuon's Traditionalism, then, was more universalist than Guénon's, as he found truth in many religions, whereas Guénon had sought a single truth primarily in Vedanta, and then in Sufism.

SMITH AND WISDOM TRADITIONS

When Huston Smith published *The Religions of Man* in 1958, he was a perennialist on the model of Aldous Huxley, not a Traditionalist, but some years later he encountered the work of Schuon and joined the ranks of the Traditionalists, following Schuon in seeking the primordial tradition in religion as well as the esoteric. In 1987 he published an article in a leading American academic journal, the *Journal of the American Academy of Religion*, responding to scholarly criticism of perennialism not by attacking scholars' lack of metaphysical understanding, as Guénon would have, but by following the norms of mainstream Western intellectual discourse.[19] While Guénon either ignored or attacked mainstream scholarship, Smith attempted to engage with it, doing so more explicitly than Eliade.

Smith started by responding to the standard criticisms of perennialism: that there is no universal mystical experience because all experience is mediated by culture; and that perennialists minimize or ignore the differences between traditions. Smith agreed that there was, indeed, no universal mystical experience, but pointed out that this was a criticism of the perennialism of James and Otto, not of the

Traditionalists, since Traditionalist perennialism proposed not universal *experience* as James and Otto had, but universal *metaphysics*. That is, experience may be mediated by culture, but the primordial tradition is not. In response to the second criticism, he pointed out that there are always both differences and similarities. 'Everything obviously both resembles and differs from every other thing: resembles it in that both exist; differs or there would not be two things but one.'[20] The question is when we should look for difference, and when for similarity. When dealing with religion, we need to look for similarities, argued Smith, not just difference. 'The perennialist finds the unity of religions *in* the religions in the way s/he finds beauty in paintings and song.'[21]

Smith then advanced his own understanding of perennialism. His first point was that it was a philosophy, not an empirical science. Like other philosophies, it provided a way of looking at things, a way of understanding. As such, it was not appropriate to judge it by the standards of the empirical sciences.

Perennialism, Smith argued, draws on 'the world's enduring religious or wisdom traditions'. 'In theistic terminology', he added, 'these traditions stem from divine revelation, but if that way of speaking closes rather than opens doors, one can think of them as wisdom reservoirs. They are tanks, or in any case deposits. Distillations of the cumulative wisdom of the human race.'[22] Traditionalism did not draw on science or reason, the limitations of which were now obvious: 'science registers only a fraction of the real', and as for 'the autonomous reason of the Enlightenment . . . what defenders does it still have among frontline philosophers?'[23] Smith was overstating his case slightly, as many philosophers still defend reason and the conclusions of the natural sciences, even if they no longer share the optimism of the Enlightenment thinkers, which now appears somewhat naive.

Finally, perennialism coexists with other approaches. Religion also exists, and is enough for most people, rather like the fact that most people can deal with reality without any knowledge of Einsteinian physics. The mystical is always a minority pursuit, as is understanding Einsteinian physics, and that is fine. 'Profundity is not determined by headcount.'[24]

Smith's article did not succeed in changing the minds of many professional scholars of religion, but it did succeed in recasting the Traditionalist understanding of the primordial tradition in terms that are easier for some readers than those used by Guénon. It became part of the range of Traditionalist understandings of the primordial tradition, though never as influential as Evola's and Schuon's understandings.

Conclusion

Traditionalist perennialism, the single most important foundation of the Traditionalist philosophy, builds on historical perennialism. René Guénon's primordial tradition is perennial philosophy, esoteric and distinct from exoteric religion; a central part of Traditionalism's paradigmatic matrix, the conceptual model that can be used for many purposes. The values that are inserted into this matrix, however, are different from those of historical perennialism. They are not Christian, Deist, or occultist. They claim to be based only on authentic sources, and may thus circumvent the wastebasket problem. Traditionalism's claim to authenticity is enhanced by its criticism of occultists and Theosophists, from whom Traditionalists distance themselves, regarding them as in-authentic and their conclusions as 'quite imaginary'. Trad-itionalism also avoids criticism from historians, partly by avoiding such historically problematic claims as chains of transmission including Noah, and also by questioning the competence of scholars, who lack metaphysical understand-ing. Huston Smith, however, simply pointed out that Trad-itionalism is a philosophy, and so should not be judged in the way one would judge the claims of an empirical science.

Guénon emphasized the distinction between the prim-ordial tradition and religion, which he identified with social order and the 'sentimental', always a negative term. Meta-physics, in contrast, was 'intellectual', a term meaning some-thing close to 'esoteric'. One consequence of the way in which Guénon distanced Traditionalism from religion, not-ably Catholicism, is that Traditionalism could still be attract-ive to the many who were disenchanted with religion. The plausibility of Traditionalist metaphysics is also enhanced by its difficulty, which, Guénon held, explains why, although of overwhelming importance, it is so little known. Metaphysics is not for everyone.

The sources Traditionalists use to provide the values for the Traditionalist matrix vary, but are all in some way reli-gious (using the general sense of that word, not the Trad-itionalist sense). Guénon looked to Vedanta and the religions of the East. Julius Evola looked to myth in general. Mircea Eliade looked to myth, and especially to shamanism, which predates later, monotheistic religions. Frithjof Schuon, unusually, looked to exoteric religion as well as the esoteric, and Huston Smith looked to 'the world's enduring religious or wisdom traditions', stating explicitly that these could be understood either in terms of divine revelation or as 'distillations of the cumulative wisdom of the human race'. Traditionalist understandings of the primordial tradition, then, do not depend on religious faith. Many Traditionalists have such a faith, but it is not required.

As an explanation of reality, Traditionalism is a development of a line of thought that goes back to the Renaissance and addresses, among other issues, the problem of the variety of religions, the triumphs of the Enlightenment, reason, and natural science. It echoes earlier systems, like Deism and Theosophy, that had at one point been widely popular, but had then declined – and it does so while avoiding some of the major reasons for their decline. It also echoes the view of myth held by psychoanalysts such as Sigmund Freud and Carl Gustav Jung, and the perennialism of scholars of religion like William James and Rudolf Otto, even though Huston Smith took pains to distinguish Traditionalist perennialism from the perennialism of those who suppose a universal mystical experience. Traditionalist perennialism is a version of a well-established feature in Western thought.

Perennialism is Traditionalism's single most important foundation, but it is not its only foundation. Almost as important, though in a different way, is its historical narrative, to which we will now turn.

CHAPTER 4
Traditionalist History

A particular historical narrative is fundamental to Traditionalism. This narrative has something in common with the two dominant historical narratives that Westerners are most familiar with – the tripartite narrative of ancient, medieval and modern, and the myth of the Fall – but comes with an important twist.

One reason that the Traditionalist historical narrative is so important is that historical narratives are fundamental to the way in which people make sense of the world they live in. People have always used narratives to make sense of events. We construct narratives about our own lives, and these narratives – what psychologists call 'autobiographical memory' – are an important source of identity. Nations need national histories as much as they need flags, and there are also universal histories, which seek to make sense of large events over long periods. These narratives are all, in some sense, fictional. Just as the same event can be remembered and recounted differently by different people, so can national histories vary from person to person and from group to group.

In this chapter, we will see how Traditionalism builds on the two historical narratives mentioned above. The first, the tripartite periodization that divides history into ancient, medieval, and modern periods, is commonly taught in schools. In the standard version of this narrative, the Middle Ages are also the dark ages, and modernity represents a recovery from darkness. The other dominant historical narrative is the Jewish and Christian account based on the myth of the Garden of Eden and the Fall, leading to the current postlapsarian age, which will be succeeded by a messianic age in which a messiah will preside over a world of peace and plenty. Both these narratives start with a Golden Age, which is terminated by a fall (the fall of the Roman Empire in the tripartite periodization and the 'fall of man' in the Jewish and Christian account), and end with a recovery, either current (modernity in the tripartite periodization) or future (the messianic age in the Jewish and Christian account).

Traditionalism combines elements of the tripartite narrative and of the mythical narrative and tells a story of its own that is quite as powerful as the better-known versions, though coming to a somewhat different conclusion. For Traditionalists, modernity represents not recovery, but a continuation of the Fall. This scheme of history is one of the most important aspects of the Traditionalist philosophy. It is also one that many people find persuasive. Guénon's translator into English, Marco Pallis, referred in 1945 to 'the impending disaster that so many dread but feel powerless to prevent'.[1] The impending disaster that people dread today is not quite the same as the one they dreaded in 1945, but the dread is still there, now attached to ecological issues and the threats posed by climate change. It is not only Traditionalists, then, who feel we are on the edge of disaster.

This chapter will start by looking at the general Western

narratives on which the Traditionalist narrative builds, and then at the basic narrative established by Guénon, and the role it assigns to the Renaissance. It will then look at how this scheme was modified by other Traditionalists, and the way in which racism, which was absent from Guénon's narrative, crept into some other Traditionalist narratives.

Mythical, tripartite, and universal history

Before we consider the Traditionalist narrative, we will review the other main Western narratives – mythical and tripartite, and also 'universal' – on which the Traditionalist narrative builds. Of these, the mythical and tripartite narratives will be immediately familiar, and the universal narrative somewhat less familiar.

MYTHICAL NARRATIVES

Ancient narratives of human history were part of religious myth. The Judaeo-Christian version of history, with which Islam does not disagree, proposes, as we have seen, three periods: the paradise of the Garden of Eden up to the Fall; the current age (which can be divided into periods before and after the Flood); and then a messianic age, which will see the restoration of the perfection of paradise. The underlying dynamic of decline and (future) recovery is not shared by the Ancient Greek mythical narrative, which had five stages, starting with a Golden Age, which in some ways resembles the Jewish paradise. In the Greek Golden Age, humans and gods are understood to have lived together, and the harmony of sacred order ruled. This Golden Age is followed by a Silver Age of disharmony and a Bronze Age of warfare, which ends with a flood. Then comes a Heroic Age in which much of Greek myth happens, and then an Iron Age, the current age, characterized by injustice and suffering. The dynamic here is one of decline *without* recovery. This Greek chronology, which is found in the *Works and Days* of the poet Hesiod, from about 700 BC,[2] was slightly modified by the Romans, notably by the poet Ovid in his *Metamorphoses* in AD 8.[3] Ovid eliminated the Heroic Age, leaving only four ages (Golden, Silver, Bronze, and Iron). Again, the dynamic is of decline without prospect of recovery, unlike the Judaeo-Christian version of history.

Similar systems can be found in most civilizations. Of particular interest for René Guénon was the Hindu narrative, which has four ages or *yuga*s. It starts with the Age of Truth (*satya-yuga*), in which, once again, humans live in harmony with the gods – and which is, in effect, a Golden Age. This is followed by the Age of Three (*treat-yuga*), in which evil makes its appearance, then the Age of Two (*dvapara-yuga*), in which deceit and suffering grow, and finally the Age of Strife (*kali-yuga*), the current age, in which the gods are absent, and disorder, immorality, and chaos grow. At the end of the *kali-yuga*, a new cycle begins, with a new *satya-yuga*. The Hindu narrative, then, resembles the Judaeo-Christian narrative in offering the prospect of recovery, though with a new cycle rather than a (messianic) new age at the end of one single, linear narrative.

The Hindu narrative is cyclical, and Mircea Eliade maintained that such narratives were once standard. This was the basis of the idea of the eternal return. In the cyclical narrative, history behaves like the seasons of the year, with summer following spring after winter, and then autumn and winter following summer, over and over again. Nietzsche also accepted the cyclical narrative, but it has not generally been popular in the West. This may be because the Christian mythical narrative is not cyclical: the sacrifice of Jesus happens once and once only, and so does the messianic age and the end of the world.

Unlike most versions of the Judaeo-Christian and Greek chronologies, the Hindu chronology assigns durations to its different ages, though there is some disagreement about how long these periods actually are in terrestrial years. According to all reckonings, however, they are extremely long – probably 432,000 years for the current *kali-yuga*. But perhaps these durations are not to be taken literally.

TRIPARTITE PERIODIZATION

The tripartite periodization of ancient, medieval, and modern first emerged in the fourteenth and fifteenth centuries. Before this, the dominant form of historical writing in Europe was annals and chronicles, which recorded events in sequence, and did little to interpret them, save to emphasize the greatness of a particular royal house or pope, or the importance of divine providence. Around 1330, however, the Italian humanist scholar Petrarch proposed a chronology with an ancient age and a new age, divided by Constantine's conversion to Christianity in 312, and suggested that the start of the new age had been dark. This idea was further developed during the fifteenth century by other Italian scholars like Matteo Palmieri and Giovanni Andrea Bussi until the familiar tripartite scheme of ancient, medieval, and modern emerged, with the Renaissance as the dividing line between medieval and modern. This scheme, like the

Judaeo-Christian and Hindu schemes, has recovery following decline, but the recovery is now, in the modern age, not in a hoped-for messianic age or in a new *satya-yuga*. What we think of as the main modern historical scheme, then, actually has a certain amount in common with earlier mythical schemes, but differs from them in placing recovery in the present, not the future.

The tripartite periodization has proved remarkably resilient, even though historians of Europe now tend to divide the Middle Ages into early, high, and late, and the dividing lines have shifted somewhat. The dark ages are now more likely to start with the fall of the Western Roman Empire than with the conversion of Constantine, and modernity may now start with the Enlightenment or even the French Revolution rather than the Renaissance. Some now propose an early modernity, a late modernity, and postmodernity.

Despite its popularity, there are problems with the tripartite scheme. It fits Italian history better than the history of areas like Greece, where the Eastern Roman Empire (known as the Byzantine Empire) survived the Western Roman Empire by many centuries, or Finland, which was never part of any Roman Empire. The Renaissance was a distant event of no immediate significance for Finland and Greece and did not herald modernity for either country. These problems only get worse when one looks beyond Europe. It is hard to fit Egyptian history, where Pharaonic, Hellenistic, and Islamic empires all flourished one after another, into a tripartite scheme. Finally, as has already been noted, all such narratives are ultimately constructions and so, in the end, fictional anyhow.

UNIVERSAL HISTORY

Although not as immediately well known as the tripartite periodization and the Judaeo-Christian mythical account, a number of alternative historical narratives were developed in the form of 'universal' histories, of which the earliest and most influential was published in 1681, some three hundred years after the death of Petrarch, by the French bishop and courtier Jacques-Bénigne Bossuet. This was a *Discourse on Universal History* that started along biblical lines at the beginning of the world with Adam, proceeded through Abraham and Moses to leave the biblical narrative with the Trojan Wars, and thence proceeded via Rome and Carthage to Jesus, Constantine, and Charlemagne.[4] Bossuet's narrative follows a more complex system than the tripartite periodization, and leads up to a different triumph: not the end of the dark ages, but the era of Charlemagne and thus the rise of the Franks, from whom the French claimed descent. Bossuet's *Universal History*, then, was also concerned with recovery following decline, and was in many ways more national than universal, as part of the point was to celebrate the French.

Bossuet's *Universal History* was challenged by Voltaire, who in 1756 surveyed the rise of various civilizations in his *Essay on Universal History*, starting not with Adam but with the Chinese and Indian civilizations,[5] breaking from the biblical narrative. From these beginnings developed an alternative scheme of truly universal history, in which multiple ages coexisted. The rise of Islam, for example, happened a little after the fall of the Western Roman Empire. A similar model was followed by the great German philosopher Georg Hegel, who in 1830 also started with the Chinese and Indian civilizations before moving on to the Greek and Roman. This model differs from the tripartite scheme both in its complexity and in not having any simple narrative of decline and recovery. For Hegel, once a civilization has fallen, it does not rise again.

HISTORY AS PROGRESS

An alternative form of universal history with a stronger narrative that echoed at least the last two parts of the tripartite periodization was also developed during the Enlightenment. In 1751, the French politician and economist Anne-Robert-Jacques Turgot drafted a 'Plan for Two Discourses on Universal History' that gave no space to Adam or the Trojan Wars, and defined universal history as 'the consideration of the successive advances (*progrès*) of humanity and the details of the causes which have contributed to it'.[6] The consideration of advances also included a consideration of obstacles to progress, which included bad and despotic government, oppressive laws, and inequality. Turgot's views were close to those of the Scottish philosopher and economist David Hume, who had written on 'The Rise and Progress of the Arts and Sciences' in 1742.

History as progress, which ended not with Charlemagne and the kingdom of the Franks but with the present day, became well established during the nineteenth century. The pioneering French historian and liberal politician François Guizot delivered his celebrated lectures on the History of Civilization in Europe at the Sorbonne in 1828, demonstrating and explaining European progress from the dark ages through the rationalist rejection of superstition and tyranny to the freedoms and prosperity of nineteenth-century France. These lectures were widely read in many languages. In Great Britain, a genre of what is known as 'Whig history' became established, demonstrating and explaining progress towards the liberties of nineteenth-century Britain. The Whig (liberal) politician Thomas Babington Macaulay was one of the most influential historians of this school.

The progressivist narratives of Guizot and Macaulay were not universally popular, of course. Some saw them as too simple, and today's historians now consider them teleological, often anachronistic, and fundamentally ahistorical. At the time, they were associated with the liberal politics they indeed supported, and were thus rejected by many conservatives. They were also unpopular with many Christians, who rejected the strong connection they made between progress and the decline of religious authority.

Two other historical narratives achieved great popularity during the late nineteenth and early twentieth centuries. One was that developed by Karl Marx with the help of Friedrich Engels. This proposed a prehistoric age in which there were matriarchal 'communist societies' and 'communist households', now often referred to as 'primitive communism'. This was succeeded by slavery, feudalism, and capitalism. These periods were to be followed by socialism and, finally, communism. The Marxist model, then, resembles progressivist universal history in some ways, but is actually closer to the Judaeo-Christian model in starting with a form of primitive paradise and ending with the hoped-for return of paradise in a sort of messianic age.

Very few universal histories of this kind were published in the years after the end of the First World War, which had shattered many people's faith in progress, or after the Second World War. Faith in progress was still to be found in the Soviet Union, at least at an official level, but the Marxist model declined in popularity as Marxism itself did, and the notion of a golden age of primitive communism is now almost as discredited as the idea of Atlantis.

The only widespread post-Second World War model that stressed progress was the astrological one that looked forward to an Age of Aquarius, which became ever more popular during the 1960s. The Age of Aquarius belongs in a model of astrological ages that is based on what astronomers call 'axial precession', the gradual change in the orientation of the earth's rotational axis over cycles of approximately 26,000 years, which means that the equinoxes move through the constellations. From this, astrologers derive 'ages' of about 2,160 years each, one for each zodiac, and there is general agreement that we are living at the end of the Age of Pisces and the start of the Age of Aquarius, though there is much disagreement about exactly when the change from one age to another happened or will happen. The Age of Pisces was widely associated with hierarchy and Christianity, and the Age of Aquarius – also known as the New Age – with peace and harmony, and spiritual and social progress. Faith in the coming Age of Aquarius, however, declined along with the hippy movement, and the term 'New Age' came to be applied primarily in a pejorative sense to the spiritual ideas of the hippies, understood (rightly or wrongly) as woolly-minded and inconsistent.

HISTORY AS DECLINE

Another once-popular model was developed by the French diplomat, journalist, and novelist Count Arthur de Gobineau, who published his *Essay on the Inequality of the Human Races* in four volumes between 1853 and 1855. This long 'essay' was in fact another universal history, arguing that the rise and fall of civilizations could be understood in terms of race, and also arguing for the superiority of the Germanic Aryan race. Gobineau's model was one of decline, not progress. After an 'age of the gods' when races were pure came an 'age of heroes' with limited racial mixing, then an 'age of nobilities' without renewal, and then 'the era of unity', now well under way, in which there would finally be only one single human race, which would inevitably die out, so that 'the globe, become quiet, will continue, though without us, to describe its impassive circuits in space'.[7] In the twentieth century, Nazi racial ideology enthusiastically adopted Gobineau's view on Germanic Aryan superiority and the undesirability of racial mixing, without adopting his apocalyptic conclusion. Gobineau's model then vanished more or less entirely with the defeat of Nazism and growing awareness of the horrors of the concentration camps. Before then, however, Gobineau's model was more popular than one might think.

After the First World War, universal histories of progress were mostly replaced by universal histories of decline, like that advanced by Gobineau, of which the most widely read was Oswald Spengler's *Decline of the West*. With its first volume published in 1918, *Decline of the West* was translated into many languages and was widely discussed, often by people who had not actually read it. It is one of those books that owe much of its fame to an inspired title.

Many people who have never read Spengler believe that he saw the West as being in decline. In fact, he did not – or at least not in his own time. His book built on the model of rise and fall developed by Hegel, and recorded the rise and fall of successive cultures, starting with those of the Ancient Egyptians and Babylonians before passing through the Indian and Chinese cultures (reversing Voltaire's and Hegel's sequence) to arrive at the Graeco-Roman culture and then, via the Arabs and Aztecs, at the Western culture. The Western culture could be expected sooner or later to decline as all its predecessors had, but that was not Spengler's main point.

Although grand narratives such as Spengler's are no longer favoured by historians, a more recent scholarly work that paints on a canvas almost as vast as Spengler's is Samuel Huntington's 'The Clash of Civilizations', first published in 1993. This focuses on contemporary and future history and understands civilizations as large units similar to Spengler's cultures. Huntington was a political scientist, not a historian, and his theory has been attacked by scholars almost as much as it has been appreciated by large sections of the general public. One of the main criticisms of his work is that it is essentialist – civilizations as he conceives of them, as great, homogeneous, and clearly defined entities, do not actually exist. Also, *civilizations* do not *do* things: states do things, as do people, as do the vast impersonal forces beloved of historians – demography, economics, technology, ideology, and so on. But not civilizations.

The Traditionalist scheme

The Traditionalist historical narrative is a history of decline, not progress. It builds on the familiar tripartite scheme, with some modifications, and also on mythical accounts, including the Judaeo-Christian one. The Traditionalist historical narrative comes in four versions, of which the most important is that of René Guénon.

GUÉNON'S HISTORICAL NARRATIVE

Guénon's main frame of historical reference was, following his emphasis on the Vedas, the Hindu one. He did not adhere literally to the durations of the different Hindu ages, which he saw as symbolic rather than to be taken literally. His conception of history was thus based on the scheme of the four *yuga*s, and the current age is the *kali-yuga* or Age of Strife, as far as it is possible to be from the *satya-yuga* or Age of Truth. Like many other schemes, but unlike the progressivist universal histories of the Enlightenment, his essential dynamic is one of decline. Increasing materialism leads to increasing fragmentation, as division is characteristic of matter, whereas the spiritual or universal is not divided. The starting point is unity and quality, and the end point is quantity. Like the Jewish and Marxist schemes, however, Guénon's scheme offers a prospect of recovery in the future.

Given the great length of the *yuga*s in the Hindu system, even if the number of years assigned to them is not taken literally, almost the whole of the recorded history of humanity, from the sixth century BC onwards, has been spent in the *kali-yuga*. For practical purposes, then, additional systems or subdivisions are needed, and here Guénon used the standard tripartite scheme, but with an important modification: the superimposition on to it of the dynamic of decline, since in Guénon's view subdivisions of great periods like the *yuga*s 'reproduce . . . the general course of the greater cycle in which they are contained'.[8] As in a fractal, the same patterns are reproduced at smaller scales, and the decline that is found from *yuga* to *yuga* is also found within individual *yuga*s, and within their subdivisions.

While for the followers of Petrarch the Renaissance marked recovery from a dark age, a move towards restoring the light of antiquity, for Guénon the Renaissance marked decline from a medieval period where something of the primordial tradition had still been known, and when there had been periodic transfers of that tradition from the East, as when Arabic texts were translated into Latin. Guénon is here referring to the many translations made during the twelfth and thirteenth centuries, when Arab philosophical, medical, and scientific works became available to Latin-reading European scholars. Yes, the Renaissance had renewed the authority of ancient philosophy, as in the standard narrative, but ancient philosophy had not been a repository of primordial truth – rather the opposite. The Greeks had borrowed from the East, but they had then – as quintessential Westerners – changed the ideas that they had borrowed in such a way as to negate much of their value, even if their esoteric teachings may have remained closer to the Eastern originals. They achieved certain aesthetic triumphs, but also the 'individualization of conceptions, the substitution of the rational for the truly intellectual, and of the scientific or philosophical for the metaphysical point of view'.[9] As always for Guénon, 'intellectual' refers to the separate faculty that can perceive the absolute, and 'the metaphysical' refers to the primordial tradition. The 'individualization of conceptions' is bad because the primordial tradition is one, and individual conceptions are multiple: quantity of conceptions thus replaces quality. For Enlightenment philosophers and their successors, the growth of individualization, the rational, the scientific, and the philosophical were all improvements. For Guénon, what mattered was the loss of the truly intellectual and of the metaphysical. Guénon, then, did not challenge the standard tripartite historical narrative, but rejected the meaning commonly attached to it.

Guénon, like Voltaire and Hegel, conceived of multiple ages coexisting. In Traditionalism's universal history, of the Middle Ages, the Renaissance, and modernity were purely Western events. Guénon felt that modernity had not arrived in the East in the way that it had in the West, though he regretted that even so there were an increasing number of Westernized Easterners, individually as far away from primordial truth as were most Westerners. The East was not modern but unchanging, which some Westerners saw as a sign of inferiority. They were wrong. Fascination with change and novelty was a Western problem, not an Eastern one. The collapse that comes at the end of the *kali-yuga* – and thus at the end of Western modernity – will affect the West, not the East.

One factor that Guénon did not bring into his analyses was race. Like most people of his time, he never took issue with the idea that there was such a thing as race in the abstract, but he attached little importance to it, and took issue with the way that certain specific races had been identified.

He denied that there was such a thing as a European 'race', as Europeans were too varied, even though there was certainly a European (Western, modern) *mentality*. He also denied the existence of an 'Aryan' race, describing this as 'an invention of the over-fertile imagination of the orientalists'.[10] Guénon, then, was not a racist. Other Traditionalists, however, were.

EVOLA'S HISTORICAL NARRATIVE

Julius Evola kept Guénon's basic historical scheme but made some modifications that were crucial for some of the views that are discussed in later chapters. At the higher level, he preferred the Graeco-Roman mythical narrative to the Hindu one, and, at the smaller scale, he moved from a simple tripartite scheme to another form of universal history. Generally, he added new details that derived from sources other than Guénon.

In his key early work, *Revolt against the Modern World*, Evola identified the Golden Age with a northern, 'primordial Hyperborean civilization', the Silver Age with a matriarchal or 'gynaecocratic' southern civilization, the Heroic Age with the Heroic Age of Greek and Roman myth, and the Iron Age with modernity. The first two of these associations were less bizarre in the 1920s than they are today. The idea of a Hyperborean (Arctic, 'beyond the north') civilization, now almost entirely abandoned, was popularized in 1903 by *The Arctic Home in the Vedas*, a book by the Indian nationalist Bal Gangadhar Tilak. Tilak relied on imaginative readings of the Vedas to argue that the Aryan race, which included Indians, had originated at the North Pole and had then been forced south. The same idea was then further popularized by the

Nazi historian Herman Wirth in his *The Dawn of Humanity*. Evola was sceptical about this idea from a historical perspective, but felt it worked well at a mythical level.

The idea of a primitive matriarchy derived from the research of the Swiss legal historian Johann Jakob Bachofen and his 1861 book *Mother Right: An Investigation of the Religious and Juridical Character of Matriarchy in the Ancient World*. Although the idea of a historical matriarchy is nowadays more popular than ideas relating to the Aryan race, enthusiastically embraced by some feminists and especially in the Neopagan Goddess movement, Bachofen's book is now as discredited as Tilak's, but was for a long time very influential. It was a major source, for example, of the Marxist idea of primitive communism, which was also seen as matriarchal. The idea of ancient matriarchy lies behind the enthusiasm of some feminists for paganism and shamanism, which are seen as matriarchal rather than patriarchal. Evola's idea of a matriarchal Silver Age retains an appeal today beyond Traditionalists, then, even if his idea of an Arctic Golden Age does not.

Evola's adaptation of Guénon's large-scale historical scheme was the source of three theoretical pairs that were important for his Traditionalism: a male–female pair, corresponding to a solar–lunar pair, borrowed from Bachofen; a warrior–slave pair, borrowed from Nietzsche; and a north–south pair, which he sometimes expressed as an Aryan–Asiatic pair and which sometimes became a northwest–southeast pair. While Guénon denied the existence of an Aryan race, then, Evola did not. Such a position was then still relatively mainstream, as the horrors of Nazi anti-Semitism had then not yet driven the word 'Aryan' out of general use. Evola's anti-Semitism is considered in more depth later on, but it should be noted here that it is not central to his work. He allocated both the Jews and the issue of race in general only a minor, secondary role in most of his analyses. This does not mean, of course, that his anti-Semitism can be morally excused, and he was certainly more of a racist than Guénon. But what was central were the north–south (or northwest–southeast), male–female, and warrior–slave pairs. The last modified Nietzsche's theoretical distinction between the noble master morality of the strong-willed, which he associated with paganism, and the emasculating slave morality of the weak, which he associated with Christianity and democracy.

Just as Evola modified Guénon's large-scale historical scheme, he also modified his smaller-scale, tripartite scheme, adding extra stages. Evola's European history starts with a Golden Age of warriors in the Roman Empire. Then comes decline with Christianity, which, following Nietzsche, he viewed as a religion for slaves, succeeded by a temporary recovery for warriors with the medieval ideal of chivalry, especially during the twelfth century under Barbarossa, the Holy Roman Emperor Frederick I Hohenstaufen. Then comes a further decline through the Renaissance and, especially, the Reformation, finally leading to modernity.

Within Evola's modified, smaller-scale scheme, there is also a north–south dynamic. Firstly, Greek civilization, which was originally Aryan and so northern, adopted democracy from Asia Minor, to the southeast. Those southeastern influences were the elements of the ancient world that the Renaissance revived. Secondly, the Hohenstaufens were, as

Nordic-Germanics, less compromised by southern influences than were other Catholics.

Evola's historical narrative, like that of Guénon, was a narrative of decline. It moved away from Vedanta towards the Graeco-Roman model, however, and incorporated a north–south pair drawn from Tilak (also used by the Nazis) and a female–male pair drawn from Bachofen (also used by the Marxists). It further incorporated ideas of warriors that, as we will see in later chapters, occupy an important place in his thought.

SCHUON'S HISTORICAL NARRATIVE

Frithjof Schuon, in contrast, kept very much to Guénon's tripartite scheme, but merged his Vedanta-derived mythical account with the Judaeo-Christian narrative, sometimes using the concept of the Fall in place of Guénon's concept of decline, and sometimes predicting a form of messianic age rather than a new cycle. This reflects Schuon's general rehabilitation of religion.

'Traditional civilizations,' wrote Schuon, 'despite their inevitable imperfections, are like sea walls built to stem the rising tide of worldliness, error, subversion, of the fall that is ceaselessly renewed; this fall is more and more invasive, but it will be conquered in its turn by the final irruption of divine fire, the very fire of which the traditions are, and always have been, the earthly crystallizations.'[11] 'Having shut himself off from access to Heaven and having several times repeated – within ever narrower limits – his initial fall, man has ended by losing his intuition of everything that transcends himself.'[12]

Some descriptions of the end of the cycle were also closer to the Judaeo-Christian than the Hindu narrative. At the end of the cycle, wrote Schuon, 'separating barriers between the different traditional worlds will have disappeared; in other words, we can say that "Christ", who for the Hindus will be the Kalki *Avatāra* and for the Buddhists the *Bodhisattva* Maitreya, will restore the Primordial Tradition'.[13] 'Christ' may be in inverted commas and compared to the Kalki *Avatāra* and the *Bodhisattva* Maitreya, but the basic idea is still the Christian one of Christ as messiah, not Guénon's idea of a new cycle of *yuga*s.

Schuon, like Evola, used the pair of Aryan and Semitic, but, like other Traditionalists, made little use of the concept of race in his historical narrative. He saw Aryan and Semitic as linguistic groups, as scholars of philology still do, though they now generally refer to 'Indo-European' languages rather than Aryan ones (Hebrew and Arabic are still classed as Semitic). He also went beyond language, however, seeing speakers of Aryan or Semitic languages as 'a psychological group and even a racial group, at least originally'.[14] He associated particular characteristics with these two groups – Aryans were metaphysicians, while Semites were mystics and moralists – but this variety of analysis was not connected with any particular understanding of history. Schuon specifically rejected Gobineau's model, arguing that the mixing of races can have both good and bad consequences. Nor did his analysis fit well with standard anti-Semitic stereotypes, which tended to assign thought to Aryans (metaphysics) and law to Semites (moralists). Schuon divided Semites between Jews and Arabs, and felt that 'the soul of the first is richer but more turned in on itself whereas that of the second is poorer but more expansive, more gifted from the point of view of radiance and universality'.[15] It could be said that Judaism is indeed more 'turned in on itself' than Islam, in that (unlike Islam and Christianity) it does not seek to convert as many people as possible. Moving in the other direction, Schuon considered both Aryans and Semites to be 'white', sharing characteristics that differed from those of the 'yellow' and 'black' races.

Schuon's racial theories, expressed above all in an art icle on 'The Meaning of Race', first published in 1957,[16] make for strange reading now. He discusses the significance of prognathous (projecting) and orthognathous (straight) jaw types, drawing on nineteenth-century racial anthropology, and his stereotypes of different races included discussion of the importance of dancing and tom-toms for the 'black' race, which is envisaged living in a state of innocence in Africa. As remarkable (and indeed objectionable) as these discussions are, they neither draw on nor contribute to Traditionalist theory. Guénon was not a racist, while Evola was, and integrated racism into his Traditionalism. Schuon was perhaps more of a racist even than Evola, and it is remarkable that he was still using the term 'Aryan' in 1958, but he did not integrate racism into his Traditionalism.

NASR'S HISTORICAL NARRATIVE

A final version of the Traditionalist historical narrative was produced by a younger Traditionalist, Seyyed Hossein Nasr, an Iranian philosopher educated in America and a follower of Schuon. Nasr studied at the Massachusetts Institute of

Technology and then did a PhD at Harvard in 1958 on medieval Islamic cosmology. He was trained in modern scholarship in a way that no earlier Traditionalist had been. He refined the Traditionalist narrative of the ancient world and the Renaissance, bringing it much more in line with generally accepted scholarly understandings.

Nasr understood the early period of Greek civilization as being in line with a more general pattern, as 'the ancient Greeks possessed a cosmology similar to that of other Aryan peoples of Antiquity'.[17] The Greeks then moved towards rationalism with Aristotle, but rationalism was never entirely triumphant, and traditional doctrines re-established themselves in late-antique Alexandria. In Nasr's narrative, two tendencies thus became established: a Neoplatonic metaphysics of Alexandrian origin, further developed in the work of the eleventh-century Muslim philosopher Avicenna (Ibn Sina), and an anti-metaphysical rationalism represented in the work of the twelfth-century Muslim philosopher Averroes (Ibn Rushd). While the approach of Avicenna triumphed in the Muslim world, the approach of Averroes triumphed in the Christian West, preparing the way for the development of a natural science and a modern philosophy that entirely excluded the metaphysical and, having severed the connection between the world and the transcendent, proceeded to contribute to the destruction of the environment.

Nasr's version of the Traditionalist narrative of decline, as proposed in a series of lectures given at the University of Chicago in 1966, built on his deep knowledge of the history of philosophy, and led to much the same conclusions as Guénon had reached, while remaining academically respectable. Nasr later returned to the question of the Renaissance, again adopting a more complex understanding. The Renaissance, he conceded, saw 'the rediscovery of Platonism and Hermeticism, and intense interest in the esoteric dimensions of Greco-Alexandrian thought in general and yet [also] movements against the esoteric perspective, interest in the philosophy and practice of magic, and at the same time strong opposition to it. The Renaissance intellectual life seems like a chariot driven by several horses moving for a short period together until the chariot is overturned and each horse gallops off in a different direction.'[18] In the end, however, the Renaissance still sowed the seeds for modernity.

It might have been expected that Nasr's modifications would have made the Traditionalist narrative more acceptable within Western academia, but this did not happen. Nasr himself was accepted by many academics, but not Traditionalism. His more complex narrative was also little taken up, perhaps precisely because it was so complex. This raises the question to what extent the original appeal of the Traditionalist narrative owed something to its very simplicity.

Finally, a comment is needed on Nasr's use of the term 'Aryan' even after it had largely vanished from scholarly use. This may reflect Schuon's use, and it may also reflect Nasr's Iranian origins. Early twentieth-century Iranian nationalism stressed that Iranians were Aryans (the two words even have a common root), and one of the titles of the Shah was *Aryamehr*, 'Light of the Aryans'. During the 1970s Nasr had even been president of Aryamehr University in Tehran. Despite his use of the term 'Aryan', racism is only very occasionally visible in his work.

Conclusion

The Traditionalist historical narrative is second only to Traditionalist perennialism as a foundation of the Traditionalist philosophy. It is the basis of the critique of modernity that we will consider in the next chapter, and is fundamental to Traditionalism's political project. It is both quite standard and quite original. It is standard in that it builds on two of the best-known narratives, the tripartite scheme of periodization (though Evola complicated this) and various mythical schemes: the Graeco-Roman for Evola and the Judaeo-Christian for Schuon. It is unusual in that it is a narrative of decline rather than progress. This is of great importance, given that so many people regard the present and future with a sense of dread.

The Traditionalist narrative is not unprecedented, as narratives of progress belong especially to the period before the First World War, since when narratives of decline, from Gobineau to Spengler and Huntington, have predominated. The Traditionalist narrative builds in part on these universal histories of decline. It is original, however, in that it defines the modern age in contrast to a Golden Age of harmony and sacred order in which humans and gods lived together. This is also a description of the Golden Age of other schemes, including the Graeco-Roman and the Judaeo-Christian, but by Guénon's time neither of these classic descriptions was taken very seriously any longer. The Traditionalist narrative is also original in that the mythical scheme used by Guénon is the Hindu one, giving rise to the term *kali-yuga* to describe the coming age. This term is as important for Traditionalists and their sympathizers as the term 'Age of Aquarius' once was for the hippies.

Finally, the Traditionalist narrative is sometimes somewhat racist. Guénon denied the existence of an 'Aryan' race, and Nasr used the term occasionally, but neither incorporated racism into Traditionalism. Schuon wrote a remarkably objectionable article on 'The Meaning of Race', but again did not incorporate racism into his Traditionalism. Evola, in contrast, did. Even so, his historical narrative is far less reliant on racism than is that of Gobineau.

The Traditionalist historical narrative is, as has been said, the basis of the Traditionalist critique of modernity. We will now consider this critique.

CHAPTER 5

The Traditionalist Critique of Modernity

Traditionalism's historical narrative leads to a critique of modernity that is as fundamental to Traditionalism as is perennialism. This critique builds on a long tradition in Western thought, just as Traditionalism's perennialism and its historical narrative do. But it is more total, more all-encompassing.

Ever since the establishment of the tripartite periodization of ancient, medieval, and modern, there has been discussion and disagreement about the main characteristics of modernity. At first, some emphasized the recovery of ancient learning. Since the Enlightenment, and especially since the mid-nineteenth century, social scientists have often emphasized rationality and individualism, seeing both as enhanced by secularization, and have looked forward to further progress towards modernity, or even postmodernity. In this chapter, we will first consider this positive understanding of modernity.

Not everyone is so positive, however. As we will see, the somewhat idealistic picture of modernity as secular rationality and individualism has often been challenged, including by Traditionalists, who see modernity as the *kali-yuga* or Age of Strife. That is the position that this chapter will then consider, showing how it in part agrees with the positive understanding of modernity but more fundamentally challenges this understanding, and how it also in part agrees with earlier challenges to the positive understanding, but takes these further and melds them into a complete whole.

Ideal modernity

The tripartite periodization which emerged from Petrarch and other Italian thinkers led inevitably to the question of what the characteristics of the current modern period might be, and – finally – to the use of the term 'modernity' to describe those characteristics.

During the seventeenth century, there was a famous debate about the ancients and moderns in France, which gave rise to various understandings of what might characterize modernity. Those who took the part of the ancients maintained the primacy of ancient culture, while those who took the part of the moderns maintained the superiority of modern culture. Charles Perrault, in his *Parallel of the Ancients and the Moderns*, published at the end of the seventeenth century, supported his argument for the superiority of the moderns by pointing out that Homer had no problem with the idea of Zeus beating his wife, something that a well-mannered modern Frenchman would not do.

Our current conceptions of modernity, however, appeared somewhat later. According to the great contemporary German defender of Enlightenment values, Jürgen Habermas, 'Hegel was the first philosopher to develop a clear concept of modernity.'[1] It was Hegel who developed the idea of the *Zeitgeist* or spirit of the times and asked what the current *Zeitgeist* was. Given that he was a philosopher and was especially interested

in 'spirit', the characteristics of his times that Hegel emphasized were somewhat abstract: freedom and rationality. One
aspect of freedom was individualism. In public life, thought
Hegel, civil law made space for the rational pursuit of one's
own interests. In politics, individuals could participate in the
political process. In the private sphere there was individualism, later understood by Habermas as 'ethical autonomy and
self-realization'.[2] In modernity, these three spheres – public
life, politics, and the private sphere – were becoming increasingly independent of each other, in contrast to earlier periods,
during which they had been held together by religion. This is
the basic understanding of modernity that others then developed, and which Traditionalism challenged.

A later and equally important theorist of modernity was
the German sociologist Max Weber, who distinguished between charismatic, traditional, and rational-bureaucratic
authority, and identified the last of these three with modernity. Charismatic authority is what a religious leader like
a prophet has, traditional authority is what a king has, and
rational-bureaucratic authority is what a letter from a government department has. Weber famously argued that the
Protestant ethic lay at the origin of capitalism, and associated modernity and rationality with the decline of older
(Catholic) forms of religion. He coined the term disenchantment (*Entzauberung*) to describe this.

Though the understandings of modernity of Hegel and
Weber both proceeded from the abstract and cultural, they
also considered the institutional supports of modernity: civil
law, political systems, the autonomy of the private sphere, and
bureaucracy. Another great nineteenth-century theorist, Karl

Marx, reversed this order, emphasizing first and foremost not institutions but their material and economic underpinnings, which were also the underpinnings of modernity. What underlay everything, he proposed, was bourgeois capitalism. Capitalism, also understood as industrial civilization, thus joined rationality, secularization, and freedom as a characteristic of modernity.

Marx and Engels also described modernity, which they called 'the bourgeois epoch', in terms of change. 'Constant revolutionising of production, uninterrupted disturbance of all social conditions, everlasting uncertainty and agitation distinguish the bourgeois epoch from all earlier ones. All fixed, fast-frozen relations . . . are swept away, all new-formed ones become antiquated before they can ossify. All that is solid melts into air.'[3] This view was echoed by the French poet Charles Baudelaire, for whom 'modernity is the transient, the fleeting, the contingent'.[4] Contingency and ever-increasing speed of change were thus added to the characteristics of modernity. There is, in fact, a widespread perception that change happens with ever-increasing speed, a perception that some see as an optical illusion: because we know more about events in more recent periods than in earlier periods, more recent periods seem to contain more events than earlier periods do.

It was not only Marx whose understanding of modernity focused on its material underpinnings. Others also went beyond freedom, institutions, and capitalism to factors like urbanization, means of communication, technology, and demographic change. This materially oriented approach was distinguished from the study of modernity by labelling it the study of 'modernization'. Modernization, which is material, may produce modernity, which is abstract. The distinction is not always easy to maintain, however. Scientific discoveries, for example, might be either material, and thus an aspect of modernization, or abstract, and thus an aspect of modernity. Perhaps scientific knowledge and the scientific method are aspects of modernity, while the *applications* of that knowledge are aspects of modernization.

One understanding of modernity, then, is as a state of rationality, freedom, individualism, ethical autonomy, and self-realization, all underpinned by secularism, capitalism, and rational-bureaucratic authority, and perhaps also by modernization in the form of urbanization, means of communication, technology, and demographic change. This positive understanding has often been challenged, however, first by philosophers and thinkers from Marx to Hannah Arendt, and then by the Traditionalists.

Modernity critiqued

Not all views of modernity were quite so positive. The rationalist materialism of the Enlightenment was quickly challenged by writers, poets, and artists, as Isaiah Berlin pointed out in his discussion of the 'Counter-Enlightenment', and this challenge extended to the rationalist materialist view of modernity. The Romantic movement's enthusiasm for the medieval, the Gothic Revival, and the Pre-Raphaelites were all, explicitly or implicitly, critiques of modernity. Even Hegel identified a problem with modernity: alienation. The individual might not see quite how much social, political, and economic freedoms in fact facilitated individual self-realization, and might instead just experience autonomy as separation, isolation. Weber went further, drawing attention to the risk that modern systems might trap individuals in a 'steel-hard casing' (*stahlhartes Gehäuse*), often termed an 'iron cage' in English. The negative impact of the iron cage of bureaucracy was explored in the work of the Austro-Hungarian surrealist writer Franz Kafka.

Alienation was a problem that Marx also examined in detail. For Hegel, the problem was that a modern person might *feel* alienated; for Marx, the problem was that modern people *were*, objectively, alienated. The industrial worker was in principle autonomous, but could not in practice behave autonomously within a capitalist system. Workers were alienated from the products of their labour, and so could gain no self-realization from it. Humans, in general, were ruled by vast impersonal forces that they could not control, 'like the sorcerer, who is no longer able to control the powers of the nether world whom he has called up by his spells'.[5] Marxism is generally understood as a critique of capitalism, but it was also a critique of modernity. With the help of the Marxist critique, alienation has become almost as well established a characteristic of modernity as rationalism.

A similar argument was made at about the same time by the English art critic and socialist John Ruskin, who wrote ironically that the idea of the 'division of labour' was misunderstood: what was actually divided by modern capitalism were men, 'divided into mere segments of men – broken into small fragments and crumbs of life' by industrial capitalism. Factories turned people into tools, and to do this, to 'make their fingers measure degrees like cog-wheels, and their arms strike curves like compasses, you must unhuman-ize them'.[6]

Some critiques of modernity were based not in socialism but in religion. The Danish philosopher Søren Kierkegaard lamented that the 'present state of the world' was a dis-ease. The Word of God could not be heard for all the noise that the world was making through 'empty communication [that] is designed merely to jolt the senses or to stir up the masses, the crowd, the public, noise!'. 'Everything is soon turned upside down,' continued Kierkegaard: 'communica-tion is indeed soon brought to its lowest point with regard to meaning, and simultaneously the means of communication are indeed brought to the highest with regard to speedy and overall circulation.'[7] Concern about the negative impact of the media is older than we might think.

Friedrich Nietzsche's critique of modernity was based around his understanding of the consequences of the 'death of God', a development that he, unlike Kierkegaard, did not entirely regret, as he felt that Christianity reversed nat-ural values, a process he called 'transvaluation'. However, the death of God could lead to nihilism, and to a society in-habited by the 'last human' (*letzter Mensch*), conventionally translated into English as the 'last man', the inhabitant of the modern world. In 1883 Nietzsche wrote of 'the most de-spicable human . . . the last human who makes everything small. His species is ineradicable like that of the ground-flea.' Nietzsche's last human asks in bemusement 'What is love? What is creation? What is longing? What is a star?'[8] Some-times, Nietzsche seems to have been writing poetry as much as philosophy. Alternatively (and preferably) the death of

God could lead to the development of a superior being, an *Übermensch*, free of the limitations of tradition and conventional morality.

In France, the lay Catholic theologian Jacques Maritain also critiqued modernity, notably in his 1922 book *Antimodern*. This book was contemporary with the Traditionalist critiques to which we will soon turn, and took a similar approach. There may have been technical progress since the Middle Ages, argued Maritain, but spirituality has declined, leaving 'a naturalist world, dedicated by a science that is material, mechanical and violent to the service of human pride and luxury, perfectly configured in political and economic life to the hateful will of a Master who is not God'.[9]

The Second World War led to renewed critiques of modernity. These critiques are so well known that it suffices to mention a few names. Hannah Arendt's famous critique of totalitarianism also included a critique of modernity. For Arendt, modernity involved the loss of tradition, religion, and authority, and the problematic consequences of these losses were clear in the ways in which human beings had become principally employed labourers rather than free actors and workers, and in the way that bureaucratic administration had emerged and had then facilitated the emergence of totalitarianism. A comparable critique was made by two leading theorists of the Frankfurt School, Theodor Adorno and Max Horkheimer, who confronted the problem that the advance of reason, science, and knowledge had culminated not in human liberation, as was once expected, but in enslavement and the Holocaust.

An even more fundamental critique was made by the

philosophers who gave rise to the movement known as postmodernism. These philosophers, notably Michel Foucault and Pierre Bourdieu, questioned the very concept of rationality, and demonstrated that many of the apparent achievements of modernity, from state-funded education to psychology, were in fact constructions that served the interests of power, and that modern culture sometimes served not self-realization but self-repression.

Critiques of modernity became even more general during the 1960s, as the counterculture rejected the values and certainties of Western materialism and turned to alternative models. The Beatles went to an ashram in India, yoga took off across North America and parts of Europe, and interest in alternatives to Western modernity became more and more general.

There were, then, viable alternatives to Hegel's idealistic Enlightenment-derived conceptions of modernity. An alternative to understanding modernity as a state of rationality, freedom, individualism, and ethical autonomy is to understand it as a state of alienation and nihilism in which the last human is trapped in an iron cage and is subject to uncontrollable impersonal forces, or to totalitarianism. Capitalism alienates workers from the products of their labour and breaks them into fragments or turns them into machines. A modern person cannot hear God through the empty noise of the media, knows not what love is or what a star is, and follows a master who is not God. Traditionalism's critique of modernity, to which we will now turn, is more comprehensive than any of the non-Traditionalist critiques we have now reviewed, but also echoes them in many ways.

CHAPTER 5

Guénon's modernity

Guénon's critique fitted with the historical narrative that identified modernity with the *kali-yuga*, and also fitted with his concept of the primordial tradition. The characteristics of the *kali-yuga* were known from the Hindu texts. It was a period during which humanity became ever more separated from the divine, as in Western modernity with Nietzsche's death of God or the liberation from religion celebrated by the Enlightenment. For Hegel and many of the thinkers of the Enlightenment, liberation from religion allowed reason and liberty to triumph. Guénon turned this around: a side effect of the veiling of the sacred was the triumph of reason.

For Guénon, modernity was the opposite of tradition. This, thought Evola, was what made his work so special. There were many critiques of modernity, but no other critique was organically related to a 'positive counterpart' in the way that Guénon's was.[10] As the opposite of tradition, which is the norm, modernity is abnormal – an important point that Guénon often repeated. Much that modern Westerners think is 'essential to human thought',[11] like the idea of 'progress', is in fact nothing of the kind, but merely a collection of ideas that have become current in the West since the eighteenth century.

Modernity is characterized by a particular type of mentality, and Guénon referred often (and always disparagingly) to the 'modern mentality', which is inherently anti-traditional. The modern mentality includes faith in civilization, progress, and science, and a fascination with action. The characteristics of modernity include the growth of individualism and of sentimentality, social chaos, and the general triumph of the

102

material. All of these are actually the contrary of the characteristics of traditional society, argued Guénon, but modern Westerners do not realize this. This is not just ignorance: for things to be understood as the contrary of how they should be understood, for the abnormal to be seen as normal, is also a characteristic of modernity. In the same way, the growth of materialism has a deeper cause: the increasingly material nature of manifestation. The first age was undivided, and as the undivided nature of the first age declines through increasing materialization and division, manifestation moves away from quality towards quantity. The *kali-yuga* is the realm of quantity. Guénon's critique of modernity is found throughout his work, but is most clearly expressed in his *The Crisis of the Modern World*, published in 1927, and in *The Reign of Quantity and the Signs of the Times*, published in 1945.[12]

Guénon held that in the modern West, the related ideas of progress, civilization, and science are 'idols of modern worship' and of a 'lay religion' that create a 'gigantic collective hallucination'.[13] Western civilization is thought by most to be the result of both material and moral progress, but this is not true. Material progress certainly exists, though it is worth less than is generally supposed. Hopes for increases in 'bodily comfort' are illusory, as material progress simply creates new wants. 'Modern civilization aims at creating more and more artificial needs.'[14] The struggle to fulfil these artificial and imaginary needs leads people to devote ever more time and energy to making money. Material progress, then, actually produces less leisure, not more. Material progress may also ultimately prove fatal, as many realize, seeing the great progress in armaments. 'It does not need much imagination,' wrote Guénon in

1930, 'to picture the West ending by self-destruction, either in a gigantic war compared with which the last one [the First World War] will seem negligible, or through the unforeseen effects of some product which, when unskilfully manipulated, would be capable of blowing up, not merely a factory or a town as hitherto, but a whole continent.'[15] The Second World War was certainly gigantic, and, although it did not lead to the complete self-destruction of the West, it was indeed more terrible in many ways than earlier wars had been. No continent has yet been blown up, but the unskilful manipulation of atomic weapons or carbon fuels is widely feared to be leading to consequences comparable to those that Guénon imagined.

Moral progress, unlike material progress, cannot be judged by an objective standard. It is subjective, and often a delusion, as 'those whose tendencies are in harmony with those of their time cannot be other than satisfied with the present state of things'[16] – that is, people who share in contemporary morality will inevitably understand the present state of things as progress in relation to the past.

Second only to the belief in progress and civilization, held Guénon, comes the belief in science. Those who are most enthusiastic about the progress of science are generally not scientists themselves, and in fact are often those who least understand what scientists are actually proposing. They are believers in things they do not actually know about. The West has certainly excelled at science, but as a form of knowledge it is extremely limited. Science is valid in its own sphere, but only because that sphere is so limited. What lies beyond that sphere – the spiritual and the transcendent – is either ignored or said to be unknowable or even nonexistent. That the West has excelled in the natural sciences reflects partly the materiality of modernity, and partly the way in which modern Westerners have lost all interest in the traditional sciences, those that – like numerology (the symbolism of numbers) – are connected to metaphysics. They excel at things which traditional civilizations would have regarded as trivial, like chemistry.

For Guénon, science is of limited significance, dependent upon quantity (often statistics) and experimentation, and interested in realities that are less universal than those described by metaphysics. And to the extent that it is also dependent on reason, modern philosophy is no better. It cannot access the metaphysical. Modern philosophy, like modern science, first ignores realities that cannot be directly perceived, then denies their existence, and finally contributes to a situation in which modern Westerners are increasingly incapable of perceiving anything that lies beyond their senses. The nonphysical world that was of such importance to all other human civilizations, past and present, simply vanishes. What instead becomes important is that which is most purely quantitative: money. Economics becomes the supreme science.

Science is also within the realm of action, in contrast to the traditional metaphysical sciences, which are within the realm of contemplation. The modern Western inclination towards action is overdeveloped, and modernity is thus characterized by the 'need for ceaseless agitation, for unending change, and for ever-increasing speed, matching the speed with which events themselves succeed one another'.[17] Marx and Baudelaire would not have disagreed. This ever-increasing speed, holds Guénon, is characteristic of the end of the *kali-yuga*: time is actually passing faster. That is why all that is solid vanishes into air.

Guénon not only condemned the idols of progress, civilization and science, but also attacked belief in originality, individualism, and sentimentality. He agreed with Hegel that an emphasis on the individual is a crucial characteristic of modernity, but interpreted this very differently. For Guénon, truth was ancient, not new, and certainly not individual or 'original' in the modern sense. Those who value what is new thus miss the value of ancient truth. Emphasis on the originality of individual ideas blocks access to true metaphysical ideas, which are neither original nor the creation or property of any one individual.

The growth of individualism is combined with the growth of uniformity. This applies both to people and to societies. Modern centralized administrations treat all persons as identical, and actually do their best to make them identical. 'The democratic ideal . . . demands that one and the same education shall be given to individuals who are most unequally gifted, and who differ widely both in talents and temperament.'[18] Democracy and equality, in practice as well as in principle, try to make every individual as similar as possible to every other individual. Uniform education is more effective in burying the unusual abilities of the few than in encouraging abilities that the majority do not have. Knowledge is reduced to the mediocre, to the lowest level of understanding.

In modernity, craftsmanship is replaced by industry, the products of which are standardized and uniform. Guénon lamented, echoing Ruskin, that 'the workman in industry cannot put into his work anything of himself, and a lot of trouble would even be taken to prevent him if he had the least inclination to try to do so'.[19] The ideal industrial worker is actually a human machine. 'Servant of the machine, the man must become a machine himself, and thenceforth his work has nothing really human in it.'[20] Identical workers live in identical apartments, consuming identical goods. The industrial worker becomes almost 'a body without a soul'.[21] Furthermore, the modern Westerner 'wants to impose [uniformity] on other peoples, together with the whole gamut of his own mental and bodily habits, so as to make all the world uniform, while at the same time he imposes uniformity on the outward aspect of the world by the diffusion of the products of his industry'.[22] Weber's 'steel-hard casing', Kafka's vision of bureaucracy, and Marx's alienation make similar points.

Not only is action valued over contemplation in the modern West, but 'feeling [is] stronger than intelligence'.[23] Modern Western civilization is sentimental. Some consider the material and the sentimental as opposites, but Guénon argues that in fact they are closely related, as sentiment is 'bound up with matter'.[24] This is one cause of the decline of religion, as is seen most clearly in Protestantism, which is a very modern form of religion. Protestantism is exclusively sentimental and moralistic, with almost no interest in doctrine, and no interest at all in the metaphysical. Protestants regard the simplicity of religious doctrine as a measure of its truth, 'as if religion ought to have been made for idiots'.[25] Those who wish to reduce religion to its most democratic form necessarily deny its esoteric element, which is inevitably difficult to grasp. The morality of such religion has nothing to do with the esoteric. There is often no significant difference between Protestant morality and lay morality, in fact. Protestantism claims to be a religion, but questions revelation to the point where it in effect denies it, and then provides the critical tools that allow others to attack other religions in similar ways. Guénon is referring to the advanced textual criticism carried out most of all by German Protestant theologians that turned Christianity's sacred texts into problematic historical documents.

Another cause of the decline in religion in modernity is compartmentalization. In contrast to traditional societies such as those of the Islamic world, where many aspects and acts of everyday life have a religious quality, the religious and the everyday are rigidly separated from each other in the modern West. Religion is assigned its own distinct place and restricted to that place.

For Guénon, the decline and withdrawal of religion contribute to social chaos. In the absence of a hierarchical system, and under the influence of the modern ideal of equality, it is thought that 'any man may exercise almost indifferently the most diverse functions, including those for which he is not in the least fitted, while material riches are generally accepted as the only real mark of superiority'.[26] Democracy means 'the exclusion of all real competence, which is always at least a relative superiority, and therefore belongs necessarily to a minority'.[27] Democracy is incompatible with sacred order.

The 'idols of modern worship' are, of course, the contrary of what should be worshipped, and Guénon developed the concept of 'inversion' to understand this, echoing Kierkegaard's concern that things were turned upside down and

Nietzsche's concern that natural values were reversed. Inversion is characteristic of the final phase of the *kali-yuga*, since 'the most complete absence of all principle implies a sort of "counterfeit" of the principle itself'.[28] This is why modernity, which is abnormal, appears normal. 'The modern world has precisely reversed the natural relations between the different orders of things', for example in valuing the material and the sentimental over the intellectual,[29] and in valuing the lesser aspects of the traditional sciences, like chemistry, which were developed into the modern sciences, over their higher, metaphysical aspects, like alchemy. Decline is seen as progress, slavery as freedom, uniformity as individualism, and so on. Most of the iconic values of liberalism are actually the opposite of what they seem. The overriding importance attached to economics and to the material is also a form of inversion. Social relations are reversed in the name of equality, which, being in fact an impossibility, leads instead to false hierarchies, for example when it is alleged that the people are sovereign and rule themselves. Democracy gives power to the lowest, while legitimate power can in fact derive only from the highest, that is to say from spiritual authority.

The 'secular religion' that worships the 'idols' of progress, civilization, and science is really a 'counter-religion',[30] worse than Protestantism, which is merely a 'pseudo-religion'.[31] Even worse, there is also further subversion of tradition in the form of 'counter-initiation', which is not just a counterfeit of the true initiations that lead to self-realization – which we will discuss later – but the parody of true initiation. Counter-initiation gives rise to spiritualism, the once-very-popular occultist attempt to communicate with the spirits of the dead, and to the identification of intuition with the subconscious, the lowest aspect of the human being, rather than with the highest, spiritual (in Guénon's terms, 'intellectual') aspect – this modern misunderstanding of the term 'intuition' being an example of the falsification of language, also a characteristic of inversion. It also gives rise to psychoanalysis, which privileges the inferior, and takes its victims on a descent into hell.

Later Traditionalist views

Evola's understanding of modernity followed Guénon, and was again influenced by Nietzsche, so that modernity for Evola was characterized not only by the problems that Guénon identified – especially democracy – but also by the triumph of the slave mentality and the disappearance of the noble warrior. Instead of noble warriors, there are so-called 'aristocrats', and 'the hands of modern aristocrats seem better fitted for holding tennis rackets or cocktail shakers than swords or sceptres'. Similarly, 'the archetype of the virile man is . . . a boxer or . . . a movie star . . . or the busy and dirty money-making banker and the politician',[32] not the warrior. Evola was even harder on money-making than was Guénon, and his criticism of bankers and businessmen sometimes becomes anti-Semitic, which Guénon's never did. Dirty money-making is identified with the Jews once in passing in *Pagan Imperialism*, and once at more length in *Revolt against the Modern World*. He never thought that modernity was mainly the fault of the Jews, however. During the 1920s and 1930s, his principal criticism of modernity was that the modern state is 'socialistic, democratic, and anti-hierarchical'. The fundamental problem was the secular nation-state. Evola's critique of modernity, then, was more explicitly political than Guénon's.

Evola differed from Guénon regarding the relationship between modernity and the West. Modernity was indeed an expression of the Western spirit, but for Evola the Western spirit was capable of more than this, and so should not be rejected just because of its responsibility for modernity. Science was not always bad, as 'methodical knowledge' was superior to irrationalism, and even technology had value, if it was understood as 'the exact knowledge of obligatory laws in the service of action'.[33] The laws with which technology engaged were also worth understanding, and technology could be put to good uses.

Evola brought gender into his critique of modernity, which Guénon had not. One consequence of the disappearance of hierarchy and of virile men was the emancipation of women, who have 'claimed for themselves a "personality" and a "freedom" according to the anarchist and individualist meaning usually associated with these words'.[34] Instead of having real men and real women – concepts that will be further examined in a later chapter – modernity had 'mixed beings lacking all contact with the forces of their deepest nature . . . for whom sex is reduced to the physiological plane . . . beings who, in the deepest recesses of their souls, are neither men nor women, or who are masculine women or feminine men'.[35] This, and the related 'universal and feverish interest in sex', was characteristic of 'the terminal phase of a regressive process'.[36] Further, 'In a civilization where equality is the standard, where differences are not linked, where promiscuity is in favour . . . it is in no way a surprise to see the alarming increase in homosexuality and the "third sex".[37]

Evola pointed to a further problem with modernity that he felt Guénon had ignored, the 'deconsecration of nature'.[38] He blamed this on the dualism of Christianity, which separates the natural from the supernatural. He did not go into this question in much detail, but, as we will see in a subsequent chapter, this view was developed further by later Traditionalists.

After the Second World War, Evola sharpened his critique of modernity, at first focusing especially on economics, the modern emphasis on which had already been criticized by Guénon. Evola went further, labelling the economy as 'demonic', and arguing that 'modern capitalism is just as subversive as Marxism. The materialistic view of life on which both systems are based is identical.' 'As long as we only talk about economic classes, profit, salaries, and production,' he wrote, 'and as long as we believe that real human progress is determined by a particular system of distribution of wealth and goods, and that, generally speaking, human progress is measured by the degree of wealth or indigence – then we are not even close to what is essential.'[39] Then, as the 1960s began, Evola added an analysis of alienation to his anti-capitalism, noting the increasing numbers of '"rebels without a cause", the "angry young men" with their rage and aggression in a world where they felt like strangers, where they saw no sense, no values worth embracing and fighting for'.[40] The rebellion against modernity was understandable, but the lack of a cause was problematic. 'Global protest,' wrote Evola,

'lacks any higher principle: it is irrational, anarchic, and in-
stinctive in character',[41] appropriate for a society made up of
a 'shifting mass of "individuals", devoid of organic connections, a mass contained by external [exoteric] structures or
moved by collective, formless, and unstable currents'.[42]

Evola's critique of modernity, then, built on and extended Guénon's, adding the decline of virility, socialism, female
emancipation, the deconsecration of nature, and capitalism.

Schuon similarly built on and extended Guénon's critique. Modernity for Schuon was 'the final cyclic phase',[43]
as it was for Guénon. Schuon tended to explain modernity,
however, not only in terms of the veiling of the sacred, but
also in terms of the unfortunate consequences of the triumph of science and industry, 'the social consequences of
mechanization and the human condition this engenders'.[44]
Science, he claimed, has led to relativism:

> man's mind more and more depends on the climate
> produced by its own creations: man no longer knows how
> to judge as a man, namely in function of an absolute which
> is the very substance of the intelligence; losing himself in
> a relativism that leads nowhere he lets himself be judged,
> determined and classified by the contingencies of science
> and technology.[45]

Industrial society, which Schuon followed Guénon and
Ruskin in understanding as the triumph of the machine, also
dehumanizes us. 'Since we cannot humanize the machine,
we are obliged, by a certain logic at least, to mechanize man,'
wrote Schuon.[46] Modernity has lost its transcendent character, and so 'society's entire reason for being is removed, and

there remains only an ant heap in no way superior to any other ant heap since the needs of life and thus the right to life remain everywhere the same, whether it is a question of men or insects'.[47]

The Traditionalist fellow-traveller Jordan Peterson's critique of modernity builds not on Guénon or the idea of the *kali-yuga* but on Arendt and, especially, on Nietzsche's understanding of the 'death of God'. He has often used the Nietzschean term 'nihilism' to characterize the crisis of modernity. His critique, however, echoes Guénon with regard to the consequences of the veiling of the sacred, or at least of the mythical, and the consequences of the triumph of reason and of modern science. His 'modern mind' differs little from Guénon's 'modern mentality'.

For Peterson, the growth of 'experimental science' has led to the loss of access to the 'mythic universe' and of understanding of symbolic meaning. 'The formal object, as conceptualized by modern scientifically oriented consciousness,' writes Peterson, 'might appear to those still possessed by the mythic imagination . . . as an irrelevant shell, as all that was left after everything intrinsically intriguing had been stripped away.'[48] Instead, 'Nihilism, alter ego of totalitarianism, is response to experience of the world, self and other, rendered devoid of certain meaning, and therefore allowed no meaning; is reaction to the world freed from the unconscious constraints of habit, custom and belief.'[49] This, aided by contemporary 'radical leftists', has produced chaos, conflict and 'psychological and social dissolution'.[50]

Conclusion

The Traditionalist critique of modernity builds on both Traditionalism's own historical narrative and on a long tradition in Western thought. Many of the aspects of modernity that Traditionalism lamented had been lamented before. What was new was, as Evola noted, the pairing of a critique of modernity with a positive alternative to modernity – tradition. Evola was right, though there are other examples of such a pairing that he did not mention, for example that by Marx, whose communist utopia once provided a compelling alternative to capitalist modernity.

The dominant Western understanding of modernity, one might think – following Habermas, Hegel, and the Enlightenment – is a positive one of rationalism, liberty, and secularism. In fact, however, this positive understanding has been repeatedly challenged. The critiques of Marx and Ruskin abhorred the consequences of modern capitalism for the industrial worker, while Kierkegaard and Nietzsche noted the negative consequences of the death of God. Weber saw a steel cage, and Kafka shone a light on it. Foucault and Bourdieu saw self-repression where others had once seen liberty. Arendt saw rational bureaucracy leading not to self-realization but to the Holocaust.

Guénon agreed with those who proposed a positive understanding of modernity that there was a relationship between secularism and the rise of reason, but saw what was gained through the rise of reason as being far less valuable than what was lost with the veiling of the sacred. This was itself a consequence of the *kali yuga*. In the *kali-yuga*, quantity reigned and the material triumphed over the metaphysical. As a result of a gigantic collective hallucination, the modern mentality worshipped false idols, notably material and moral progress, and science. Science indeed brought some material progress, but at a cost: industrial production turned workers into machines. Moral progress was an illusion. Inversion led people to think the abnormal was normal, and to mistake slavery for freedom, and uniformity for individualism.

This is a more all-encompassing criticism than most, as, while other critics condemned aspects of modernity, Guénon condemned all of it. Aspects of modernity that others had noted and critiqued in isolation were all explained by one ultimate cause. While Marx paired his critique with a future utopia that might one day exist, Guénon paired his critique with a past that, he contended, had once existed, and still might exist in the East.

Guénon's counterpart to modernity, tradition, was of course also a construct. There was no real evidence that his traditional world had ever existed. In some ways, it might be argued, it was simply the contrary of what he most disliked about modernity. If modernity was materialist, tradition must have been spiritual. If modernity was uniform, tradition must have been hierarchical.

Later Traditionalists built on this critique. Evola made it more political, taking aim at the modern nation-state, and lamenting the disappearance of hierarchy and of virile men. Schuon focused especially on the triumph of science and industry. Jordan Peterson placed modern ideology in opposition to myth, and did not refer to the *kali-yuga*. For Evola and Schuon, Guénon's placing of modernity in opposition to tradition remained central, as did his placing of the material in opposition to the sacred. So too his identification of the deepest cause of modernity: not capitalism and industry as for the Marxists, not a steel cage or the death of God, but time itself, the *kali-yuga*.

This, together with Traditionalist perennialism, is what is most foundational to the Traditionalist philosophy. One other foundation, however, needs to be considered before we can move on to the Traditionalist project itself, and that is the difficult question of what, if anything, should be done about all this.

CHAPTER 6

Traditionalism, Thought, and Society

The last of the foundations of Traditionalism is its position on how and when thought can change society. This is not a question as old or as fundamental as the questions of religious variety, the rise and fall of civilizations, or modernity. But it is still a well-established question. Does thought change society directly, addressing and convincing everyone, or does it change society indirectly, by changing the terms of a debate, or through the minds of a powerful few? The answer to this question determines what actions people who want to change society take. The great mass ideologies of the twentieth century addressed all of society directly, when possible establishing control over the mass media to do so. Traditionalism, in contrast, is not a mass ideology. It addresses the few, who may then change society indirectly. This approach is the basis of the Traditionalist project, except in the case of the Traditionalist fellow-traveller Jordan Peterson. It was also the approach taken by the French Enlightenment philosopher Denis Diderot and recommended in the early twentieth century by the Italian communist Antonio Gramsci, and was finally adopted by today's radical right.

Direct and indirect

One of the earliest discussions of the impact of thought on society is found in the New Testament, where the disciples are commanded to go into the world and preach, since 'he that believeth and is baptized shall be saved; but he that believeth not shall be damned'.[1] This is the starting point of the dominant Western view on the topic. Thought is understood to have a decisive direct impact on the individual. However, it is not only the individual who is important. The community also matters. Saint Paul advised the early Christians to 'consider how to stir up one another to love and good works, not neglecting to meet together . . . but encouraging one another'.[2] The community, then, also has an impact on the individual. Thought changes the individual directly, and also indirectly, by changing the community, which in turn changes the individual.

During the Middle Ages, preaching directly to individuals to secure their salvation was widespread. The Catholic order that is generally known as the Dominicans is in fact officially called the Order of Preachers. This preaching was generally oral, given that those who were being preached to were almost always illiterate. The focus was on the direct impact of thought on the individual more than on any indirect impact on the individual through the community.

New approaches to the impact of thought on society emerged with modernity, however. One of the great achievements of the early Enlightenment thinkers was the *Encyclopaedia* edited by Denis Diderot, which was as much a manifesto as a reference work. Diderot's *Encyclopaedia* includes a long article by Diderot himself in which he discusses its purpose. Certain entries, Diderot wrote, might 'covertly attack, unsettle, or overturn certain ridiculous opinions which one would not venture to disparage openly . . . The silent effects of [this] would necessarily be perceptible over time.'[3] A respectful but critical approach to certain prejudices 'acts very quickly on good minds, and ineluctably and without any disagreeable consequence, silently and without scandal, on all minds', with the ultimate effect 'of changing the common mode of thinking'.[4] Diderot, like other Enlightenment thinkers, sees thought having an impact on society in two stages: first on 'good minds', and then on 'the common mode of thinking'.

Diderot's approach to the impact of thought on society can be identified with a stage of modernity that is called 'bourgeois', because it impacted primarily the new class of comfortably wealthy laymen who were then replacing ecclesiastical scholars as the centre of European intellectual life. While during the Middle Ages manuscripts had been the concern of a small group of professional scholars working in Latin, by Diderot's time the spread of printing and literacy, as well as of wealth and so of leisure, meant that books such as the *Encyclopaedia* were read in local languages like French by a much larger group, not as part of their work as professional scholars, but for their own private interest. Some see in this development the emergence of a 'public sphere' in which there could develop a public opinion that could have an impact on the actions of the state, leading over time to participatory political systems and ultimately to democracy.

Bourgeois modernity was followed by what some call

'mass modernity', in which the crucial group was the new class of urban industrial workers, increasing numbers of whom could be reached by the new mass media: newspapers, radio, and then television. These mass media differed from the books read by Diderot and his followers, which, though cheaper than medieval manuscripts had been, were still expensive. The new mass media reached everyone, not just the bourgeoisie.

The possibility of addressing large numbers of people directly brought a new approach to the impact of thought on society: the attempt to organize and direct the masses. Socialists were among the earliest to grasp the new possibilities. The proletariat, when fragmented, was at the mercy of the capitalist system. Once class consciousness had been achieved by propaganda and agitation, the proletariat could become a force that might change history.

There was, however, a paradox: while ideas could change society, the ideas which were dominant in any society served the interests of the dominant classes. In a capitalist society, the dominant ideas served the interests of the bourgeoisie, or so the communists felt. For the Nazis, ideas produced by the group that the Nazis believed to be dominant – the Jews – also impacted general ideas. For both communists and Nazis, then, although ideas impacted individuals directly, social groups also impacted ideas, and sometimes these were the wrong social groups, impacting ideas and individuals in the wrong way. What mattered most was not the ideas, but the underlying social groups, and structures of power. Totalitarian regimes were therefore careful to limit or eliminate particular social groups, and to place the mass media under their own control.

Mass modernity has now been replaced by something else, as media technologies have changed and as service economies and automation have replaced large-scale industry. This has led to yet another approach to the impact of thought on society. Now, one of the most influential theorists of the relationship between thought and society is the early twentieth-century Italian communist Antonio Gramsci, who went beyond the classic Marxist view that those in power determined what is thought, and argued that the ways in which things are understood have a direct impact on how things are done. This perspective is one of the things that lie behind current concerns about how particular groups are named, since (following Gramsci) how we name a group has an effect on how we conceive of it, and thus in the end also on how we treat it. Gramsci was close to Diderot in emphasizing how the common mode of thinking can be changed indirectly. His ideas have been adopted by the radical right, which uses the term 'metapolitics' to describe how political change may be produced by changing the terms of a debate.

Understandings of the relationship between thought and society, then, have varied over time. The early Christians and medieval Christian preachers emphasized the direct impact of thought on individuals, though they also recognized the indirect impact of the community. Diderot, writing for a small bourgeois class, emphasized the indirect impact of thought. The mass media brought a new focus on direct impact, followed by a renewed emphasis on indirect impact today, typified by Gramsci and the radical right's idea of metapolitics.

The Traditionalist model

The Traditionalist starting point is closer to the communists and the Nazis than to Diderot or Gramsci: it is not so much the ideas that matter as the structures that produce them. The key structure, however, is not capitalism or the Jews, but the *kali-yuga*. Guénon saw the *kali-yuga* as having a decisive impact on both society and ideas, though he did also sometimes speculate that individuals or groups were promoting modernity to serve their own interests. Given that the nature of modern society was characteristic of the *kali-yuga*, there was little possibility of changing the common mode of thought. This is why Guénon, unlike the thinkers of mass modernity, never directly addressed either overtly political issues or the masses. The masses, by definition, were incapable of understanding truth, given that they were the victims of Western modernity. Truth was, again by definition, accessible only to the few. To the extent that there was any possibility of changing society, this was by changing underlying attitudes, not by addressing political issues directly; here, Guénon was moving a little towards Diderot and metapolitics. 'Modifying the mental outlook of a people is the one and only means of bringing about any deep or lasting change, even in the social sphere.'[5] The Traditionalist project, as a result, is essentially intellectual.

Guénon's position did not, however, exclude all hope. Thought had two possible impacts. One was on the individual: like the early Christians, Guénon regarded understanding as a path to the divine for particular people. The other possible impact was not on modern society as it now stands but on the coming transition from the *kali-yuga* to the new cycle. Here Guénon saw a possible role for an 'intellectual elite' that was in some ways the counterpart of Diderot's 'good minds'. Guénon's intellectual elite, of course, was not intellectual in the normal sense of that word, but in the sense that the primordial metaphysical tradition is intellectual. In some ways, Guénon's elite might be better labelled a spiritual or metaphysical elite, or an esoteric elite. His discussions of this intellectual elite and its role, first advanced in his *Introduction to the study of the Hindu Doctrines* in 1921, are elaborated especially in his *East and West* in 1924.[6] What mattered was quality, not quantity, as 'spiritual power is in no way based on numbers'.[7]

Guénon saw the collapse that comes at the end of the *kali-yuga* as happening in three possible ways. It might happen that Western civilization would sink into barbarism and vanish, like other vanished civilizations of the past. In this case, there was nothing to be done. Alternatively, 'Eastern peoples, in rescuing the Western world from this incurable decay, would assimilate it by consent or by force, either as a whole or in respect of some of its component parts.'[8] Under these circumstances, the presence of an 'intellectual nucleus, even if consisting of a small elite' that understood tradition, might act as intermediaries between West and East.[9] A third possibility was that Western civilization would succeed in reconstituting itself, in relearning from the East what it had forgotten of perennial truth, and perhaps even in using this to smooth the transition to the new cycle. Again, this could only be the work of an intellectual elite. A fourth possibility, less often floated than the three outlined above, was that there might be a temporary recovery before the end of the *kali-yuga*. While real recovery can be expected only with the start of a new cycle, the dynamic of decline is not only a straight line. There is thus always a possibility that, 'at moments when the downward tendency seems on the point of prevailing definitively in the course of the world's development, . . . some special action intervenes to strengthen the contrary tendency, and to restore a certain equilibrium'.[10] This special action would, once more, be the work of an intellectual elite.

This, then, is the analysis that motivated Guénon to recover the primordial tradition, even though the nature of the *kali-yuga* is such that modernity cannot be changed. An intellectual elite may help the transition to the new cycle, or perhaps temporarily restore a certain equilibrium. But it is not the only motivation; there is also the direct impact of thought on the individual. The attempt to re-establish the West on an Eastern metaphysical basis would not succeed quickly, even if it were to succeed. However, those who attempted it, 'while having no hope of ever seeing it come outwardly to flower . . . would reap many other satisfactions from it, gaining for themselves inestimable benefits'.[11]

In principle, any Eastern system might be used to reconstitute the West. In practice, certain systems are easier than others for Westerners to understand. Guénon's preferred solution was at first for Westerners to return to their own Catholic tradition, given that differences in traditional forms reflected differences between the mentalities of different peoples. Westerners would always have a need for exoteric religion, which neither the Chinese nor the Hindu tradition could supply. However, the Chinese tradition is easier for

Westerners than the Tibetan, and the Indian is easier than the Chinese. Hence Guénon's reliance on the Hindu tradition in his writings. There was also Islam, of course, but in the 1920s Guénon felt that, although Islam is closest of all to the Western mentality, it was unsuitable because there was more prejudice against Islam in the West than there was against Hinduism, and this prejudice and fear might well attach to any intellectual elite organizing itself on an Islamic basis.[12] He later changed his mind on this point.

Guénon devoted considerable effort to establishing his intellectual elite, partly through the Traditionalist journal *Études traditionnelles*, and also through an extensive correspondence that he maintained over many years with readers of his books and of the journal. The journal and the correspondence established and sustained a global network of Traditionalists. In a way, then, Guénon's main project was successful. What he would have recognized as an intellectual elite did actually come into existence.

This elite was always informally organized. Guénon considered that metaphysical doctrines could never be reduced to one single system, and that any attempt at formal organization would fail, as any organization would inevitably be joined by unsuitable persons, who might 'be led astray by the prospect of some immediate social action, perhaps even political in the narrowest sense of the word, which would be the most disastrous thing that could happen'.[13] Guénon was probably thinking of those who sympathized with Fascism.

Later developments

Later Traditionalists agreed with Guénon regarding the difficulty of changing anything in the *kali-yuga*, the pointlessness of appealing directly to the masses, and also the possible impact of a small elite. Julius Evola, however, looked for a rather different elite from Guénon's, not so much intellectual as activist, while Frithjof Schuon had little hope for any change in society, and saw the function of a spiritual elite as being primarily the transmission of esotericism.

EVOLA'S ARISTOCRATIC ELITE

When Evola first discovered the writings of Guénon, he was already active in groups that were on the fringes of both Italian Fascism and the German right. He was thus already engaged in attempts to influence the thoughts of political actors and the development of society. This engagement was reflected in the three possible approaches to the coming collapse of the West that he outlined in *Pagan Imperialism* in 1928. One was to do nothing and withdraw into isolation, an idea which he considered more seriously in the post-war period than in 1928. Another was to hasten the triumph of 'progress', and thus the end of the current cycle and the start of a new cycle. This is an idea that he did not explore much further. A third possible approach was for a small number of people to 'unite . . . in the call to consciousness and to revolt'.[14] This is the project that he himself engaged in, and which is most associated with his name in Traditionalist thought.

Two weapons, he argued, were needed to fight modernity. The first was an elite, which differed somewhat from Guénon's intellectual elite, as Evola felt that the mere presence of 'an elite acting behind the scenes of history' on Guénon's model would not make any difference. 'Tradition has always existed in this subterranean sense and it still exists today . . . yet the presence of Tradition in this sense has not prevented the decline of Western civilization.'[15] Instead, the elite that was needed was 'an aristocracy, a race of masters, of rulers', to be created by 'inner renewal' and 'bringing out, conscientiously and tenaciously, new differences, interests, and new qualities from the undifferentiated substance of the individuals of today'.[16]

The second weapon was 'a movement, a revolt from the depths',[17] led perhaps by the aristocratic elite. This revolt would break the existing system and make way for a new one. Quite how is discussed in a later chapter, on Traditionalist politics. It was not, however, to be brought forth by a direct appeal to the masses. Yes, 'action and control are exerted by means of ideas' and may be 'applied to the task of awakening energies, movements, and social currents . . . of exerting on the masses', but such ideas are purely instrumental. A ruler must not believe them himself, 'he must not accord to them any absolute value whatsoever, but instead must regard them coldly as means, as fascinating tools'.[18]

SCHUON'S SPIRITUAL ELITE

Schuon, in contrast, wrote much less of an elite or of social change than either Guénon or Evola, but did establish a sort of elite that had more impact on society than either Guénon's or Evola's did. Schuon's elite consisted of the members of the Sufi order that he founded and ran, and also of followers who were committed to him and his teachings, but were not members of his Sufi order. This was his central project.

That Schuon wrote less about an elite was in part because he did not concern himself with the possible impact of Traditionalism on society. He broadly agreed with Guénon that society could change only if mentalities changed. 'The error of modern man is that he wants to reform the world without having either the will or the power to reform man, and this flagrant contradiction, this attempt to make a better world on the basis of a worsened humanity, can only end in the very abolition of what is human.'[19] But even if reforming mankind was impossible, 'one should in any case reform oneself'. However, one should 'never believe that inward realities are of no importance for the equilibrium of the world',[20] as 'bad example is not alone in being contagious'.[21] This appreciation for the impact of good example, however, falls far short of Guénon's hopes of an elite guiding the West through the transition to a new era. When Schuon writes of the spiritual elite, his point is not its possible impact on the equilibrium of the world, but its function in transmitting esotericism, and the fact that the spiritual elite is, always and everywhere and of necessity, small.

Schuon also took issue with Guénon's views on the possible impact of the East on the West. Firstly, he challenged Guénon's idealized picture of the East, which he thought 'was already in a state of great decadence at the time when Western expansion began, though this decadence can by no means be compared with the decadence of the modern West'.[22] This decadence, 'the decay of a physical organism worn out with age', meant that Hinduism had 'los[t] some of its actuality or vitality', though it still retained its original spirituality.[23] Secondly, he insisted that Western civilization was based on Christianity and should remain Christian. 'One cannot set aside this intellectual and mental formation, however weakened it may be.'[24]

Schuon's group had a rudimentary, informal organization, as certain favoured followers devoted themselves full-time to accompanying and assisting Schuon. Beyond this, the standard Sufi model was followed, with a *khalifa* or representative established in each country in which Schuon had a following – which was, by the end of his life, most of the major countries in Europe, the Americas, and parts of the Muslim world. Unusually in Sufism, both the existence of this order and its membership were kept secret. This practice, which is closer to Western initiatic societies like Freemasonry than to anything that is known in the Muslim world, has begun to be relaxed somewhat in recent years. Even so, the size of the Sufi order that Schuon founded is unknown. Its impact is now probably less significant than it was during the second half of the twentieth century.

Both the followers of Guénon and those of Schuon included a number of ordinary people who simply read Traditionalist works and followed Traditionalist norms. Many followers also contributed to the Traditionalist corpus, writing in Guénon's journal and its successors, and also writing books, some of which were aimed at other Traditionalists and had a small circulation, while others were aimed at the general public and on occasion had a wide circulation. Huston Smith's *The World's Religions* was a long-time bestseller in the United States, though less popular in Europe, and books by Seyyed Hossein Nasr, such as *Islamic Life and Thought* and *The Need for a Sacred Science*, were also widely read, though never quite bestsellers. We will consider some of these books in more detail later on. Schuon's followers were generally more influential than those of Guénon, given both the number of books these followers wrote and the size of their readerships. Some of them also held influential positions, mostly in academia but occasionally also in political life, for example in Bosnia and Jordan, as we will see in a later chapter. This may not have been exactly the elite that Guénon had envisaged in the 1920s, but it was still an elite of sorts. Other Traditionalists, who did not follow Schuon, may also have felt part of an elite. This in itself has contributed to the impact that they have had over the years: self-confidence and a sense of mission make people more effective.

PETERSON'S YOUTUBE FOLLOWING

The single exception to the rule that Traditionalists do not address the masses directly is the Traditionalist fellow-traveller Jordan Peterson, who started putting recordings of his University of Toronto lectures online in 2013, and in 2016 published a video entitled 'Professor against Political Correctness' that brought him a wide general audience. Over the following five years, this video was watched over 500,000 times, and several later videos each collected five million views on YouTube. His book 12 *Rules for Life: An Antidote to Chaos* sold five million copies in the first few years after its 2018 publication, and his accompanying video had been watched 19 million times by the end of 2022.

This was not exactly a mass audience of the sort that the communists and the Nazis once addressed. The earlier lectures were originally aimed at university students, and even the later ones would be hard to follow for those who came to them without some preparation. *12 Rules for Life* was aimed at a wider audience than Peterson's earlier work, but was still not always easy reading. If not exactly a mass audience, however, the following Peterson attracted was far larger than the sort of small elite proposed in Guénon's model, and after 2016 Peterson became a direct and prominent participant in the public political debate. In 2018, the American economist and blogger Tyler Cowen was cited in the *New York Times* as saying that Peterson was 'the most influential public intellectual in the Western world'.[25] This was something of an exaggeration, but Peterson was certainly very visible. His direct approach to the public was very different from the indirect approach of other Traditionalists.

Peterson's books and videos, which have attracted more public attention than the work of any other Traditionalist, have also attracted more opposition. His videos and his combative sound bites have made him a major target for opponents of 'hate speech', and thus also a subject for disputes over free speech. He has been defended as well as condemned. He is more often ridiculed than taken seriously in such media as the *Guardian* and the *New York Times*, and a visiting fellowship that he had been offered at Cambridge University was withdrawn in 2019 (though then restored in 2021). He was banned from Twitter in 2022 after refusing to delete a post that Twitter judged offensive. All this has, of course, added to his fame.

CHAPTER 6

Conclusion

The question of thought and society presents a central paradox for Traditionalism. On the one hand, modernity, with all its abnormalities and its blindness to tradition, is inevitable, explained by the *kali-yuga*. There is no point in addressing the masses, as they will never understand. Nothing can be done save to look to oneself and await the new era. On the other hand, Traditionalists have often been very active, especially in recovering and spreading knowledge of the tradition. This knowledge, however, is not aimed at the masses but at an elite: intellectual for Guénon, aristocratic for Evola, and spiritual for Schuon. Here the Traditionalists come close to the position of Diderot, who hoped that 'good minds' might absorb the views of the Enlightenment and then change 'the common mode of thinking', and of Gramsci, who argued that the ways in which things are understood have a direct impact on how things are done. The views that the Traditionalists value, of course, are very different from those that Diderot or Gramsci valued.

The Traditionalist position on the impact of thought on society, then, is fundamentally different from that of modern mass ideologies. This is partly because of the absoluteness of the Traditionalist critique of modernity, which is seen as the opposite of the sacred tradition, and this follows in turn from the Traditionalist view of history as decline. Traditionalist perennialism might in principle be combined with different approaches to the question of how and when thought can change society, and might in theory be the basis of some kind of mass ideology, but in practice this has never happened, as

Traditionalist perennialism has always been combined with the Traditionalist view of history and modernity.

The Traditionalist view of history and modernity, like Traditionalist perennialism, is distinct from the views taken by others on central questions relating to myth, religion, history, and the nature of modernity. Traditionalist perennialism is a version of a philosophy that goes back to the Renaissance, and exists also in universalist and academic forms. What Guénon added to perennialism was the insistence that understandings of the esoteric primordial tradition must be drawn from authentic sources, and that these were absent from Western modernity. Guénon looked outside the West to Vedanta and the East, while later Traditionalists looked outside modernity to myth, religion, and (in the case of Huston Smith) 'wisdom traditions'. This gave rise to a very fundamental and absolute critique of modernity, paired with a positive alternative: tradition. The pair of tradition and modernity was explained in terms of a view of history as decline that, again, was not entirely new, but which tied the two parts of the pair neatly together.

So much, then, for the foundations of the Traditionalist philosophy. They are interesting in themselves, partly because they present such a radical alternative to more established views. They are also interesting because they are the basis of the Traditionalist project, and it is to this that we will now turn.

PART II

Core projects

CHAPTER 7
Self-realization

The earliest application of the foundational ideas of Trad-itionalism was to the project of self-realization, which Guénon simply called 'realization'. As we will see, understandings of quite what self-realization was differed from one Traditional-ist to another, but all agreed on the importance of this project, and also agreed that it involved the fulfilment of one's true nature through some form of consciousness of the transcend-ent. In contrast, non-Traditionalist understandings of self-realization, of which there are many, often omit the sacred.

The two other major applications of the foundational ideas of Traditionalism, discussed in subsequent chapters, are to Traditionalism's religious and political projects, and individual realization always runs parallel to these other applications. In religion, Traditionalism tends towards Islam (though not ex-clusively); Islam at the exoteric level is generally accompanied by esoteric realization through Sufism. In politics, Tradition-alism tends towards the radical right, but this is also gener-ally accompanied by esoteric realization, though not through Sufism. Julius Evola identified three alternative paths to real-ization: the path of action, the path of asceticism, and the path of devotion. The path that fitted best with politics, he thought, was the path of action.

Non-theistic paths to realization

Paths to self-realization and the models of existence on which they depend can be broadly classified as naturalistic, theistic, or non-theistic. Naturalistic models and paths rely on laws that are not supernatural – that is, they are 'natural'. The Big Bang is a naturalistic model of the origin of existence. Naturalistic explanations tend to be materialist, and do not generally imply any particular path to self-realization, other than, perhaps, the maximization of well-being or the minimization of income inequality. They will not be considered further.

Theistic explanations are often taken as the main alternative to naturalism. An explanation of existence in terms of creation is a theistic model, whether it is monotheistic, as when the Creator is the one true God, or polytheistic, as when Gaia emerges from the void and gives birth to Uranus. Theistic models and theistic paths depend on a deity or deities. They are not the only alternatives to naturalism, however. There are also non-theistic models and paths that are not naturalistic, as in the case of the Advaita Vedanta, which Guénon took as the basis of his understanding of the primordial tradition. Guénon also referred to other systems, notably Sufism, Taoism, and Scholasticism. Taoism is non-theistic, while Sufism and Scholasticism integrate non-theistic models and paths into theistic religions. Traditionalist understandings of self-realization are generally non-theistic. This derives from Guénon's rejection of Catholicism in favour of Vedanta, and reflects the general rejection of theistic models that accompanied the general Western loss of faith in Christianity.

Before turning to Guénon's understanding of the path to

self-realization, this chapter will discuss its sources in Advaita Vedanta, Sufism, and Neoplatonism, the late antique development of Plato's work that survived the advent of Christianity in various, often hidden, forms. Neoplatonism is our starting point because it is the non-theistic system best known to Westerners and is the basis of the technical vocabulary used in Western languages. Even so, it is not now widely known, though once it was. Neoplatonism is also important for Sufism, which is the basis of much later Traditionalist thought and practice, and for Scholasticism. It also has something in common with Advaita Vedanta, which was the main basis of Guénon's thought. A full survey of non-theistic systems of self-realization would take a book in itself, so for Taoism this chapter will simply repeat the famous opening lines of its central text, the *Tao Te Ching* (literally, The Book of the Way and Virtue):

> The Tao that can be told is not the eternal Tao
> The name that can be named is not the eternal name.

That Neoplatonism, Advaita Vedanta, Sufism, and Scholasticism all have something in common in their views of reality and prescriptions for self-realization is an important support for the perennialist view of the relationship between religions and traditions. It is relatively easy to explain in historical terms in the cases of Neoplatonism, Sufism, and Scholasticism, because we know that Neoplatonic texts were translated from Greek into Arabic and Latin, so that the discussions started by the Neoplatonists were continued by Arab Sufis and Latin Scholastics. It is less easy to explain the relationship between Neoplatonism and Advaita Vedanta, as no comparable translations have survived, but Greeks and Indians were in contact in the Persian capital, Persepolis, at the time of the early Greek philosopher Pythagoras, whose influence on Plato is visible, in the sixth and fifth centuries BC so a possible, if unproven, route does exist. There are also, as we will see, two further possible, though also un-proven, historical explanations of how Neoplatonism and Advaita Vedanta have much in common. Traditionalists, of course, prefer metaphysical explanations to historical ones.

NEOPLATONISM AND SCHOLASTICISM

Neoplatonism is a later development of the Ancient Greek philosophy of Plato and Aristotle. The most important Neo-platonist philosopher was Plotinus, who was born in Hellen-istic Egypt in about AD 204 and died in Rome in 270, and wrote in Greek. He never used the term 'Neoplatonic' and in fact drew on Aristotle as well as Plato. It has been suggested that he may also have been drawing on the Vedanta, as his own teacher in Alexandria, about whom almost nothing is known, is reported by one source to have inspired in him a desire to learn more of the teachings of the Persians and Indians. This is one of the two further possible historical explanations of simi-larities between Neoplatonism and Vedanta: that Plotinus may have been drawing on a teacher who drew on Vedanta.

Scholastic Neoplatonism emerged in Europe when An-cient Greek and Neoplatonic texts became available in Latin translation just as the European university system was be-coming established in the thirteenth century. Universities were at first called 'schools', and 'scholastic' thus really means 'academic'. Philosophers at the University of Paris were especially important, as they were reading texts by Plato, Aristotle, Plotinus, and followers of the latter. Scholasticism is thus a non-theistic system within a (Christian) monotheistic framework. It is not always Neoplatonic, and the leading Scholastic philosopher Thomas Aquinas was in fact hostile to many Neoplatonic ideas. Scholastic Neoplatonism, like Scholastic philosophy as a whole, ended when modern philosophy became established. Modern philosophy uses different methods and texts to debate different questions.

To understand Neoplatonism, we have to go back to the original Plato. He wrote on many topics, but what is of most import for Neoplatonism is his theory of 'forms', which are part of the Platonic model of existence or cosmology. This theory proposes that, in addition to the familiar world of things we can touch and feel, there is another world, or sphere, of 'forms' or ideas. As well as a red rose and a red traffic light in this 'sensible' world (sensible because we can sense it, not because it necessarily makes any sense) there is the form of redness in the world of forms. The redness of my rose is just one of many instances of redness on earth, and is not perfect redness. Redness in the world of forms, however, is perfect, and one. The same principle applies to shapes as to colours – the triangle, for example – and also to objects. A triangular pastry combines two forms, the triangle and the pastry. Pastry, too, has a form.

Plato was also convinced that the human soul (*psyche*) is immortal, has a transcendent or divine origin and – under certain circumstances – can remember its origin and what it once knew, including the forms. This was also part of his model, and gives rise to a path: 'A man who employs such memories rightly is always being initiated into perfect mysteries and he alone becomes truly perfect; but since he separates himself from human interests and turns his attention toward the divine, he is rebuked by the vulgar, who consider him mad and do not know that he is inspired.'[1] Plato is here using the term 'initiated' metaphorically, comparing the philosopher to the actual initiates of the Eleusinian Mysteries or the Orphic Mysteries of Dionysus. Quite what their admission or initiation involved was secret and has never become known, but it was thought to lead to a special position in relation to the divine. This is the origin of the concept of initiation, which is of great importance to Traditionalists.

Plotinus took Plato's system and added to it the idea of the 'First Cause', which came not from Plato but from Aristotle. The idea is that if every result must have a cause, and if each such cause must itself be caused, then either the chain of causation goes back indefinitely, or there is, somewhere, a first, self-caused cause. If the first cause is the cause of everything, it is also the cause of the forms; and the forms are the cause of the sensible world. The First Cause cannot be investigated further; it contains everything in itself; it is singular. It can thus be called 'the One', and this is what Plotinus, and perhaps also Plato, did call it. Plotinus also called the sphere where the forms are, which is clearly not a world like the sensible world, *nous*, 'the Intelligence' or 'the intellect'. This gives rise to a simple model of the One → the Intelligence → the sensible world. Put differently, the sensible world emanates from the Intelligence, which emanates from the One.

The next stage in Plotinus' work was to introduce the soul into this structure. A person consists of body and soul, and the soul has a form, just as the body does. The human soul, however, does not reflect a form directly in the way that a triangle does. Instead, there is another intermediary, also (confusingly) called soul, which may also be termed 'Universal Soul' for the sake of clarity, so that the model now becomes the One → the Intelligence → the Universal Soul → an individual person's soul. The individual soul is then divided into a higher and lower soul. The higher soul is in touch with the Universal Soul, while the lower soul is in touch with matter. The number of emanations thus increases, as does the complexity of the cosmological model.

Connecting this model with Plato's understanding, Plotinus then argued that any individual soul, which is part of the Universal Soul, may move in either of two directions: towards matter in the sensible world, or towards the One. And the individual soul that moves towards the One may perhaps actually meet the One, in which case it becomes part of the One – which of course is what it was in the first place, as all proceeds from the One, and the One contains everything in itself. This is union (*henosis* in Greek). The starting point of the journey back to the One is knowledge, as a means to the soul remembering what it once knew, as it was for Plato. What characterizes the later stages of the journey is not explained in the texts that have survived. Putting this slightly differently, the Platonic path to self-realization begins in understanding the model, but does not end with this understanding.

The Scholastic philosophers who encountered the Neoplatonic system, which is really non-theistic as its references to 'the divine' are not to any particular deity, could either reject it or attempt to reconcile it with the monotheistic system of Christianity. Aquinas ultimately rejected it, as did many Catholic theologians who were not philosophers. Some Scholastic philosophers, however, reconciled Neoplatonism and Christianity, including Anselm of Aosta, an Italian monk of the Benedictine order who became Archbishop of Canterbury in 1093; Albert of Lauingen, better known as Albertus Magnus, a German friar of the Dominican order who became Bishop of Regensburg in 1260; and Eckhart of Hochheim, better known as Meister Eckhart, a German Dominican monk who was condemned for heresy and died around 1328. All these Christian Neoplatonists, in one way or another, identified the First Cause with the Christian conception of God. They used the term 'mystical union' (*unio mystica* in Latin) to denote the Neoplatonic union (*henosis*), giving rise to one sense of the modern term 'mysticism'. All, as monks and friars, were already ordained, which is a form of initiation comparable to initiation into the Eleusinian or Orphic Mysteries, not a metaphorical initiation as in Plato's usage. They all engaged in a variety of ascetic practices – poverty, celibacy, prayer, fasting, retreat, and so on. The communal life of the monastery, in which they participated, is also a form of spiritual practice. Scholastic Neoplatonists did not explicitly identify the start of the path to self-realization as being an understanding of the model, but their version certainly does not exclude this.

Since the First Cause contains everything in itself, once it is understood as God, it becomes difficult to maintain an absolute separation between Creator and created. The idea that God and the world are not separate is sometimes described as 'pantheism', but this is a difficult term, which means very different things for different people. It was at one point used as a euphemism for a form of atheism that was developed from the work of Baruch Spinoza, which has nothing at all to do with Neoplatonism. For some, it means that God is in the world – and nowhere else. This is not a Neoplatonic position.

The Scholastics developed a terminology to distinguish the Neoplatonic higher and lower soul. The two Latin words *spiritus* and *anima* had previously been used more or less interchangeably, but *spiritus* now came to be applied especially to the upper soul, and *anima* to the lower soul. The *anima* animates the physical body. This distinction is central also to the Sufi understanding, and thus to Traditionalism.

ADVAITA VEDANTA

Advaita Vedanta (literally, the end of the Veda) is an interpretation of the Upanishads, ancient Hindu texts from between the eighth and third centuries BC. The most important philosopher of Advaita Vedanta is Shankara, who lived during the eighth century AD, and is said to have been born in Kerala in southwest India and to have died in Kedarnath, high in the Himalayas. He wrote in Sanskrit. It is not certain that the texts now attributed to him are all entirely by him, and it has been suggested that his later followers may have been in touch with Sufis, which is the second of the two further possible historical explanations of similarities between Neoplatonism and Advaita Vedanta. In this case, Advaita Vedanta would be drawing on Sufi Neoplatonism. Again, this is unproven.

Shankara, like nearly all Hindu philosophers, worked with the pair of *brahman* (ultimate reality; literally, growth) and *atman* (soul; literally, breath). In this model, *brahman* has no origin, is beyond time, space, and thought, and is the essence of everything. It resembles the One of Neoplatonism. The *atman* is the eternal essence of the individual, following a logic found also in Hebrew and Arabic, where the word for 'soul' is also the word for breath. A living thing breathes; when it no longer breathes, it is dead.

One of the questions that occupied Hindu philosophers was whether *brahman* and *atman* are separate or the same. A parallel question related to *prakriti* (nature) and *purusha* (soul, like *atman*). Dualists maintained that *prakriti* and *purusha* are separate, whereas non-dualists like Shankara maintained that *brahman* and *atman* are the same. Only *brahman*, taught Shankara, is real. The conclusion of this argument is the same as that of the Neoplatonists, that the soul is ultimately contained within the One. Reality, then, is one, a position that differed from the standard dualistic approach, which is also the approach of the monotheistic religions, which emphasize the absolute distinction between humanity and God. Shankara emphasized the difference between *brahman* and the sensible world in terms of unity and plurality – *brahman* is single and the world is multiple – and in terms of action – *brahman* is unchanging, and the world is characterized by change. He also saw *purusha* as a principle from which things are born, and *prakriti* as matter, in a formulation comparable to Platonic form and matter. The final and crucial pair is of *paramatman* (supreme soul) and *atman*. *Atman* is the individual soul, and *paramatman* gathers all *atman* together, making it the equivalent of the Universal Soul of Neoplatonism.

For Shankara as for other Hindus, a person seeks *moksha* (liberation), freedom from the cycle of death and rebirth and associated sufferings. *Moksha*, in Shankara's view, could be achieved even in life, and involved *yóga* (union) with *brahman* – rather like Plotinus' *henosis* and the Scholastics' mystical union. The Sanskrit term *yóga* is the origin of the English term 'yoga' to denote a popular relaxation process that is derived mostly from *hatha yóga* (forced *yóga*, focusing on control of the body). The starting point of Shankara's path to self-realization is again knowledge, as it was for Plotinus. Thereafter, Shankara recommended a form of contemplation that merged the particular into the general. This leads to an awareness of *brahman* that actually is *brahman*.

Shankara belonged to the Hindu *sannyasa* (ascetic) tradition, and is seen as the organizer of the Dashanami ('ten names') group of ascetic lineages. *Sannyasins* (ascetics) commonly start the ascetic path with a *diksha* (initiation), and then follow a number of ascetic practices, including poverty, celibacy, prayer, fasting, and retreat that are similar to those followed by Christian monks in the Scholastic period. The communal life of the *ashram* (monastery) is also a form of spiritual practice, as is the communal life of the monastery. The model and path provided by Advaita Vedanta, then, are comparable with those provided by Scholastic Neoplatonism and, as we will now see, by Sufism.

SUFISM

Sufism (a term of obscure origin) is an interpretation and application of Islam, originating about one hundred years after the death of the Prophet Muhammad in AD 632. One of the most important philosophers of Sufism is Muhyi al-Din Ibn Arabi, who was born in Murcia in Spain, then part of the Muslim world, in 1165, died in Damascus in 1240, and wrote in Arabic. He is contemporaneous with the Scholastic philosophers of Europe, with some of whom he has much in common. It was Ibn Arabi whose texts and theories were studied in Cairo by Abdul-Hadi, the Sufi of Swedish origin who passed his understandings to Guénon.

Sufi theology is a branch of Islamic theology and draws both on Islam and on Islamic philosophy, which is itself a development of Greek philosophy, and especially of Neoplatonism. Just as Scholastic philosophers in Europe used Ancient Greek and Neoplatonic texts in Latin translation, so Islamic philosophers used much the same texts in Arabic translation. The Arabic translations were made three or four centuries before the Latin translations, and many of the early translations into Latin were actually made from Arabic, not from the original Greek.

Islam is very much a monotheistic religion, so the great problem facing Arab Neoplatonists was how to reconcile the non-theistic conception of the One with the conception of God. This was solved by understanding the One as the Necessary Being (necessary because a first cause is necessary), and equating the Necessary Being with God, a solution that was later adopted by the Scholastic Neoplatonists. The Intelligence and the Universal Soul could then be translated into Arabic without much difficulty, and their details discussed and debated. *Henosis* was variously understood as union, inhabitation, and knowledge. Again, the details were much discussed and debated.

The idea that God and the world are not separate, which follows from the idea that the One contains everything, proved controversial. The doctrine of the Unity of Being (*wahdat al-wujud*, sometimes translated into English as 'pantheism') has been much discussed, both in terms of to what extent it is compatible with mainstream Islamic theology, and in terms of what different people who used the term actually meant by it. This is not always clear, partly because the idea is so controversial.

For Ibn Arabi, there were two parallel models with two parallel paths. Following the Quran, God created the world and humanity, and revealed through His prophets the rules that, if followed, will lead a person to paradise, avoiding the fires of hell. Alternatively, following Neoplatonic philosophy, the world and humanity are connected through the Universal Soul and the Intelligence to the Necessary Being or One, and the soul can follow a path to return to the Necessary Being and achieve union – that is, *henosis* or mystical union or *yoga*. The different terms mean much the same thing.

For Ibn Arabi and most Sufis, that which may achieve union is the spirit (*ruh*), not the ego (*nafs*). The distinction here is essentially that between the Neoplatonic higher and lower soul, labelled *spiritus* and *anima* by the Scholastics. The *ruh* is the *spiritus*, immortal and in touch with the Universal Soul. The *nafs* is the *anima*, in touch with matter. The distinction is important for Sufi practice, which aims to conquer the ego/*nafs*/*anima* in order to liberate the spirit/*ruh*/*spiritus* from the clutches of the material world.

Sufis, like Catholic monks and Hindu *Sannyasin*s, join an order, in this case called a *tariqa* (path), normally giving an oath of allegiance (*bayat*) to do so, as a form of initiation. The oath is given to a teacher or *shaykh* who once gave a similar oath to his own teacher, who had also given an oath, in a chain (*silsila*) going back through the ages, ideally to the Prophet Muhammad and thus to God. Sufis in a *tariqa* follow ascetic practices, notably prayer and fasting, sometimes including retreat and poverty, but not usually including celibacy. Likewise, the communal life plays a role, though a reduced role, as Sufis rarely live permanently in their *zawiya* (chapel), and normally just visit and meet there. Sufi practice, then, is similar to other versions aiming towards mystical union, but not identical.

Given the remarkable similarities between different mystical systems, both as regards model and path, it is easy to see why many people have come to accept versions of the perennialist position. Many contemporary scholars of religion, however, reject that position, doubting that there can be one single experience of the numinous that is independent of culture and stressing that descriptions of mystical experiences in human languages inevitably reflect the cultures in which they have developed, as we saw in an earlier chapter.

Traditionalist understandings

Some discussion of these issues, which Guénon called metaphysics, is found in everything he wrote. Certain books were devoted especially to metaphysical questions. These included *Man and His Becoming according to the Vedanta* (1925), *The Symbolism of the Cross* (1931) and *The Multiple States of the Being* (1932). In his earlier works, Guénon explained his metaphysics in terms of Vedanta; in later works, he used more abstract terms, with less reference to Sanskrit terminology. In both earlier and later works, he referred to Taoism and Sufism as well as Vedanta, and sometimes used

Scholastic terminology. This, he stressed, was 'synthesis', not 'syncretism'. Syncretism assembles elements of different systems in a more or less random fashion, while synthesis 'consists in envisaging things in the unity of their principle, in seeing how they are derived from and dependent on that principle, and thus uniting them, or rather becoming aware of their real unity, by virtue of a wholly inward bond, inherent in what is most profound in their nature'.[2]

What follows below will, in general, use Scholastic rather than Sanskrit terms. It will draw on one of Guénon's later books, *Perspectives on Initiation*, published in 1946 as an edited compilation of earlier articles.[3] This book is more representative of Guénon's later positions, which are the ones that passed into mature Traditionalist doctrine.

Guénon's metaphysics addresses two large questions. The first of these is the model: how the universe is structured. The second is the path to self-realization: what the human being should do within this structure. In asking these two questions, Guénon was asking two central questions that have been asked many times before, by Plato and Plotinus, among others.

THE GUÉNONIAN MODEL

Guénon understood the universe in the same terms as Shankara, as structured around an unlimited and infinite universality – *brahman*, the 'Supreme Principle' – finding expression in the limited materiality of being and manifestation, *atman*. He used the Scholastic terms 'form' and 'matter' and 'essence' and 'substance', and the Sanskrit terms *brahman* and *atman* and *purusha* and *prakriti*, more or less interchangeably.

Brahman and *atman* are ultimately one and the same, an understanding which Guénon compared with the doctrine of the Unity of Being in Islam (which he called the 'Supreme Identity', following an unusual alternative translation of the Arabic *wahdat al-wujud*). Manifestation is limited, temporary, and changing. Non-being is not just the opposite of being, but actually more permanent than being. The infinite, naturally, contains all possibilities. Manifestation, in contrast, contains only certain possibilities.

Guénon then followed Sufi understandings, especially, in his division of the soul into spirit and ego. He explains that the individual person can be understood in terms of 'self' and 'ego', and that the self is the *ruh* or *spiritus*, defined as 'the transcendent and permanent principle of which the manifested being, the human being, for example, is only a transient and contingent modification'.[4] The self (spirit) is the *atman*. No Sanskrit equivalent is given for the ego.

The Guénonian model, then, is essentially Neoplatonic, though Traditionalists generally regard it not as Neoplatonic but as primordial, or just 'traditional'. With the important exception of the American-trained Iranian philosopher Seyyed Hossein Nasr, discussed below, most Traditionalists would resist an identification of the Guénonian model as Neoplatonic, since such an identification places Traditionalism squarely within human intellectual history. Traditionalists prefer to find the origins of the tradition outside human history, in the transcendent. Even Nasr puts things the other way round in relation to this chapter, and argues that Neoplatonism corresponds to the primordial, not that the Traditionalist understanding of the primordial is Neoplatonic.

GUÉNONIAN REALIZATION

Guénon also follows Shankara, the Neoplatonists, and the Sufis in understanding the objective for each person as being what he calls the 'realization [of] unity' – though the French term *identité*, which here means unity, is often mistranslated into English as 'identity'. Elsewhere, he writes of 'the intimate and essential union of the being with the Divine Principle, or, if it is preferred, with the Universal'.[5] 'Divine Principle' here denotes *brahman*, or the One. The realized yogi of the Hindu tradition, he says, is the 'Universal Man' of the Muslim tradition,[6] 'Universal Man' being his translation of the Arabic term *al-insan al-kamil*, which literally means 'perfected human'. This is the term applied by Sufis to those who have reached union with the Necessary Being. Once someone has reached union, Guénon explains, they are 'released from all the limiting conditions of individuality'. 'The "ego" has effaced itself and disappeared completely before the "Self".'[7] This is very much the Sufi understanding.

Guénon distinguished sharply between realization and 'mysticism', a term which he did not understand in the Scholastic sense of mystic union but in the looser, contemporary sense of 'religious experience'. For Guénon, the mystical religious experience was both passive and random, involving sentiment and imagination, resulting from no particular method, and found only in the West. He objected to the many scholars of religion who identified the realization that is enabled by initiation, which he called the 'initiatic', as 'mysticism' – an error on Guénon's part, as those scholars were, in fact, simply referring to the older sense of the word 'mystical'. The dispute, then, is about nomenclature. Guénon's realization is, actually, mystical union, and what he contrasts it with is, actually, unstructured religious experience. In the older sense of the word 'mystical', Guénon was a mystic.

In answer to the question of how to proceed towards union, Guénon, like Plotinus and Shankara, suggested that the path starts with knowledge, which he added can be grasped only through intellectual intuition (with 'intuition' understood as above reason, not as below reason, as some psychologists and modern philosophers understand it). There may be an intermediate stage, as 'Union with Universal Being may be looked upon as constituting a necessary stage on the way towards ultimate union with the supreme *Brahma*.'[8] Here he was probably drawing on Sufism, which in some versions identifies intermediate stages on the path towards the Necessary Being.

Even more important than knowledge, however, was initiation. Initiation was the start of the path, not the path itself; it was 'the transmission of a spiritual influence', starting with certain 'preparatory methods', and continuing with things that cannot be transmitted verbally.[9] 'The individual is the source of the initiative toward "realization"', 'pursued methodically under rigorous and unremitting control', though never achieved by the individual alone.[10] There is thus a need for 'the work that must be accomplished subsequently in order that this initiation, at first virtual, may become more or less fully effective'.[11] This work is 'inner work', which Guénon also called 'effective initiation' to distinguish it from the earlier stage of 'virtual initiation'. It might, for example, include *mantras* in the case of Hindus, and *dhikr* in the case of Sufis (the two are similar, both being phrases repeated many times as a form of prayer that leads to particular mental or spiritual states, quite distinct from the prayers of exoteric religion). It might also include teaching conveyed using symbols, which can place seeds 'in the intellect of the initiate who must thereafter bring them from potency to act', as the initiate then follows 'the plan that he will afterward have to realize within himself in order to come to the effective possession of the initiation that he has received only virtually from the outside'.[12] The idea of the role of symbolism in realization is found in many traditions, including some Western esoteric traditions.

Guénon's model was a 'synthesis' of Vedanta and other, similar systems, as he himself recognized. Such a synthesis was not, however, possible when it came to actual initiation, he argued, as, although all paths end up in the same place, they have different starting points, appropriate to the nature of each person – if, that is, the person is suited for initiation in the first place, which not everyone is. Initiation could not come from texts; skilled teachers adapt their teachings to the needs and capabilities of the individual being taught, so teaching must always be both direct and oral. Attempts to merge paths were syncretism, and syncretism tends to assemble elements that do not belong together, and 'such an aggregation cannot really constitute a doctrine any more than a heap of stones makes a building'.[13] Syncretism is never more than pseudo-initiatic, and may even be counter-initiatic. In the same way, one individual can follow only one initiatic path at a time; one should not attempt to assemble one's own heap of stones.

What was needed for realization was therefore 'attachment to a regular, traditional organization'.[14] Such an organization must be regular in the sense that it is long-established

and is not either an attempt to recreate a vanished traditional form such as those found in ancient Egypt or Chaldea, or a
syncretic combination of other traditional forms. Ideally, as
in Sufism, the initiator is 'a link in the "chain" of which the
starting-point lies outside and beyond humanity'.[15]

The early Traditionalists devoted much effort to trying to
identify such regular, traditional organizations, and Guénon
wrote at length on what such organizations were not. In the
end he concluded that there were only two regular, traditional organizations in the West, Freemasonry and Compagnonnage. Both are fraternal associations, one found throughout
the West and the other found mainly in France. Freemasons
focus on symbolic ritual and mutual assistance, and Compagnonnage uses different rituals and was once built around
particular trades. Not all forms of Freemasonry were regular, however, concluded Guénon, and Compagnonnage was
an even more difficult issue, as it had vanished with the Industrial Revolution. Both Freemasonry and Compagnonnage were originally craft organizations, Guénon stressed.
The crafts were understood by him to have originally been
connected with the universal, derived from first principles.
Participation in the crafts 'constitutes for those who carry it
out an effective means of participation in the tradition, and
this is as much as to say that it takes on a truly "sacred" and
"ritual" character'.[16] Historically, Guénon was right about
Compagnonnage, but perhaps not about Freemasonry. The
Freemasons themselves trace their origins to medieval stone-
masons, but there is little historical evidence for this, and
much that points to a seventeenth-century origin.

Other regular, traditional organizations existed outside

the West, thought Guénon, and of these it was Sufism that was most important. It was Sufism that Guénon took as his own path, being initiated into the Hamdiyya Shadhiliyya order in Cairo in the 1930s.

Just as the Guénonian model is essentially Neoplatonic, the Guénonian path to realization is essentially Sufi. Comparisons are made to other traditions, and the possible existence of other initiatic organizations is considered, but nothing in the Guénonian path departs significantly from Sufi norms. Traditionalists do not generally identify the Guénonian path in these terms, and would put things the other way round: the Sufi path is the same as the primordial esoteric path, and that is the path that Guénon identified.

EVOLA'S PATHS

Julius Evola was less interested than Guénon in the question of how the universe is structured, but was still very much interested in paths to self-realization. His understanding of these occasionally coincided with Guénon's, but more often differed. He at first agreed with Guénon on the importance of initiation and studied Eastern paths to self-realization, but then concluded that no regular initiations survived, at least in the West. Compagnonnage was of 'very slight importance' and anyhow unknown outside France, and Freemasonry was mostly 'a fantasy system . . . built on the basis of an incoherent syncretism', and, when it was not, was a pseudo-esotericism of the worst sort, as could be seen from its support of anti-authoritarian revolutionary causes.[17] Freemasonry in France and Italy was, indeed, closely associated with republicanism. Given the absence of regular paths as envisaged by Guénon,

thought Evola, 'we also need to consider paths that are themselves exceptions'.[18]

The first paths that Evola investigated and wrote about,
which he seems to have regarded as essentially one, given
that they all lead to the same conclusion, were mostly Hindu:
the paths of Tantra, Shakti, and the 'Secret Way' of sexual
rituals (in *Man as Potency*, 1926, republished as *The Yoga of
Power* in 1949), alchemy (in *The Hermetic Tradition*, published in 1931), and Buddhist asceticism (in *The Doctrine of
Awakening*, published in 1943). All these books focused on
the details of practice, considering knowledge only to the
extent that it was needed for practice. In the case of alchemy,
the need for knowledge was considerable, as the first step
was to understand the meaning of alchemical symbols, which
could not be achieved simply by reading a book, even Evola's.
It was also necessary to reflect on the symbols until they had
been truly understood.

Evola then turned away from Eastern paths, which he
thought required 'a transplantation into a different psychic
and spiritual soil', given differences of race, ancestry, mentality, and even language.[19] Such a transplantation was not
easily achieved. Nor was it really necessary, as there was also
value in the Western spirit, which was admittedly responsible
for modernity, but was also capable of more than that, most
importantly in seeing 'the value of the personality, capable of
an active initiative, aimed at autonomy'.[20] The West offered a
path of 'absolute action and true personality' through which
'the living values on this plane can escape, reaffirm themselves, and integrate themselves into a higher order'.[21]

Without initiation, Evola saw two paths to realization for

men, and one path for women – his understandings were usually very gendered, much more so than Guénon's, and this aspect of Traditionalism will be discussed more fully later on. For men, the two possible paths were the path of action and the path of asceticism; for women, there was the path of devotion. What these paths all had in common was heroism: active heroism for men and passive heroism for women. And what the two paths available to men had in common was that the warrior or the ascetic both 'affirm themselves in a life that is beyond life, the former through pure action and the latter through pure detachment'.[22]

Through both paths, 'those who have mastered themselves', those who are not 'tied to earth and matter, to man and humanity', become 'man-gods' and gain 'the bright calm of the Seers, the superb "solar" reality of those in whom the idea has become blood, life, and power'.[23] This path, the 'solar' path, allows men 'to develop a link directly to the divine, transforming themselves into it and possessing it as a living and real state of their own experience'.[24] Evola's understanding resembles Guénon's understanding of mystical union, but also differs from it. The idea of the man-god, which Evola also sometimes called the 'absolute individual', comes not from Neoplatonism but from sources such as Nietzsche. For those who have not mastered themselves, 'every need, every desire, and every passion expresses a deficiency of being'.[25] For those who have mastered themselves, both paths – action and asceticism – also confer power, and make an individual fitted to rule. While Guénon's metaphysical realization is essentially otherworldly, Evola's realization also has worldly ends. His politics is discussed in a later chapter.

The path of asceticism is not explained in detail. In Evo-la's early *Pagan Imperialism*, it was much the same as the path that Guénon had identified, with a man aiming at 'free-ing himself from the human, i.e., from the sensory, the ra-tional, and the emotional, and . . . identifying himself with one or another form of "metaphysical" experience . . . which, as its limit, culminates in a state of perfect identity, spirit-ual vision, full suprasensual and suprarational accomplish-ment'.[26] 'Perfect identity' is Guénon's phrasing, and may be better understood in general terminology as 'perfect unity'. Guénon envisaged unity with the *brahman* or the Necessary Being. Evola did not specify what he envisaged unity with, but it was not Guénon's Necessary Being. In *Revolt against the Modern World*, written a few years later, Evola objected to the very idea of such union, which he called 'pantheistic' and identified as religious and feminine rather than metaphysi-cal. In pantheism, 'ultimate reality is conceived as a great sea into which the nucleus of an individual merges and becomes dissolved like a grain of salt. In pantheism, personality is an illusory and temporary manifestation of the one undifferen-tiated substance, which is simultaneously spirit and nature as well as the only reality; in this weltanschauung [world-view] there is no room for any authentically transcendent order.'[27] For Evola, personality was not illusory. This runs very much against Guénon's view.

The path of action is explained in more detail. It is the path of the warrior, of him who 'evokes in himself the tran-scendent power of destruction; he takes it on, becomes trans-figured in it and free, thus breaking loose from all human bonds'.[28] In an unusual reinterpretation of Islamic theology, which distinguishes the lesser jihad (Evola's path of the warrior) from the greater jihad (Evola's path of the ascetic), Evola argues that the greater jihad may be experienced within the lesser jihad, i.e. that the warrior is also an ascetic.

Evola stressed that the warrior is not the same as the 'soldier', a word that is derived from *solidus*, the name of a late Roman coin, and which originally meant 'mercenary'. A soldier is not necessarily a warrior, and a mercenary is certainly not a warrior. A medieval knight was a warrior, and chivalry was a path to self-realization – and a better one than Christianity. It was based on 'the ideal of the hero rather than of the saint, and of the conqueror rather than of the martyr; regarding faithfulness and honour, rather than *caritas* and humbleness, as the highest virtues'.[29] The saint whom Evola sees unfavourably is a Christian saint, and it is the Christian virtues of charity and humbleness that are the problem, not the idea of sanctity.

Evola's idealization of the knight was not quite an idealization of aristocracy. In all great civilizations, he wrote, 'nobility was not characterised by the simple fact of having ancestors, but by the fact that the ancestors of the nobility were divine, unlike those of the plebeians'. By 'divine' he meant ancestors 'who had actually followed a transcendent form of life . . . transmitting to the lineage a blood made divine, and, along with it, rites'.[30] The right sort of ancestors, then, might help, but ancestry on its own did not produce nobility. In traditional civilizations, 'it was necessary for the quality virtually conferred upon a person at birth to be actualized by initiation' and 'an individual became a member of the group of true men who control the community only through the new life awakened in him by initiation'.[31] This is a slightly different view from Guénon's, as it sees initiation as actualizing inherited qualities – that is, in Guénon's terms, as 'effective', not just 'virtual'. At one point, Evola proposed that the initiation of warriors had been a feature of the *Männerbünde* (male brotherhoods) that the Nazi medievalist Otto Höfler had identified as a feature of ancient Germanic tribes, an identification which is no longer generally accepted. For Evola, those brotherhoods had both 'an initiatory (i.e., sacred) and a warrior meaning'.[32]

In 1955, Evola presented the path of action as a viable solution for the West. It could, he wrote, be termed 'magical', and he looked forward to 'a magical epoch' that would allow the West to 'cut the knot of the "dark age" – the Kali Yuga . . . The new traditional form that the West will make its own will arise from the spirit of its most ancient tradition: from the ancient Arctic-Atlantic spirit . . . the legacy of heroic, active, and conquering races.'[33] Evola is here referring to his Arctic Golden Age, the origin of the Roman Empire and of medieval chivalry.

The optimism of 1955 did not last. In his last major book, *Ride the Tiger*, published in 1961, Evola explored the question of how one might somehow remain untouched by the 'utter dissolution' of late modernity, even in the absence of any traditional paths.[34] In theory one might simply withdraw into isolation, but that required a certain sort of character, and also financial resources that were beyond most people's reach. The remaining possibility was 'self-unification', to 'discover the supreme identity with oneself',[35] again using the phrase that Guénon used to translate the Arabic *wahdat al-wujud*, but meaning something different by it. For Guénon, as for the Sufis, union was with the Necessary Being or *brahman*. Evola, passing through the divinization of the self, ended with self-unification.

To discover the supreme identity with oneself, one might follow a version of Nietzsche's 'self-overcoming' and 'self-creation', and – in Nietzsche's words – 'become who you are'.[36] One approach was to start by identifying and stabilizing one's own 'internal form', thus giving oneself a firm base, and then establish 'a direct and absolute relationship between . . . what one is . . . and transcendence'.[37] Finding one's own internal form 'in an age of dissolution' was not easy. It might be done 'through an experiment . . . the search for, or the acceptance of, those situations or alternatives in which the prevailing force, one's own "true nature", is compelled to manifest and make itself known'.[38] No particular experiments are mentioned but 'experiencing life to the maximum', Evola wrote in his intellectual autobiography, was a path he had followed himself as a young man.[39] He had particularly favoured mountain-climbing, as 'in the most difficult climbs, the will to power is affirmed and realised in the purest way'.[40] Evola also referred to 'self-awareness' as understood by the twentieth-century Armenian-French mystic George Gurdjieff, who, like Nietzsche, did not follow any traditional path, and has therefore generally been regarded by Traditionalists with great suspicion. Gurdjieff's path to self-awareness included placing people in bizarre or extreme situations – not exactly traumatic, but tending in that direction. Evola's implication is that such situations might lead the true self to manifest itself.

Another way in which a solid base could be built to achieve

'self-overcoming' and 'self-creation', wrote Evola in 1961, was through what was almost a version of existentialism, the philosophy associated especially with Jean-Paul Sartre and the 1960s that holds that existence precedes essence, and that how we choose to exist – our acts – thus determines our essence – who we are and what our life means. For Evola, self-creation could result from devotion to a cause or activity, 'the objective perfection corresponding to a given function and a given meaning'. Through a 'function or superior vocation . . . the personality is summoned to a higher obligation (for instance, royalty and pontificate, monastic orders, and so on)'.[41] The only example of such a function that was examined in any detail was political, as we will see in a later chapter. Again, this was a path that Evola said he had himself once followed. It is not clear to what extent Evola's final understanding of transcendence resembles Guénon's realization – it is specified at one point to be 'transcendence *in oneself*'[42] – but Evola may have been coming close to this.

Evola's understanding of self-realization, then, matches Guénon's understanding in that both Traditionalists agreed on the importance of reaching what both called the 'supreme identity' (though they may not have meant exactly the same thing by this unusual term). They also at first agreed on the importance of initiation and the relevance of non-Western paths (Sufi, Hindu) and pre-modern paths (alchemy). Evola, however, then concluded that in the absence of any surviving traditional initiation, one had to look to non-traditional paths: Nietzsche, perhaps even Gurdjieff, and something resembling existentialism. The late Evola, then, might be called a non-traditional Traditionalist.

SCHUON'S METAPHYSICS

Schuon, like Guénon, was interested in both models and paths. Like Evola, his views were in some ways broadly similar to Guénon's, and in other ways quite different. While Guénon derived his cosmology from Vedanta and often used Sanskrit terms, Schuon's metaphysics was often presented in Christian terms, though he also drew on Vedanta and on Guénon's understanding of Vedanta. While Guénon emphasized realization through initiation and the esoteric, neither of which is really a Christian concept, Schuon wrote of salvation and gnosis, and combined initiation with religion. Though it was still the esoteric aspects of religion that mattered, Schuon partly rehabilitated religion as a path to realization, as we will see in more detail in a later chapter.

Schuon's cosmology was essentially the same as Guénon's, though generally expressed more poetically:

> The world is not only more or less imperfect or ephemeral, but cannot even be said to 'be' at all in relation to absolute Reality, since the reality of the world would limit God's Reality and He alone 'is'. Furthermore, Being Itself, which is none other than the Personal God, is in its turn surpassed by the Impersonal or Supra-Personal Divinity, Non-Being, of which the Personal God or Being is simply the first determination from which flow all the secondary determinations that make up cosmic Existence.[43]

This paragraph would make little sense to many readers, but for those who understand Guénon's metaphysics, it summarizes them elegantly enough – though with the addition of

God, who is not found in Guénon's own model, which is primarily non-theistic.

Schuon also sometimes explores alternative cosmologies, however. In *Gnosis: Divine Wisdom* he explains two models, one in which 'the world is comparable to concentric circles which, while reflecting the centre, never attain it, so that there is absolute separation', and one in which 'the world is like a star, every ray of which unites the periphery to the central point', a perspective that 'sees God in everything that exists'.[44] Both models, suggests Schuon, should be combined.

Realization is, for Schuon as for Guénon, union, but it is expressed in more monotheistic terms, as union with God, named as such. This union may be achieved not only through knowledge and practice, as for Guénon, but also through love: 'If love is the inclining of one being toward another, with a view to union, it is Knowledge that, by definition, will bring about the most perfect union between man and God, since it alone appeals to what is already divine in man, namely the Intellect.'[45] Love, however, is still necessary. Schuon distinguishes two 'spiritual types', one based around knowledge or truth, which he calls contemplative and labels with the Sanskrit term *jnana* (knowledge or gnosis), and one based around love, placed in opposition to egotism, which he labels with the Sanskrit term *bhakti* (devotion or attachment). Although many people identify the way of love with Christianity, and Schuon does often make that identification, the way of the conquest of egotism is also Sufi – Sufis speak of the conquest of the ego or *nafs*. For Schuon, the *bhakti* way is the way of religion in general. Schuon also identified the way of knowledge especially with Islam. This is the esoteric way.

In practice, realization or union is to be achieved through initiation, and here Schuon follows Guénon in emphasizing Sufi orders and craft initiation, and also in mentioning initiatory possibilities within Hinduism. In practice, Schuon devoted much time and effort to running his own Sufi order, though he never wrote about this, as the existence of the order was kept secret until after his death. He echoes Evola in considering the 'cosmic' aspect of sexuality, and noting that 'the sanctification of sexuality confers upon it a quality that transcends its carnal aspect and neutralizes or even abolishes the latter',[46] and that sexual intercourse has a 'quality of Platonic *anamnesis* [recollection]',[47] reminding the soul of primordial divine union; however, he does not explore this possibility in any detail in his published work. He modifies the understanding of the Sufi order slightly, though, noting that in practice Sufi orders are composed of large numbers of people, which they indeed are – they are part of popular culture in the Muslim world. This does not fit well with the idea of the spiritual elite as necessarily restricted. Schuon therefore divides the membership of Sufi orders into a small inner circle and a larger outer circle, and argues that the participation of the outer circle is, actually, exoteric. This is a perspective that a religious-studies scholar who knew Sufism might well endorse.

Schuon breaks with both Guénon and Evola in arguing that contemporary Christian monastic orders also represent the initiatory tradition. He argues that Christianity is esoteric as well as exoteric, citing the doctrine of the Trinity, which is comprehensible only to 'those who are capable of conceiving the Divinity under other more or less relative aspects'. 'Expressions such as "Son of God" and especially "Mother of God"' are, in fact, 'purely esoteric.'[48] Grace 'is initiatory in its kernel or essence';[49] and the great example of Christian esoteric practice is found in the Eastern Orthodox tradition of Hesychasm (Quietism) and its use of the Jesus Prayer ('Lord Jesus Christ, Son of God, have mercy on me, a sinner'), which Hesychasts repeat continuously, in the manner of a Hindu *mantra* or Sufi *dhikr*. Again, a religious-studies scholar might well endorse this view, as Hesychast theology is also influenced by Neoplatonism. That Schuon finds his Christian initiation especially in an Eastern Orthodox tradition in some ways reduces the contrast with Guénon and Evola, as it was Catholicism that Guénon so often argued was purely exoteric. Even so, it is invariably Christianity as a whole that Schuon describes as esoteric, not just Eastern Orthodox Christianity.

Schuon also found esotericism and initiation in a religious tradition that had never interested Guénon, though it had interested Mircea Eliade: Native American religion. 'Among the American Indians,' wrote Schuon, '. . . something primordial and pure has been preserved despite all the obscurations that may have been superimposed in certain tribes, perhaps mostly in relatively recent times.'[50] Native Americans, like other nomadic peoples such as Bedouins, Tuaregs, and ancient Mongols, shared in the nobility of the warrior. And foremost among the rites of the Native Americans was the Sun Dance, 'a virtual union with the solar Spirit, hence with the Great Spirit'.[51] Schuon was not the only outsider to develop an interest in the Sun Dance, which, like the Sweat Lodge (a practice that Schuon also praised), has become ever more popular outside Native American communities, to the extent that this is now often understood as a case of problematic 'cultural appropriation'.

One thing about Native American practice that appealed to Schuon was its apparent primordial simplicity, the importance of which Schuon often emphasized, and also found in other areas. 'There is a concordance between the *religio perennis* and virgin nature,' wrote Schuon, 'and by the same token between it and primordial nudity, that of creation, birth, resurrection, or the high priest in the Holy of Holies, a hermit in the desert, a Hindu *sâdhu* or *sannyâsin*, a Red Indian in silent prayer on a mountain.'[52] This was one basis of the importance that Schuon attached to nature, discussed in a later chapter. Schuon himself also practised primordial nudity, a practice that at first passed unnoticed, but then became more widely known among his followers, especially after a disaffected follower complained about it to the police. This caused much confusion and distress.

Schuon was interested not only in realization, but also in the way in which 'any man is able, within the limits of his own home and family life, to effect something like a traditional restoration by deliberately reversing the process of alienation'. This 'has a real spiritual value for the person concerned'.[53] Schuon and some of his closest followers lived as far from modernity as possible, in unspoiled woodland outside Bloomington, Indiana, avoiding modern clothing such as jeans and modern vulgarities in ways of speaking, focusing on the spiritual and the beautiful.

NASR'S METAPHYSICS

Subsequently, Seyyed Hossein Nasr, the American-educated Iranian philosopher who was a follower of Schuon and who knew Islamic, Scholastic, and modern Western philosophy as well as anyone, reintegrated Traditionalist metaphysics with scholarly understandings of the history of philosophy and also with Neoplatonism. Nasr identified Plotinus as the main bearer of the metaphysical tradition that had survived the triumph of Aristotle. He traced the survival and periodic visibility of Neoplatonism through European history, ending with Henry More, a seventeenth-century philosopher at Cambridge and one of the last notable Neoplatonists. In Nasr's narrative, as we have already seen, 'the ancient Greeks possessed a cosmology similar to that of other Aryan peoples of Antiquity', a cosmology that he compares with that of Samkhya, one of the schools of Veda Hinduism, but Greek religion then declined, moving towards 'naturalism and empiricism' and thus rationalistic philosophy.[54] In Alexandria, however, there developed Neoplatonic metaphysics, Neopythagoreanism and Hermeticism. Nasr also argues that while rationalism triumphed in Europe, as it did after the decline of Scholasticism, the metaphysical and Neoplatonic approach of Alexandria remained strong in Islam, so that 'the Christian emphasized the nature of God, the human soul and salvation while the Greek [and thus the Islamic] emphasized the "divine" quality of the cosmos and the "supernatural" status of intelligence itself'.[55] In Islam, 'the gnostic, illuminationist dimension associated with Sufism had been alive from the start and continued as the inner life force of this tradition. In fact, Islam turned more and more to this direction during its later history.'[56]

This narrative fits comfortably with modern scholarly understandings, save in the final point, that Islam turned more and more towards the metaphysical and Neoplatonic approach of Alexandria. Islam, like any great world religion, comes in many forms, and while some did indeed turn towards the metaphysical and the Neoplatonic, some also turned away from it, often decisively. There is nothing metaphysical or Neoplatonic about the puritan and scripturalist understandings of Islam found among the Wahhabis of Saudi Arabia.

Nasr's metaphysical narrative reconciled Traditionalism with historical knowledge. He did not, however, develop or alter pre-existing Traditionalist ideas of self-realization.

PETERSON'S HEROIC PATH

Once again, the Traditionalist fellow-traveller Jordan Peterson takes a very different approach. His understanding of self-realization reflects his experience as a clinical psychologist and his dismay at modern nihilism more than it does his understanding of tradition and myth. Some of his advice is very practical, and for this reason he has sometimes been identified as a conservative. Although some of his conclusions may indeed be conservative, however, their basis is still Traditionalist.

Peterson's view of life is bleak: 'We are not equal in ability or outcome, and never will be,' he writes. 'A very small number of people produce very much of everything. The winners don't take all, but they take most, and the bottom is not a good place to be. People are unhappy at the bottom.

They get sick there, and remain unknown and unloved. They waste their lives there. They die there.'[57]

Given this, what is needed is that one should avoid dying of alcoholism or drug abuse, and then 'shoulder the burden of Being and . . . take the heroic path'.[58] This starts with 'standing up straight with your shoulders back', the first rule in *12 Rules for Life*, his bestselling book. Standing up straight, writes Peterson,

> is not something that is only physical, because you're not only a body. You're a spirit, so to speak – a psyche – as well. Standing up physically also implies and invokes and demands standing up metaphysically. Standing up means voluntarily accepting the burden of Being . . . You respond to a challenge, instead of bracing for a catastrophe. You see the gold the dragon hoards, instead of shrinking in terror from the all-too-real fact of the dragon. You step forward to take your place in the dominance hierarchy, and occupy your territory, manifesting your willingness to defend, expand and transform it. That can all occur practically or symbolically.[59]

Much of the advice Peterson gives in *12 Rules for Life* is very practical: work hard at your job, and do not allow bitterness to eat away at you. Get your life in order, and accept responsibility. Stop saying the wrong things to people. But Peterson also tells his readers to 'do only those things that you could speak of with honour'.[60] He may never have read Evola, but in some ways he understands self-realization similarly.

Conclusion

The foundational idea with which this book started is perennialism, which in Traditionalism becomes the idea of the
primordial tradition. All Traditionalists agree that there
is a primordial tradition. There is also general agreement
that the primordial tradition indicates both a metaphysical
model or cosmology and a path to self-realization. There is
less agreement about the precise details of the primordial
tradition, however. The model that Guénon found in Advaita
Vedanta, Scholasticism, and Sufism was essentially Neoplatonic, as Seyyed Hossein Nasr later realized, though other
Traditionalists prefer to see it simply as primordial. The path
that Guénon described was essentially Sufi, and compatible
with his Neoplatonic model because Sufism, like Scholasticism and possibly even Advaita Vedanta, draws on Neoplatonism. That Sufism, Scholasticism, and Advaita Vedanta
have so much in common is, incidentally, an important
argument for the perennialist position. There is also a non-
metaphysical, purely historical explanation, at least in the
cases of Sufism and Scholasticism: the Islamic philosophers
on whom Sufi theology drew, like the Scholastic philosophers, had been reading Neoplatonic texts.

Julius Evola, however, agreed with Guénon regarding the
path to self-realization only in part. The early Evola seems
to have understood self-realization in terms of union with
the transcendent, just like Guénon, but then moved away
from this idea towards an understanding of self-realization
as 'blood made divine' and then as 'self-unification'. The
early Evola also accepted the importance of initiation and

the usefulness of non-Western systems, especially Hindu ones, but the later Evola despaired of traditional initiation and turned instead to paths of Western origin, including one that resembled existentialism. At all stages, rather than turning to Sufism, Evola emphasized the warrior, giving rise to understandings of 'spiritual warriors' that later became widely popular. Evola's understanding of the path to self-realization, then, has important political implications, which will be discussed in a subsequent chapter.

Frithjof Schuon, again, agreed with Guénon only in part, accepting Guénon's esoteric path to self-realization through Sufism, but also finding a comparable path in contemporary Christian monasticism, where Guénon had been convinced that nothing of the sort could be found. Schuon's interest in Native American practice marks a new departure for Traditionalism, but did not contradict Guénon's views in the same way, and continued the Traditionalist investigation of the non-Western and pre-modern. Schuon's rehabilitation of Christianity has important implications for the Traditionalist understanding of religion, which will also be discussed in a subsequent chapter.

Seyyed Hossein Nasr, who was a follower of Schuon, agreed with his shaykh's understanding. As a well-trained philosopher, however, he recognized the Neoplatonic basis of the Traditionalist model and path, and in recognizing this healed the rift between Traditionalism and academia that went back to the Sorbonne's rejection of Guénon's PhD thesis. Despite this, Traditionalism and academia have generally continued to look askance at each other.

Finally, Jordan Peterson's practical advice was very

different from the metaphysical paths charted by other Traditionalists, but in the end was in some ways not so different from Evola's vision.

Self-realization, Traditionalism's first and major project, was an individual project. It is impossible to say to what extent individual Traditionalists have succeeded in this project, precisely because it is so individual. You cannot see my degree of self-realization, and I cannot see yours. The project of self-realization, however, led to the Traditionalist engagement with religion, the consequences of which were more evident, and it is this to which we will now turn.

CHAPTER 8
Religion

One of the major Traditionalist projects has been in the area of religion. It is this project that first made Traditionalism important, even though religion was not originally a major concern of René Guénon. His original project was not religious; it was the creation of an 'intellectual' (i.e. spiritual and esoteric) elite and the achievement of self-realization. Both these projects, however, required initiation, which in practice meant either Freemasonry or Sufism, and Sufism required Islam. The religion of Islam thus became part of the Traditionalist project, and Traditionalism consequently became important for Islam, initially in Europe and then globally.

Unlike self-realization, religion has not had the same importance for all Traditionalists. Guénon was initially hostile to it, and was careful to distinguish his metaphysics (good) from religion (bad), at least until he came to Islam through Sufism. Julius Evola was even more hostile to it. It was Frithjof Schuon who developed the idea of 'the transcendent unity of religions', discussed in this chapter, and made possible the wider Traditionalist engagement with religion that remains important today.

As we have seen, religion, like myth, has lost much of its authority since the Enlightenment, at least in most parts of the West. That Guénon did not align himself with the Catholic Church avoided collateral damage to Traditionalism in a period when the Church was fast losing credibility. Evola followed Nietzsche in condemning Christianity as a religion for slaves. Schuon, however, aligned himself with religion in general, and his followers became influential in the public presentation and understanding of religion towards the end of the twentieth century, especially in America and among Western Muslims. Traditionalism thus came to have an impact on society, or at least on some forms of contemporary religiosity, for the first time. Much of this impact persists today.

Earlier Traditionalist views

Two somewhat different views of religion can be found in Guénon's work, an early view that was mostly anti-religious and a later view that assigned religion an important role in the achievement of metaphysical realization.

Initially, as we have seen, Guénon carefully distinguished traditional metaphysics from religion, which he saw as exoteric and as serving primarily social purposes. In his view, while metaphysics was intellectual, religion was primarily sentimental. In modernity, religion tended towards moralism, and the extreme example of this was Protestantism, which was purely moralistic and sentimental, and not really a religion at all. Catholicism, too, had lost its esoteric content.

As we have also seen, Guénon understood the various initiatic paths as having one single point of arrival but different points of departure, and this included different exoteric religions. As a result, 'those who, having penetrated to the principial unity of all the traditions, are no longer tied to any particular traditional form'.[1] Exoteric religion, then, could be dispensed with. Guénon later altered this position slightly, accepting that, though exoteric religion might in principle be dispensed with, in practice it often was not. Although a person who has reached the end of the initiatic path is no longer tied to any particular traditional form, he noted, such a person 'will generally continue to confine himself outwardly to a given form even if only as an "example" to those around him who have not yet reached the same point'.[2]

Towards the end of his life, however, Guénon changed his position, giving exoteric religion an important and even indispensable role. This change of view coincides with the period during which he got to know Egyptian Islam and Sufism as actually practised in Egypt. Egyptian Sufis are invariably devout Muslims. Guénon began to emphasize the necessity of an orthodox exoteric religious frame for the metaphysical realization that was the aim of the primordial tradition. This was stressed most clearly in a short article on 'The Necessity of Traditional Exoterism' that was published posthumously in 1952, but prefigured in an article published in 1947. In the posthumous article, Guénon made two arguments. One was a development of the earlier view that an initiatic path might start in an exoteric religion, and stated that the gap between the 'profane' nature of modern life and the metaphysical had grown so great that anyone hoping to prepare themselves for initiation needed exoteric religion, or rather what Guénon called 'traditional exoterism', to bridge that gap. 'Adherence to an exoterism,' Guénon asserted, 'is a preliminary condition for coming to esoterism.'[3] Exoteric religion is the foundation on which esoteric metaphysics can build, he argued, as is clear to everyone who knows a tradition where the exoteric and esoteric are directly linked; Guénon was here thinking of Islam, and footnoted the standard Sufi metaphor of shell and kernel, which he had used as the basis for an article in 1931. In this metaphor, the shell that is the Sharia protects the kernel that is the *haqiqa* (the esoteric truth).

The other argument was a pragmatic one, and was that if any master within an esoteric tradition seemed happy to initiate someone who was not following the appropriate exoteric tradition, one should doubt the qualifications of the master in question, since 'every true spiritual master must necessarily exercise his function in conformity with a definite tradition'. This, Guénon stressed, applied only to initiation proper, not to merely giving 'doctrinal clarifications . . . [and] practical counsels'.[4] An exception was made only for an 'exclusively esoteric' tradition, by which Guénon probably meant Vedanta.

Guénon also further revised his views on whether or not those who have penetrated to the unity of all the traditions are or are not still tied to a particular traditional form. In the same posthumous article, Guénon states that

> One must not believe that this exoterism can be rejected once initiation has been obtained, any more than the foundation can be removed once the building has been constructed. Exoterism, far from being rejected, must in reality be 'transformed' in the measure corresponding to the degree attained by the initiate, for he becomes more

and more qualified to understand the profound reasons for it; and as a result the doctrinal formulas and rites take on for him a significance much more genuinely important than they could have for the mere exoterist who in the end is by definition always restricted to the exterior appearance alone.[5]

The esotericist, then, may become an exoteric religious authority.

A related question that Guénon also discussed towards the end of his life was the question of conversion. He distinguished between conversion proper and 'adopt[ing] a [different] traditional form' for esoteric reasons. It was entirely appropriate for someone who could find no possibility of metaphysical realization within their own tradition 'for reasons of an esoteric and initiatic order, [to] adopt a traditional form different from that to which they would seem to be linked by their origin', as Guénon himself had. However, conversion for purely exoteric reasons – 'the exterior passage from one traditional form to another' – was unfortunate, since as well as showing a 'lack of mental stability', it showed metaphysical ignorance, since it implied 'the superiority of one traditional form over another'.[6] Anyone with metaphysical knowledge realizes that no traditional form is superior to any other. Conversion of this sort also tended to increase sectarianism, and the disunity between followers of different traditions. Guénon did not say this, but in Egypt conversion from Christianity to Islam, or Islam to Christianity, which may, for example, happen in connection with marriage or divorce, often leads to conflict, as the community which loses a member frequently feels that one of their own has been kidnapped and brainwashed by the other community.

EVOLA AND RELIGION

Guénon, then, moved from an earlier position that dismissed religion to a later position that recognized its importance, but mostly as a means to an (esoteric) end, not as an end in itself. Evola, in contrast, was at least as anti-religious as the early Guénon, and remained anti-religious to the end. As we have seen, he identified Christianity as one of the most problematic aspects of the period since the Roman Empire. He did, however, concede that religion, or at least 'theism', might serve some purpose for those who were not suited for metaphysical realization, and perhaps especially for women, as we will see in a later chapter. On one occasion, he conceded that 'a return to Catholicism can play a positive role as the first step along a path that must necessarily lead beyond Catholicism proper',[7] a view similar to Guénon's understanding of the path to realization starting in exoteric religion.

In general, however, Evola remained implacable in his opposition to religion in general and to Christianity in particular.

The Transcendent Unity of Religions

Schuon, in contrast, was never anti-religious in the way that Evola and the early Guénon were, and granted religion a much larger and more important place than even the later Guénon. He saw the path to realization as not only starting in exoteric religion, but also in some respects remaining within it. Beyond this, all the main religions shared in what he called

'transcendent unity'. This was an important shift from Guénon's position, where unity was found in the esoteric, primordial tradition. In the end, there was one single tradition.
For Guénon, exoteric religions were united to the extent that
they were connected through the esoteric to the primordial
tradition, but the unity was in the primordial tradition, not
in the exoteric religions. For Schuon, in contrast, the exoteric religions *themselves* shared in unity. Where Guénon had
written of the perennial tradition, Schuon often wrote of the
religio perennis, the 'perennial religion'.

This development of the Traditionalist philosophy was
of importance because it made possible an alliance between
Traditionalism and religion, instead of the confrontation resulting from the positions of Evola and the early Guénon,
or the slightly uncomfortable truce made possible by Guénon's later position. Schuon's position allowed the esoteric to be introduced into the exoteric. This was his single
most important contribution to the development of Traditionalism, and makes him the most important of the Traditionalists when it comes to religion. While for Guénon
metaphysics was primary, and religion of interest only from
a metaphysical perspective, for Schuon religion was also primary, and primary for metaphysical reasons. His views on
self-realization, considered in the previous chapter, derive,
in large part, from this understanding of religion. His work
appreciated, valued, and used all the grandeur and majesty of
religion. This was, however, religion in general, not any one
particular religion. His conceptions were never constrained
or subject to any single religion.

Schuon's starting point was that exoteric religion reflects

the esoteric and makes it visible. 'Religion translates meta physical or universal truths into dogmatic language.'[8] Thus, 'religion, by its very nature and independently of any wish of its representatives, who may be unaware of the fact, contains and transmits this purely intellectual knowledge beneath the veil of its dogmatic and ritual symbols'.[9] While Guénon had sought and found the metaphysical in Vedanta, and Evola had sought and found it in myth, Schuon also sought and found it in religion – with or without the agreement of religion's 'representatives'. And it was not just the reflection of universal, metaphysical truths that gave meaning and authority to religion: Schuon also recognized the importance of revelation and prophecy, the classic legitimation of monotheistic religion, which Guénon had ignored. Exoteric religion thus became valuable in itself. Another consequence was that the esoteric connection between different religions became more visible, and the different religions thus drew closer together.

One consequence of Schuon's conviction that exoteric religion reflects the esoteric and makes it visible was that the important things that exist in one religion also exist, in one form or another, in other religions. A leading example of this was the Christian doctrine of incarnation, whereby God becomes flesh in Jesus. 'What is "incarnation" for Christianity is "revelation" or "descent" for the other two monotheistic religions,' wrote Schuon.[10] In the case of Islam, that which is understood to have been revealed is the Quran, which Schuon frequently equated to Jesus. From an academic perspective, he was not wrong, as the Quran is a form of incarnation to the extent that the words of the Quran are understood by Muslims as coming directly from God. The Quran, alone of all that is in creation, is actually not created; rather, it precedes and transcends creation. The Arabic term for incarnation, *tajasud*, is never applied to the Quran by Muslims, however, and Muslims see not the Quran but Muhammad as the counterpart of Jesus, as Muhammad was a divinely appointed prophet, which is what Muslims consider Jesus also to have been.

The concept of 'descent' is found in Hinduism, which Schuon, like some Hindus, understood as monotheistic. The Sanskrit for 'descent' is *avatar*, and the god Vishnu, for example, is understood to have had several *avatar*s or 'descended forms'. The god Rama is seen as an *avatar* of Vishnu. This concept is close to the Christian doctrine of incarnation. Schuon extended it to include the Prophet Muhammad, who he argued was actually an *avatar*, even though the nature of Islamic theology, which focuses on the absolute, could not put it in these terms. An *avatar* is, in the end, the manifestation of the divine in creation, and in the Prophet 'a certain Divine Aspect took on under particular cyclic circumstances a particular terrestrial form'.[11] This explains how Islam and other religions are actually expressions of the transcendent, not just reflections of primordial tradition.

Schuon, unlike Guénon, wrote well, and his investigations of the commonalities between religions were often quite poetic:

In Christianity the soul is 'freezing to death' in its congenital egoism, and Christ is the central fire that warms and restores it to life; in Islam on the other hand the soul is 'suffocating' in the constriction of the same egoism, and Islam appears as the cool immensity of space that allows it to 'breathe' and 'expand' toward the boundless. The 'central fire' is denoted by the cross, the 'immensity of space' by the Kaaba, the prayer-rug, the abstract interlacings of Islamic art.[12]

Although Schuon generally emphasized the transcendent unity of religions, he also accepted that there were important disagreements between religions. The teachings of individual religions do not include 'the validity of other orthodox religious forms, because the idea of religious universality is of no particular usefulness for the purpose of salvation and may even exert a prejudicial effect on it, since, in the case of persons not possessing the capacity to rise above an individual standpoint, this idea would almost inevitably result in religious indifference'.[13] This, then, is why no religion taught the transcendent unity that Schuon himself taught.

Schuon minimized disagreements between religions in two ways. On the one hand, he argued that religions did not actually dismiss other religions as much as seemed to be the case. When negative things about Jews and Christians appear in the Quran, for example, they 'have primarily a symbolic meaning . . . and their mention by name is simply a means of describing certain conditions affecting humanity in general'.[14] They are not actual criticisms of Judaism or Christianity. Schuon gave no evidence to support this particular understanding of Islamic theology, but an argument for it could be constructed, though with difficulty. Such an understanding is rarely, if ever, found among Muslims. Similarly, Schuon writes that 'when the Quran appears to deny the death of Christ, it can be understood to mean that in reality Jesus vanquished death, whereas the Jews believed they had killed the Christ in his very essence'.[15] It is true that the Quran *can* be understood in this way, again with difficulty, but it is commonly not understood in this way.

Schuon's other way of minimizing disagreements between religions was to argue that religions had traditionally been true *in their own spheres*, and that disagreement had therefore been without much practical significance. 'A religious form is made, if not for a particular race, at least for a human collectivity determined by certain particular conditions,' wrote Schuon.[16] Christianity is the religious form that is appropriate for the West, and Islam for the Arabs. Both have expanded outside these areas, but Christianity has expanded only because of modernity – which is itself problematic – and when Islam expanded into India, Muslims did not force Hindus to convert, because they were outside Arabia. As was the case for the view of the Quran criticizing 'certain conditions' when it appeared to criticize Jews and Christians, Schuon does not give any evidence to support this particular understanding of Islamic history, which most historians would reject. In the first place, the conquering Muslim armies never actually forced anyone to convert, anywhere. It was not that Hindus were not forced to convert, but that they chose not to. In the second place, almost the whole of the population of Indonesia did convert to Islam, and Indonesia is even further from Arabia than is India. Most Muslims in the world today are not Arabs, so a view of Islam as an Arab religion makes little sense.

Both of Schuon's arguments, then, are problematic. That

has not stopped them from being attractive to many people, especially those without specialist knowledge of Islamic theology and history. And the idea that each religion has its own characteristics, its own strengths and weaknesses, its own approach to the real, is an appealing one.

Schuon, however, was not entirely uncritical of religion. Even if he did not echo Evola's polemics against Christianity or Guénon's polemics against modern Catholicism and Protestantism, he sometimes criticized certain forms of Christianity. One of the reasons for the revelation of Islam, for example, was that Christianity had by that time 'given birth in Arabia and the adjacent countries to all manner of deviations that threatened to inundate the Near East, and even India, with a multitude of heresies that were far removed from primitive and orthodox Christianity'.[17] Deviations and heresies were defined by Schuon in terms of primordial tradition: a religion that reflected primordial tradition was orthodox, and one that did not was not. 'A religion is orthodox if it provides a sufficient, if not always exhaustive, idea of the Absolute and the relative, and thus of their reciprocal relationships, and a spiritual activity that is contemplative in its nature and effectual with regard to our ultimate destiny.'[18] And problems with Christianity were not found only in the Near East at the time of the birth of Islam. In modernity, 'having failed to raise human society to the level of the religious ideal, one lowers religion to a level which is humanly accessible and rationally realizable'.[19] Science has forced religion to 'falsify imperceptibly its own perspective and more and more to disavow itself'.[20] And when a religion has lost the esoteric, it is reduced to 'literalism and sentimentality'.[21]

This is a point that Schuon did not make as often or as strongly as Guénon did, but it was a point that he did make, and that echoed Guénon's dismissal of modern Catholicism.

Schuon saw a further problem with religion. Religion could be an 'all-invading autocracy' that might stop people proceeding to the esoteric.[22] This was a special issue for Schuon when it came to Islam, since – though he did not say this in his public writing – he and most of his followers were Sufis, and so of necessity Muslims, and the Sharia of Islam can certainly seem an 'all-invading autocracy' given that it addresses not just big issues like adultery (not allowed) but also small issues like which foot to put first when entering a bathroom (the left). Here Schuon constructed an ingeni ous argument based on the status of the *sunna*, the practice of the Prophet Muhammad, which is understood in Islam to be exemplary – that is, a Muslim should follow it. Most of the Sharia is based on the *sunna*. In Schuon's view, the *sunna* could be divided into three categories: spiritual, moral, and intermediate. The spiritual *sunna* was primarily the re-membrance of God, esoteric practice, and was of the first importance. The moral *sunna*, in contrast, was essentially social – Schuon is here reverting to Guénon's understanding of religion as being primarily about social order. 'From the point of view of the *Religio perennis*,' wrote Schuon, 'the ques-tion of the Sunna implies a highly delicate problem, given that the accentuation of the intermediate and social Sunna goes hand in hand with a particular religious psychism . . . a particular mentality, one which obviously is not essen-tial to Islamic gnosis.'[23] The particular mentality was that of the Arabs, to whom Islam has been revealed, and whose mentality was by implication not the mentality of Schuon or his Western followers. Given that Schuon considered that 'the intermediate and social Sunna' were 'obviously . . . not essential to . . . gnosis', his followers generally ignored many of the *sunna*. Most Muslim Sufis would strongly disagree, and would argue that all aspects of all of the *sunna* are essential elements of the Sharia, and thus of the path to gnosis.

Schuon's answer to the question of the *sunna* is in part his answer to the question raised by Guénon of adherence to exoterism (religious forms). Schuon agreed with Guénon that Muslims who had 'attained a spiritual degree of a nature to authorize such abandonment' did not in practice abandon exoteric practice.[24] However, he then came close to justifying such abandonment. Since 'the plane of action . . . has no connection with the Path of metaphysical discernment and concentration on the Essential', what matters is not 'an imitation of the Prophet founded on the religious illusion that he is intrinsically better than all the other Prophets, including Jesus', but 'imitation of the Prophet founded on the prophetic quality in itself, that is, on the perfection of the Logos [divine word] become man'.[25] The Logos is more important than any single religion.

Finally, Schuon also addressed the issue of conversion, coming to much the same conclusions as Guénon. Firstly, 'it goes without saying that it is possible to pass from one religious form to another without being converted, which may happen for reasons of esoteric, and therefore spiritual, expediency'.[26] Secondly, although 'to pass from one Asian tradition – Hinduism, Buddhism, or Taoism – to another is in effect no great matter, seeing that the metaphysical content is everywhere quite apparent . . . inside the framework of the three Semitic traditions, a change of religion almost amounts to a change of planet.'[27] Guénon would not have agreed.

Schuon's transcendent unity of religions, then, is both a development and a rejection of Guénon's understandings. It is a development in that it is an expansion of Tradition-alist perennialism from the esoteric to the esoteric *and* the exoteric. It is a rejection in that it blurs the distinction be-tween the esoteric and the exoteric that was so important for Guénon, and values religion in its own right, not as a means to an esoteric end.

Later developments

Schuon had a larger and more influential following than Guénon, and many of his followers were active as writers or scholars. Two were especially important in the further devel-opment of Traditionalist approaches to religion: Seyyed Hos-sein Nasr and Huston Smith, both of whom we have referred to previously. Nasr moved from Iran to America after the Iranian revolution, and worked as an academic while writing for a general audience as well as a specialist one. Smith was also an American academic with a large general audience.

Nasr completed the Traditionalist rehabilitation of re-ligions, referring in his later work to 'traditional religions', a wider category than the few religions that had been dis-cussed by Guénon and Schuon. He barely mentions meta-physics or the esoteric in his writings, save occasionally and in accessible terms, for example as 'an inner dimension ac-cessible to the few who are able to penetrate from the realm of outwardness to the inward, who are constituted in such a way as to seek at all costs that pearl of great price which was forbidden by Christ from casting before swine'.[28] Those who remember Guénon's intellectual elite and his distinction between the esoteric and the exoteric can recognize which 'few' Nasr is here referring to, but, for others, the presentation is much more inclusive.

Nasr also addressed an issue that had not been addressed before: that commonalities between different religions perhaps reflected not transcendent unity but rather transfer and syncretism, as many scholars of religion would maintain. From the 'Divine Order issue forth . . . many cascades', he proposed, and some 'gush forth over similar types of formations and terrains corresponding to similar human collectivities, and thus constitute members of a religious family . . . Nor is it impossible for a tributary of one cascade to flow into another.'[29] Occasional transfers and syncretisms, then, do not invalidate the central Traditionalist argument. Nasr further strengthened this argument by making explicit what had been implicit in earlier discussions of metaphysics: that the 'Divine Reality is beyond all conceptualization . . . and is referred to by such sacred formulae as the *Lā ilāha illa'Llāh* (There is no divinity but God) of Islam, *neti neti* (Not this, not that) of the Upanishads, the "Tao that can be named is not the Tao" of the Tao Te-Ching."[30] He is here expressing in relatively comprehensible form the Neoplatonic proposition known as 'negative theology': that all that can be said of the One is what it is not, not what it is. For example, the One is not multiple. This point strengthens the Traditionalist argument because, if the divine reality is beyond conceptualization, it is also beyond discussion and disagreement. And if all religions do not disagree on this most fundamental point, then they all agree, in transcendent unity.

Although Nasr extended the discussion of religion to include all major religions, he identified himself personally with only one particular religion, Islam, in contrast to earlier Traditionalists, none of whom identified publicly with any particular religion. Islam was the religion into which he had been born, that was associated with his Iranian ethnicity, and which he had studied in great depth. He had undoubted authority as a scholar of Islam and as an Islamic theologian. Despite his perennialism, then, Nasr conformed to the standard model whereby one person belongs to, and represents, one religion. If Schuon made peace between Traditionalism and religion in general, Nasr made peace between Traditionalism and individual religious identities. In some ways he also Islamized Traditionalism, as he and most of his followers were unabashedly Muslim.

As seen previously, Huston Smith was the author of the tremendously successful book *The Religions of Man* (later *The World's Religions*), first published in the 1950s and very widely read in America, though less so in Europe. The book was originally inspired by the perennialism of Aldous Huxley rather than by Traditionalism. Smith became a Traditionalist after its first publication. His later work combined Huxley's universalism with Traditionalism's anti-modernism and Schuon's transcendent unity, reaching large audiences both among the American public, much of which welcomed and respected him, and within American academia, where his reception was often sceptical, if not hostile. Smith developed Schuon's transcendent unity by putting theory into practice, not only valuing all religions but practising several of them. Asked by an interviewer how he had spent his morning, Smith replied that he had started with the Islamic dawn *salat* prayer, then done some *hathayoga*, and ended with a chapter from the Gospel of St John. Then came coffee. 'I never met a religion I did not like,' wrote Smith on another occasion,[31] describing his own discovery and practice (on top of his original Methodism) of Hinduism, Buddhism, and Islam. Smith's example did not inspire many others at the level of practice, but served to drive home the basic idea of transcendent unity, as well as some of the Traditionalist theory on which it was based, generally re-expressed in easily accessible terms.

Smith's *The World's Religions* is one of the books that the Traditionalist fellow-traveller Jordan Peterson has recommended on his website, but ultimately Peterson's approach is, once again, very different. Recognizing that the system of symbolic meaning that was most familiar to Westerners was Christianity, Peterson moved on from a focus on the myths investigated by Mircea Eliade, which had featured prominently in his University of Toronto lectures and in his early book *Maps of Meaning*, which was published by an academic press and did not sell in the millions. Instead, he started to frame his ideas in Christian terms. His single most popular video, which between 2017 and 2022 received over 11 million views, was the opening video in a 'Biblical Series', entitled 'Introduction to the Idea of God'.

Peterson's idea of God, however, is not conventionally Christian. His introduction starts with Nietzsche and Jung, and then argues for the Bible as a repository of truth, comparable to myth, dreams, and archetypes. He asks where such things came from, and suggests that as well as revelation, there are also rational explanations: 'I don't want to say that everything that's associated with Divinity can be reduced in some manner to biology or to an evolutionary history, or anything like that,' says Peterson. 'But insofar as it's possible to do that reduction, I'm going to do that. And I'm going to leave the other phenomena floating in the air, because they can't be pinned down, and in that category I would put the category of mystical and religious experience, which we don't understand at all.'[32] Peterson's use of Christianity, then, is pragmatic.

Conclusion

The application of the Traditionalist philosophy to religion has gone in two opposite directions. Originally, Traditionalism was anti-religious, stressing the esoteric, and dismissing exoteric religion as sentimental and unimportant. This was the position of Evola and the original position of Guénon. Guénon then changed his position, recognizing the importance of exoteric religion as a means to accessing the esoteric, but still placing the exoteric in second place.

Schuon, in contrast, rehabilitated religion, blurring the distinction between exoteric and esoteric, and rescuing exoteric religion from the second place where Guénon had left it. He and his followers thus became religious figures, not esoteric ones. Schuon and Smith spoke for religion in general, while Nasr spoke for Islam in particular. Schuon was never very widely read, but Nasr was, and so was Smith, at least in America. Nasr became one of the most important Islamic theologians writing in the West, a leading member of a group that has become more and more important with the proliferation of well-educated, Western-born Muslims whose tastes in reading resemble those of other well-educated Westerners. This continues today. Nasr was also widely read in some parts of the Islamic world, including Turkey and Bosnia. Smith became one of the most important and influential writers on religion in America, despite the reserve with which he was received by academia. Even after his death, his approach remains popular, again especially in America. Peterson then expressed his Traditionalism in Christian terms, though pragmatically.

With Nasr and Smith, the Traditionalist project for the first time had a real impact on society. Sacred order was not restored, but many people accepted Traditionalist perspectives on religious matters, generally regarding these perspectives as genuinely traditional, not as the fruit of the Traditionalist philosophy that they actually were. This impact has continued with Peterson's lectures.

CHAPTER 9

Politics

The third major Traditionalist project has been political. The Traditionalist political project played a small part in the politics of Fascism and Nazism during the Second World War, and a larger (and more violent) part in Italian politics in the 1960s and 1970s. It is the Traditionalist political project that makes Traditionalism so important today: in America with Jordan Peterson, in Russia with Aleksandr Dugin, and in Europe and America with the alt-right and far right.

Politics, like religion, has not had the same importance for all Traditionalists. René Guénon was not politically active, and nor was Frithjof Schuon. Julius Evola, however, was a political activist for most of his life, both during and after the Fascist period. He is sometimes seen as a Fascist, but, as we will see, things are more complicated than that. After his death, Traditionalist politics seemed to lessen in importance, but since the 2000s this trend has reversed, and interest in Traditionalist approaches to politics has been growing.

Followers of Schuon very much downplay the political element of Traditionalism and the political significance of the work of Guénon, but an unbiased reading of Guénon shows that he himself regarded the political and the social as important. The Traditionalist political project is inherent in the Traditionalist philosophy, even if not all Traditionalists are particularly political.

Contemporary and pre-modern political theory

Contemporary Western political theory is always based, in one way or another, on the idea of popular sovereignty: it is generally accepted that the legitimacy of government depends on the will of the people and the consent of the governed. Democratic systems of one kind or another are regarded as the best way of turning the theory of popular sovereignty into practice. Only rare exceptions are made, for example for institutions like the European Union, which reflects the will of the people only imperfectly, but still – it is hoped – attracts the consent of the governed because of the benefits that derive from it.

Popular sovereignty, however, is far from being the only possible basis of a theory of politics, as we find if we look beyond the West. Some commentators think that the 'China model', which emphasizes popular welfare and quality of government irrespective of democratic mechanisms, is now increasingly attractive, and there is growing discussion of a 'New Confucianism', not only in China but perhaps beyond. In the Middle East, Islamists have proposed divine sovereignty as an alternative to popular sovereignty since the 1930s, though their model has never been successfully implemented, despite many attempts. There are still anarchists who reject all forms of sovereignty, and a few real monarchies survive in states like Jordan and Abu Dhabi.

Western political theory has generally examined three

issues: the purposes of the state, control of the state, and the organization of society. Contemporary political theory focuses on placing the state under effective democratic control and on organizing society to achieve something like the French revolutionary ideals of liberty, equality, and fraternity, with liberty now generally termed 'freedom' and fraternity generally understood as solidarity and (at least in Europe) welfare. To what extent the desired equality is social and to what extent it is economic are still disputed.

Pre-modern political theory, however, generally saw order and virtue as the objectives of the state. For Aristotle, the objective was the 'good life', defined in philosophical terms as living a reasoned life of virtue and excellence, and made possible by social harmony. Confucian political theory saw social order, personal virtue, and general harmony as the aims of the state, and classic Islamic political theory also understood the two main purposes of the state as being the avoidance of disorder, and encouraging virtue while discouraging vice. Medieval European political theory emphasized justice, order, and the common good. The emphasis on order found in so many systems of political theory may seem strange to modern Westerners, who tend to take good order for granted, but will seem less strange to those who have suffered from real disorder, whether the disorder of rampant corruption in a weak state or the chaos of a failed state, which is an obstacle to almost everything, as well as being potentially life-threatening.

Pre-modern political theory sometimes relied on limited forms of democracy to control the state, but not always. Socrates and Plato famously rejected democracy as being too dangerous, given the risk of short-sighted incompetence and populism, and emphasized justice and virtue instead. Confucianism likewise emphasized virtue, and classic Islamic political theory emphasized religion: the state was quite as subject to the Sharia as was any individual person. In medieval European political theory, the king ruled by divine right, but was also subject to God, not that this made much difference in practice, save that occasionally the papacy tried to sanction monarchs with whom it was in conflict, usually without much effect.

When it came to the organization of society, the starting point of all pre-modern political theory was not equality but difference. As a minimum, all societies that had slaves or serfs – as most did – distinguished them from free persons. Some societies then went on to establish more complicated systems. Medieval Europe distinguished priests, nobles (who were in theory administrators and warriors), free commoners (urban or rural), and serfs. India distinguished priests and teachers (Brahmins), administrators and warriors (Kshatriyas), farmers and merchants (Vaishyas), and serfs (Shudras). In addition, there were outcasts. Tokugawa Japan distinguished court nobles, warriors and administrators (*samurai*), and peasants, craftsmen, and merchants. In addition, there were priests and outcasts. The Ottoman Empire distinguished rulers – imperial functionaries, soldiers, administrators, and religious scholars – from the 'flock' of free commoners (urban or rural), and from slaves. All these pre-modern systems, then, gave special status to priests, warriors, and administrators.

The rigidity of these distinctions varied. Sometimes change was possible: the son of a medieval European artisan might become a priest, or the son of an Ottoman farmer might become an administrator. Slaves might be freed by their owners. Sometimes, however, change was impossible, as in the Japanese and Indian systems, where difference was reinforced by endogamy: people could only marry within their own class or caste.

Political theory based on the idea of difference was not only found in medieval Europe, India, Japan, and the Ottoman Empire. The socialist art critic John Ruskin, who railed against the way that modern industry turned the worker into a slave, saw this as the cause of the revolutionary fervour of his times, of the masses' hatred of the upper class, to which he belonged. The problem was not poverty or inequality, he felt, but the degrading work that workers were forced to do. 'To obey another man, to labour for him, yield reverence to him or to his place, is not slavery. It is often the best kind of liberty, – liberty from care.'[1] Ruskin's opposition to industrial capitalism did not mean rejection of hierarchy.

Pre-modern political theory, then, dealt not with popular sovereignty, democracy and equality, but with the importance of order, virtue, and harmony, and the hierarchical organization of different social groups. It will by now come as no surprise that the application of Traditionalism to politics has more to do with pre-modern political theory than with modern political theory, given Traditionalism's negative view of anything modern.

Guénon's politics

Guénon always denied any direct interest in the political, but expressed views that were in fact very political in his *The Crisis of the Modern World* in 1927 and, especially, in *Spiritual Authority and Temporal Power* in 1929.[2] His political utopia is, of course, that of the first age, the *satya-yuga*, during which 'all things, in every order of existence, are connected and correspond to one another so as to contribute to universal and total harmony; for harmony . . . is nothing other than the reflection of principial unity in the multiplicity of the manifested world'.[3] This utopia is long lost, but it is still possible for laws and systems in the manifested world to reflect it. This is the main point about Guénon's proximate political utopia: 'a traditional civilization is . . . one where the intellectual realm dominates all the others, and where all things, science and social institutions alike, proceed from it directly or indirectly, being no more than contingent, secondary, and subordinate applications of purely intellectual truths'.[4] The 'intellectual realm' is, in Guénonian terms, metaphysics. One contemporary example of such a system, thought the young Guénon, was the Muslim world, where 'the entire social order forms an integral part of religion, from which all legislation is inseparable'.[5] Guénon had at that point never been in the Muslim world, and presumably changed his mind when he later lived in Egypt, where the reality was very different from the ideal. Guénon also idealized the Confucian system:

> In order to make the natural virtues shine in the hearts of
> all men, the ancient princes first of all applied themselves
> to governing their own principality well. In order to
> govern their principality well, they first restored proper
> order in their families. In order to establish proper
> order in their families, they worked hard at perfecting
> themselves first. In order to perfect themselves, they first
> regulated the movements of their hearts. To regulate the

movements of their hearts, they first perfected their will. To perfect their will, they developed their knowledge to the highest degree.[6]

Guénon's ideal is thus a partnership between spiritual authority, which conserves and transmits knowledge (the tradition), and temporal power, which acts on knowledge and maintains order. This, wrote Guénon, is what is meant by what the Chinese called 'the mandate of heaven', and is expressed in another form by the idea of the 'divine right of kings', and visible in the way that kings are anointed by the clergy at their coronations.

Holders of spiritual authority may also carry out tasks such as performing rites, but these activities are secondary to their primary function, which is the transmission of the tradition. The function of temporal power, which may be exercised by a monarch but properly belongs to an entire class, is different: it is the maintenance of internal order through administrative and judicial actions, and the maintenance of external order through military force. This, too, requires knowledge, but the knowledge of the temporal power is a lower form of knowledge than that of spiritual authority. The actions of temporal power apply the principles that spiritual authority guards. Hence the distinction between power, which involves action, and authority, which involves true knowledge. Judges and soldiers have power; priests and scholars have authority. Action must be under the guardianship of knowledge; action without knowledge is pointless or even destructive.

Society is not only made up of the holders of spiritual authority and of temporal power, however. There are other groups, and Guénon classifies these using the Hindu concept of caste. Caste is generally (and, in fact, correctly) understood in the West as hereditary, but in Guénon's conception it is not necessarily hereditary, and certainly not random. Caste is, rather, 'a social function determined by the particular nature of each human being'.[7] It is not comparable to class in the modern economic sense. Caste in India may be generally hereditary in practice, Guénon conceded, but it is not necessarily so in principle, as, although heredity is an important influence on every person, it is not the only influence.

Guénon identified each of the four Hindu castes with equivalents in the system of the European Middle Ages. Spiritual authority resided in the clergy, which equates to the Brahmin caste. Temporal power was held by the nobility, which equated to the Kshatriyas. The lowest of the four Hindu castes, the Shudras, was the serfs; the intermediate caste of the Vaishyas was sometimes classed by Guénon as the 'commonality'[8] and sometimes as the Third Estate.[9] Although Guénon on one occasion resisted this identification, other Traditionalists have understood the Vaishyas as the bourgeoisie and the Shudras as the proletariat. For Guénon, neither the bourgeoisie nor the proletariat is a traditional social group. Guénon's scheme of castes is not always all-encompassing. In different contexts, he discusses the crafts and their initiatic significance. It is not clear to which caste he thought initiated craftsman belonged.

Modernity, of course, does not live up to this model. Guénon understood his political utopia as having vanished in Europe during the Middle Ages, as the temporal power established its dominance over sacred authority, for example as the outcome of the long struggle between the pope and the Holy Roman Emperor, which the pope lost. The next stage was for lower castes to establish their authority over the temporal power. In the case of France, Guénon blamed King Philip IV, who ruled from 1285 to 1314, and who successfully established his own royal authority against the resistance of the nobility with the support of officials of non-noble origin. Historians have seen in this the beginning of the end of the feudal system; Guénon saw in it the beginning of the dominance of the Vaishyas over the Kshatriyas. He also saw it as the beginning of the modern nation-states that broke the unity of medieval Christendom and made possible the full subjection of national Churches to national states, first in Protestant countries and then also (in effect, if not always in theory) in Catholic countries.

To complete this process of decline and inversion, the reign of the bourgeoisie was then challenged by the Shudras, and 'with the domination of the lower castes comes intellectual night, and this is what in our day has become of a West that threatens to spread its own darkness over the entire world'.[10]

The last three stages of Guénon's scheme, it will be noticed, correspond to the historical narrative of Marxism, which looks for the triumph of the proletariat over the bourgeoisie, and welcomes the earlier triumph of the bourgeoisie over the feudal aristocracy as a necessary means to this end. The last three stages of Guénon's scheme are also defensible in terms of the views of contemporary historians. The difference in the Traditionalist view of politics is not in the facts, but in the significance given to them. Few would disagree that power has passed over recent centuries from the Church and the aristocracy to the middle classes, and then increasingly to the people as a whole. Modern democrats regard this as a good thing. Traditionalists do not.

Modernity and democracy are understood by Guénon not just in terms of the inversion of castes but also in terms of the absence of caste. Individuals in modernity fill roles for which they are not suited. He goes further, making a number of critiques of democracy that derive less from Traditionalism than from other sources. Democracy, he observes, is a contradiction in terms. The basic idea that the people rule themselves, that the rulers and the ruled are the same, is an impossibility. Rulers may convince the ruled that they are ruling themselves, but this is in fact an illusion. The public opinion that government in theory respects and follows is in reality very often manufactured by those in power. That which can be most easily manufactured, of course, is that which is in accordance with the modern mentality. Popular confusion is thus 'assiduously fostered by all those who have some interest in maintaining the confusion, if not in making it worse'.[11] Whether particular people who promote confusion by promoting certain modern ideas are doing so because they are dupes who actually believe in them, or because it serves their interests, is always hard to establish.

Guénon does not specify who these people are, who pretend that the ruled rule themselves and who manufacture public opinion to maintain confusion, though he did on one occasion observe in passing that 'politics seem to be altogether controlled by finance',[12] an argument then popular among those who associated finance with the Jews. Guénon never made this anti-Semitic argument explicitly. On another occasion he speculated about the 'conscious auxiliaries' of 'malefic forces' entering through 'fissures' in modernity.[13] The early Guénon did not mention malefic forces, but later writings discuss them: not only as being behind certain aspects of modernity, but also as being engaged in some of the rituals of shamanism. Guénon did not share Eliade's positive view of shamanism, and saw it as a form of witchcraft or black magic.

A political analysis such as this, which identifies a desired utopia and elaborates a critique of the present, would normally end with a discussion of the appropriate course of action for moving from the imperfect present to the desired utopia. This is what Marxism, Nazism, and Islamism all do, usually concluding that revolution is the appropriate course of action. This third standard element in political ideology, however, is almost entirely absent from Guénon's work. Instead, Guénon simply emphasizes the importance of his intellectual elite. Since sacred authority, the guardianship of knowledge, is superior to temporal power, the first step is the restoration of knowledge and sacred authority. Any actions relating to temporal power without the prior fulfilment of this essential precondition are inevitably pointless or harmful. This is why Guénon himself did not engage in political action. The action in which he did engage – the recovery of the primordial tradition – was the precondition for social and political change.

Evola's politics

Evola took a different view of the relationship between sacred authority and temporal power, and therefore also of political action. For Evola, the Brahmin caste was not purely priestly. It was a caste that combined divine and temporal power, after the model of the god-kings of the primordial Golden

Age, of whom the best known is Pharaoh – Evola found and cited many other examples. His version of the inversion of castes, which he called the 'regression of castes', thus differs from Guénon's, and starts when the Kshatriyas take military power from the Brahmins, reducing them to a mere priesthood that then develops into a religious priesthood, as found in Christianity, which is of course the enemy and the inverse of tradition. From that point onwards, Evola's version matches Guénon's, even down to such details as the role played by Philip IV. The fundamental disagreement about sacred authority and temporal power between Evola and Guénon, however, gives rise to very different forms of Traditionalist politics. Guénon saw himself as the leader of an elite of initiated metaphysicians. Evola hoped to lead an elite of divine warriors. The function of Guénon's elite was to amass knowledge; the function of Evola's elite was to act. Guénon's objective was metaphysical; Evola's objective, at least before the end of the Second World War, was fundamentally political. It was the restoration of what he called the *imperium*, a state comparable to the Roman Empire, ruled by royal power acting with spiritual rectitude and authority.

Before we examine Evola's politics further, we must consider two further minor additions that he made to Guénon's understanding of caste. One was to recognize that the caste system is generally regarded negatively in the modern West. What people most dislike is the idea of heredity, that 'social status can predetermine the type of activity to which a man will consecrate the rest of his life and which he will not be able to abandon'.[14] However, argued Evola, traditional people did not think that birth was random; they did not think that anything was random; neither, then, was caste seen as random. Traditional people also had as their objective 'achieving one's own perfection within the fixed parameters [of] one's individual nature and the group to which one belonged'.[15] In medieval Europe, everybody was proud of what they did: the peasant was proud and happy to farm, the trader to trade, and the craftsman to craft. Every occupation was a vocation. Evola failed to note that much historical evidence actually shows that medieval peasants were not always happy.

Evola's other addition is a somewhat lyrical illustration of the regression of castes, through a historical study of architecture, the family, and ethics. The great building, which was originally the temple, became the castle, then the walled city, then the factory, and 'finally . . . the rational and dull buildings that are the hives of mass-man'. Meanwhile, the family went from the sacred to the patriarchal, to the bourgeois, to impending dissolution, and the ethical went from spiritual virility and initiation to the warrior ethics of honour, and then to the bourgeois ethics of 'pure economics, profit, prosperity, and of science as an instrument of a technical and industrial progress that propels production and new profits in a "consumer society"'. Finally, 'the advent of the serfs corresponds to the elevation of the slave's principle – work – to the status of a religion', which is one way in which Evola understands socialism, with its emphasis on the dignity of labour. 'The slave's self-congratulating stupidity creates sacred incenses with the exhalations of human sweat,' concludes Evola.[16] Except that, he adds, the last two phases are connected and mixed, so that the bourgeois search for money and profit makes slaves of the serfs as well.

Evola, as we saw in an earlier chapter, thought that two weapons were needed to fight modernity and free everyone, even mass-men enslaved in their hives. One was an elite 'race of masters', and the other was a 'revolt from the depths' to break the existing system.[17] Revolt was important for Evola: the title of his major early work was *Revolt against the Modern World*, a title that is iconic for Traditionalism as a whole. Violence, he warned, could not solve the problems of modernity, as it can only destroy; it cannot build. Violence, however, can make way for a new system.

In 1932, in the expanded German translation of his *Pagan Imperialism*, Evola was specific so far as the revolt was concerned, endorsing some of the major political developments of the period. He called for 'the union of the two Eagles, the German Eagle and the Roman Eagle'.[18] This project was for a union between two peoples, but also between Fascism, which had been in power in Italy since 1922, and Nazism, which would come to power in early 1933 as the culmination of a rise that was not too difficult to predict when Evola was writing. Such a union never took place, though an alliance between Nazi Germany and Fascist Italy was signed in early 1939, shortly before the outbreak of the Second World War. Evola could claim no credit for this development but, with the revolt of Fascists and Nazis against bourgeois liberalism, he thought his revolt from the depths had started. He expressed reservations about both systems, however. Fascism had certainly triumphed over democracy and socialism in Italy, and had created a 'new national reality' with a spirit of hierarchy, virility, and authority, but was still too attached to the centralized state. Fascist corporatism risked creating a syndicalist system, and most leading

Fascists were 'people who have risen up from below, without name or true spiritual tradition'.[19] Nazism, on the other hand, might lead to 'a true Germanic rebirth', but neither nationalism nor socialism fitted at all with what the real Germanic tradition stood for. There was a risk of Nazism becoming 'a mass phenomenon, which gathers around the momentary prestige of a leader'. There was also an issue with Nazi anti-Semitism, which was insufficient, as 'a radical anti-Semitism is possible only to the extent that there is at the same time an anti-Christianism'.[20] Dictatorship, thought Evola, was like violence: it could not solve the problems of modernity, but it could clear the way for a solution.

Evola, then, was a critic of Fascism and Nazism, but not at all from the liberal perspective from which both systems are condemned today. The purpose of this book is to explain the Traditionalist philosophy and its applications, not to pass judgement on individual Traditionalists. If moral judgement were to be passed on Evola, however, he certainly would not be excused on the grounds of his criticisms of Fascism for over-centralization and of Nazism for over-emphasizing the leader and failing to accompany its anti-Semitism with anti-Christianism. Nor would he be held innocent of the consequences of the later impact of his work.

The utopia that Evola hoped in the 1930s might result from the revolt of Fascists and Nazis was 'a new Middle Ages', 'a decisive, unconditional, integral return to the Nordic pagan tradition'.[21] Ideally, there should be a god-king, after the model of the Egyptian pharaohs – but not a mere political dictator. Beyond this, Evola looked for a 'return to the system of castes [as] the return to a system of truth, justice, and "form" in the higher sense'.[22] This would produce a social organization 'rooted in a spiritual reality',[23] and it would thus be possible to 'restore aristocratic values, values of quality, of difference, and of heroism'.[24] A state built on these bases would fulfil the function of making possible the good life (a term that Evola does not use). 'It is the task of Tradition to create solid riverbeds, so that the chaotic currents of life may flow in the right direction. Free are those people who, upon undertaking this traditional direction, do not experience it as a burden but rather develop it naturally and recognize themselves in it so as to actualize through an inner elan the highest and most "traditional" possibility of their own nature.'[25]

During this period, Evola often wrote about race, more because it was a topic in which there was much interest, especially in Germany, than because it played a central part in any of his analyses. It was his writings on race that drew Mussolini's attention and, briefly, favour, and also attracted attention in Nazi Germany. Evola's understanding of race was very far from Nazi orthodoxy, which made it especially interesting and, for some people at least, relevant in the post-war world. There were good things about racism, thought Evola, in that it was inherently anti-egalitarian and anti-rational, but he was opposed to Nazi racism for two reasons. One was practical: that in focusing their attentions on the Jews, the Nazis were missing other, more important, enemies. The other was philosophical: that Nazi racism was purely materialist, and made the elementary mistake of trying to explain the greater ('the psychic and super-biological part of man') in terms of the lesser (race).[26] Arthur de Gobineau's scheme, as expressed in his once-celebrated *Essay on the Inequality of the Human Races*, was 'an illusion, which among other things, lowers the notion of civilization to a naturalistic and bio-logical plane'.[27] Human beings are more complicated than dogs and horses, and, although blood may be of overriding importance for dog-breeders, it is only a relatively minor factor when it comes to human beings. Merit can pass down through blood, but blood alone confers no merit.

What matters most is the spirit, wrote Evola. The idea that the decline of civilizations is caused by racial mixing is historically untenable. Most great civilizations are com-posed of multiple races; if the civilization is strong, the various races are melded into one: only when the civiliza-tion becomes weak is racial heterogeneity a problem. Again, what matters most is the spirit. Given this, Evola might have simply ignored the concept of race, as Guénon mostly did, and as nearly everyone today does. Instead, he proposed a concept of what he called 'the race of the spirit' that really has almost nothing to do with biological race and is purely about the spirit. Evola's 'race of masters' is a race only in a metaphorical sense, since blood alone confers no merit.

This said, Evola was clearly anti-Semitic, and even in 1963 blamed 'the suffering of Jews in Fascist Italy' on 'the well-documented anti-Fascist sentiment of international Jewry, which intensified following Italy's alliance with Germany'.[28] To this he added the extraordinary statement that 'neither I nor any of my friends in Germany knew about the Nazi out-rages against the Jews; had we known about such outrages, in no way would we have approved of them'.[29] We do not ac-tually know what Evola did or did not know about the Holo-caust at the time, but he was not an ordinary person on the sidelines of events who might perhaps have known nothing of them. He was in close contact with senior figures in the SS and Nazi Party, and some of his 'friends in Germany' certainly knew what was going on. And to say, in 1963, that one would not have *approved* of the Holocaust is hardly to condemn it. That Evola had some Jewish friends and appreciated some Jewish religious texts, as he later pointed out in self-defence, really does not help.

Where the Jews did play an important role in Evola's philosophy was in his understanding of the origins of Christianity. The Jews, too, had had a Heroic Age, and there had been Jewish warriors, like Elijah, Enoch, and Jacob. Once the Jews had been defeated militarily, however, they adopted a slave mentality, the concepts of 'guilt' and 'sin', and a helpless dependence on an all-powerful God as illustrated in the story of the Garden of Eden. They also developed 'prophetic expectations' that 'degenerated into an apocalyptic, messianic myth and in the fantastic eschatological vision of a Saviour who will redeem Israel; this marked the beginning of a process of disintegration'.[30] All of these carried over into Christianity, and also exercised an independent 'negative influence' in late modernity. The problem was the specific history of the Jews, not that they were Semitic. Islam also 'originated among Semitic races', but does not emphasize guilt and sin, and rather than having a slave mentality has the admirable doctrine of jihad.

Inevitably, Evola's views changed after the fall of Fascism and Nazism – even if, in regard to 'Nazi outrages against the Jews', they did not change as much as one might perhaps have expected. In his first major post-war work, *Men among the Ruins*, published in 1953, Evola noted that neither

Fascism nor Nazism had been able to do what needed to be done before suffering defeat in an ill-planned and ill-timed war. In 1964, in *Fascism Viewed from the Right*, he noted growing enthusiasm for the idea of Fascism among some young Italians who had never actually known historical Fascism, and warned against such 'nostalgia' for a 'myth'. Those who had been alive at the time knew that 'not everything was in order in Fascism'.[31] He then examined the problems with Fascism at some length, at a level of historical detail that may have confused some of the younger, less expert Italians for whom he was writing.

In 1953, writing for individuals within the Movimento Sociale Italiano (Italian Social Movement), a neofascist movement that enjoyed some modest electoral success, especially in the early 1970s, Evola developed a new project with a more practical take on politics, less focused on tradition and much more directed towards a critique of contemporary issues. This included a critique of totalitarianism that was aimed against the USSR and the western European Communist parties that were then relatively popular in some countries, as 'a mechanical, all-inclusive system', and a reaction to 'libertarian-individualistic disintegration'.[32] However, the generally accepted opposition between communism and democracy (in fact, bourgeois liberalism) was false, as both were actually expressions of the primacy of the economic. What was now needed was to break that primacy, 'deproletarize the view of life',[33] and establish an 'organic state', conceived rather as the pre-war Evola had conceived the *imperium*. Quite how this was to be done was not made clear. Evola referred to 'a new radical front',[34] but did not go into details. He was probably referring to the group that split off from the Movimento Sociale Italiano in 1956 to form Ordine Nuovo (New Order), a truly radical group, as we will see.

By 1961, Evola had concluded that there was no realistic possibility of effecting any change in politics or society, and that, given this, all that could be done was to await the end – or, in theory, try to hasten it, though that was a risky course of action, given that what came next might be of no benefit to oneself. He therefore advocated 'riding the tiger' of late modernity, in the sense of the old myth that a person who is riding a tiger cannot be eaten by it, and may even benefit when the tiger becomes exhausted. This involved an attitude that he called *apoliteia*, a term that he does not gloss, but which etymologically indicates withdrawal from the public, political sphere. This, however, was an inner attitude, he stressed, and did not preclude action for the sake of action, which, as he reminded his readers, was a path to realization, the third path of 'self-unification' through 'the objective perfection corresponding to a given function and a given meaning', discussed in an earlier chapter. Political action, then, was in order, so long as it was clear that 'all that matters is the action and the impersonal perfection in acting for its own sake'.[35] This was Evola's final political project.

Quite what sort of political action was recommended was not specified. The action that was taken by Ordine Nuovo, in particular, was violent, including a 1969 bombing at the Piazza Fontana in Milan that killed 17 people and injured 88, a 1974 train bombing that killed 12 people and injured 48, and possibly also the 1980 bombing of the Bologna railway station, which killed 85 people and injured over 200. It is unclear to what extent Evola was responsible for these actions, some of which occurred after his death. His observation that the path to self-unification results in 'a vision of reality stripped of the human and moral element, free from the projections of subjectivity and from conceptual, finalistic, and theistic superstructures',[36] which owes more to Nietzsche than to Guénon, might indeed facilitate terrorism. And Ordine Nuovo's project certainly included the use of terrorism.

Evola's application of Traditionalism to politics produced a body of abstract theory that echoed Guénon, and two more practical political engagements: one with Fascism and Nazism, and one with the radicals of Ordine Nuovo. Neither of these engagements was in any sense successful, save perhaps in that they cast Evola's abstract theory in a more serious light. For many, Evola was not just a theorist, but also a warrior, and so an inspiration.

Schuon's politics

When it comes to politics, Schuon seems very different from Evola. He was not, apparently, interested in politics, and never wrote on the subject at any length, though he did make some political comments in his 'Principle of Distinction in the Social Order', published in 1957. Some of his followers have held political positions, however, so his political views still matter, even though they are little emphasized in his work. He endorsed three of Traditionalism's central political ideas: Guénon's idea of the primacy of knowledge over temporal power, Guénon's and Evola's understanding of caste, and – to some extent – Evola's understanding of empire.

With regard to the primacy of knowledge, Schuon on one

occasion condemned modern liberalism in passing, on the basis that to attempt to reform humanity on the basis of the material rather than the spiritual inevitably led to 'miseries far worse than those from which one was trying to escape'.[37]

Caste was not generally an issue for Schuon, but he dealt with it at length in his 'Principle of Distinction in the Social Order'. As for Guénon and Evola, for Schuon modernity meant the triumph of the Shudras (the lowest caste, identified with the proletariat). Schuon's concern, however, was not so much the absence of hierarchy in modernity as the negative impact of modern egalitarianism, the absence of 'social differentiation', which 'imposes a certain mental uniformity'[38] and means that 'vocations are blurred and geniuses are worn down, by schools in particular and by official worldliness in general; every spiritual element is banished from professional and public life'.[39] Here he is echoing Guénon more than Evola.

This can be avoided by a caste system, as in India, but such a system is absent, for example, from Islam, which can be understood as distinctly egalitarian. This was a problem that Guénon had not addressed. The absence of a caste system is not a problem, thought Schuon, so long as a society has a 'religious basis' and works by 'first by attaching man to God and then by recognising the presence of God in man'.[40] The 'spiritual liberty' that is destroyed by modern Western egalitarianism may, if not guarded by social differentiation, be guarded by a powerful 'code of manners', as in Islam. Schuon's understanding of Muslim society might be challenged, as, although it is true in principle that 'a poor man . . . feels at ease among the rich',[41] this is not generally true in practice.

Schuon also developed the thought of Guénon and Evola

by emphasizing the distinction between two groups that might be understood as Shudras: the peasantry and the industrial proletariat. Given Schuon's emphasis on the negative impact of the machine, it is not surprising that the peasantry is contrasted favourably with the industrial proletariat. The peasantry has an 'innate dignity when one compares them with the rootless masses of the big towns',[42] and even today (the 1950s) one can sometimes meet 'peasant aristocrats' who 'give the impression of being survivals from another age'.[43] Modernity could be contrasted with the Middle Ages, when 'the artisan drew a large measure of happiness from his work, which was still human, and from surroundings which were still in conformity with an ethnic and spiritual genius'.[44]

Empire was also not a major topic for Schuon, but he noted in passing that modernity could also be contrasted with empire, and here he mentions, as well as the Roman Empire, the Confederation of the Iroquois, a pre-European North American state, reflecting his appreciation of Native American spirituality. He does not always follow Evola, however. The 'theocratic essence of the imperial idea' is not present in all ancient civilizations, Schuon wrote. Some, like Pharaonic Egypt and Nebuchadnezzar's Babylon, were no more than 'a cult of the massive and gigantic, as well as a cosmolatry often accompanied by bloody or orgiastic rites' in which the 'divinization of the human is combined with a passionate humanization of the divine; potentates are demigods, and the gods preside over all the passions'.[45] Schuon was more critical of power, and especially of the pharaohs, than was Evola.

Schuon, then, did not make any great contribution to the application of Traditionalism to politics. He did, however, accept certain Traditionalist political ideas, notably regarding caste, which may have some importance given that some of his followers were politically engaged.

Later developments

The political views of Guénon and Evola were subsequently taken further, without reference to Schuon, by Aleksandr Dugin in Russia, and by the alt-right and far right in Europe and America. These developments need a separate chapter of their own, and such a chapter is to be found at the end of this book. The politics of the Traditionalist fellow-traveller Jordan Peterson, however, have more in common with classic Traditionalist positions, and will be treated here.

Peterson makes the same distinction between authority and power that Guénon made. The proper source of authority for Peterson is not, however, spiritual, but rather 'competence', understood in a very practical sense: one wants a competent mechanic to fix one's car, and the competent mechanic should be in charge of the trainee mechanic. Competence is the product of intelligence, conscientiousness, hard work, and orderliness. It may also be the consequence of biology and of tradition.

For Peterson as for Guénon, authority and power should ideally be combined. Peterson, however, locates the problem with modernity more precisely than did Guénon: the issue is the postmodern left. During the late twentieth century, Peterson has written, 'the barely repentant Marxists still inhabiting the intellectual pinnacles of the West' revised old Marxist understandings. 'Society was no longer repression of the poor by the rich. It was oppression of everyone by the powerful.'[46] Necessary hierarchies based on competence thus came to be misunderstood as oppressive hierarchies based on power and self-interest.

Peterson never refers to caste, but natural, traditional, and necessary hierarchies are as important for him as they were for Guénon or Evola. Order is 'the hundreds-of-millions-of-years-old hierarchy of place, position and authority. That's the structure of society. It's the structure provided by biology, too – particularly insofar as you are adapted, as you are, to the structure of society.'[47] The first rule in *12 Rules for Life* is to stand up straight, but the first discussion in the book is about lobsters and the hierarchies that they form.

In Peterson's view, then, hierarchies are not only based on competence, but also on tradition, biology, and human nature. Radical leftists, however, ignore all this and instead maintain that 'human identity is purely learned' because 'if there's no central human nature, then human beings can be transformed sociologically, politically into the image that the radical leftists would prefer . . . the reshaping of society on an egalitarian basis with equality of outcome for everyone'[48] – essentially, the utopia that Marxism promised and failed to deliver. There is, of course, argues Peterson, a central human nature, and the best understandings of that nature are to be found in tradition and myth.

Peterson's first major public application of his political understandings to contemporary politics was in his 2016 video, 'Professor against Political Correctness'. This took aim at two major postmodern concerns, gender and race. He subsequently focused on gender, which is discussed a later chapter, emphasizing biology, human nature, and the appropriacy of traditional hierarchies. He has paid less attention to race, and has never maintained that either biological or racial hierarchies exist or are appropriate. In this he agrees with Guénon and Evola. He has sometimes been called a 'white supremacist', but this is inaccurate.

Peterson's position on race is that 'white privilege' does not exist, and that, while discrimination does exist, it is generally assumed rather than proved, and the motives of those who condemn it are political and suspect. What is identified as white privilege is, according to Peterson, often simply majority privilege: a member of the Chinese majority in China benefits from it in the same way that a member of the white majority in Canada does. White privilege may also often simply be the privilege conferred by wealth. Perhaps Black people are under-represented at the University of Toronto in relation to numbers in the census, but this does not have to be because of discrimination. There are many possible explanations, thinks Peterson, and the representation of various other groups at the university does not correspond to the census either: there are disproportionately many Asians in the mathematics department, and disproportionately many Jews everywhere, 'because Jewish people tend to be over-represented in disciplines where intellectual prowess is valued'.[49] To understand difficulties experienced by those who are not members of the majority in terms of race is, in fact, racist, as 'it's attributing to the individual the characteristics of the group as if the group was homogeneous'.[50]

Denying the existence of white privilege is part of a political project to oppose what Peterson sees as postmodern leftist negation of traditional understandings of human nature and society. Peterson has done this directly in his videos and books, and viewing and sales figures suggest that he has had some success in this project.

Conclusion

The initial application of Traditionalism to politics was the work of René Guénon at a theoretical level, even though he himself was not politically active. Julius Evola was certainly politically active, which has perhaps caused his political theories to be seen in a more serious light. His development of Traditionalist politics, however, was less at a theoretical level than at the level of application to the political circumstances of two very different periods: Fascist Italy between 1922 and 1945 and then the troubled post-war Italy of the 1960s and early 1970s.

The foundation of Traditionalist politics is the idea that, just as there was a primordial tradition, there was also once a traditional society, and that the key to this traditional society is found in Hinduism, if not exactly in Vedanta, and is the idea of caste. Caste is understood in terms of hierarchy, and the higher two castes are understood in terms of spiritual authority and temporal power. Guénon and Evola differed over the precise relationship between these two, with Guénon seeing the traditional relationship as being the superiority of spiritual authority over temporal power, and Evola seeing the traditional relationship as one in which spiritual authority and temporal power combine. In both cases, spiritual authority and knowledge of the tradition are the essential bases of a traditional political and social system, and certainly not of popular sovereignty, which is seen as the final stage in the regression of castes. Jordan Peterson also believes in the existence of a traditional social system organized in hierarchical terms, though he has never used the idea of caste, and identifies authority not with the spiritual but with competence and biology.

The question of race, which was so important for Nazism and is also important for some parts of the contemporary radical right, was not important for Guénon, who dismissed Gobineau's scheme as 'an illusion'. Evola did write on race, but more because of its importance under Nazism, which he at one point saw as part of the necessary revolt against the modern world, than because it was part of his own thought. Rather than endorsing Nazi racism, Evola also dismissed Gobineau, and attempted to re-understand race in spiritual rather than biological terms. He was, however, anti-Semitic despite this. Peterson is not a racist, but objects to anti-racism, which he views as postmodern leftism.

Just as Schuon's major contribution to Traditionalism was its religious project, Evola's major contribution was its political project. This fitted with his approach to self-realization, and to two of the paths he identified. The path of the warrior fitted well with his idea of empire, and with the Fascist and Nazi period, as both Fascism and Nazism idealized strength and combat. The later, quasi-existentialist path to self-unification through devotion to a cause or activity fitted well with the post-war period, and with the activities of radical groups such as Ordine Nuovo. Both paths remain popular today. With Evola and Ordine Nuovo, Traditionalism's political project also had a real impact on society, especially in Italy. As we will see in a later chapter, the subsequent development of Traditionalism's political project had an even wider impact.

PART III

Further projects

CHAPTER 10
Art

The earliest area beyond the major areas of self-realization, religion, and politics to which the Traditionalist philosophy was applied was art. Questions of art and aesthetics do not have the same immediate and universal impact on life as questions of self-realization, religion, and politics, but they have been discussed since before Plato. The appreciation of beauty is a form of human understanding that is distinct from both reason and revelation, and yet is somehow at the same level as those two major sources of truth and, probably, independent of them. Beauty, art, and their appreciation have thus interested philosophers irrespective of their practical significance. In addition, art does also have practical applications. It plays a role in religion, and religion plays a role in art. Art also helps define what culture is, and what a cultured person is.

Many Traditionalists, including Guénon, had no great interest in either art or aesthetics. Other Traditionalists have been interested in them, however, and Traditionalist theories of art have had an impact within the field of art criticism, especially when it comes to non-Western art, Indian and Islamic, which has always been somewhat peripheral to dominant Western understandings of art. Traditionalist theories of art also inspired much of the work of a Traditionalist composer, Sir John Tavener, one of the most widely appreciated English composers of the twentieth century.

The key figure in the early development of Traditionalism's artistic project was Ananda Coomaraswamy, an Anglo-American scholar of partly Sri Lankan parentage who was nine years older than Guénon. Coomaraswamy was a towering figure in the early Western study of Indian art, and his approach in this area is still influential today. He is sometimes placed alongside Guénon as one of the founders of the Traditionalist school. He was certainly a close collaborator of Guénon, and worked through many of Guénon's ideas to give them a more scholarly basis in numerous learned publications, but his impact on Traditionalism was primarily in the area of art.

Traditionalism's artistic project then continued with later Traditionalists, including at the high-profile World of Islam Festival in London in 1976, and in later applications to architecture, Islamic geometric patterns, and music.

Earlier discussions

The Ancient Greeks were interested in questions of aesthetics, which they considered in two distinct categories: beauty and art. Discussion of what underlay natural beauty was the focus of the Ancient Greek study of perception. For Platonists, unsurprisingly, the answer lay in the forms. The closer something in the physical world came to the perfection of its form, the more beautiful it was. And beauty itself was perhaps a form. In any case, the perception of beauty was a sort of recollection of the forms, and one accessible to everyone, as everyone has experienced the forms directly before birth. Since the soul has a transcendent or divine origin, it can remember what it once knew, including the forms.

Although subsequent discussions of beauty merged with discussions of art, for Plato these were two different issues. Plato was suspicious of art, which he understood primarily in terms of poetry. Prose convinced directly, through its logic; poetry convinced indirectly, irrespective of its logic. This made it dangerous, though it could also be turned to good and moral ends. Art was also problematic because an artefact was an indirect representation of a form: a physical apple was already distant from its form, but a painting of that apple was even more distant. The artificial was not as good as the natural. One solution to this problem was for art to imitate the forms directly.

By the Middle Ages, this solution had become widely accepted: art should imitate not the physical but the ideal, the form or 'nature', as the term was used in the twelfth century in the very popular *Didascalicon* (encyclopaedia) of the German theologian Hugh of St Victor, a Christian Neoplatonist. Medieval religious art was understood by many to teach directly, giving immediate access to the transcendent in a way that arguments of the theologian or preacher could not. In an age in which literacy was the preserve of the few, religious art could reach larger audiences than logical argument. This view proved long-lasting.

During the Renaissance, European painting was transformed by technical advances in perspective, oil paints, lighting, and understanding of anatomy. Renaissance painting and sculpture were naturalistic, and naturalistic art of one sort or another remained dominant in the West until the end of the nineteenth century, when the technical perfection and finish of Neoclassicism came to be seen by many as tired and sterile. The search for alternatives to naturalism then led through movements such as Impressionism to the Futurist 'Black Square' of Kazimir Malevich, and onwards to today's modern art.

Post-Renaissance aesthetic theory developed in several directions, increasingly ignoring the forms and Platonic and Neoplatonic understandings. During the Enlightenment, beauty became increasingly understood by many as a subjective experience. What exactly was that experience? Did beauty trigger an emotional reaction? Or was there an intellectual process? If there was an intellectual process, each new perception was perhaps understood in terms of previous perceptions and understandings, and the appreciation of beauty and art might be understood as a skill. This appreciation, understood by many as 'taste', was not necessarily the common property of humanity. There was good taste and bad taste, and good taste might be learned, and so became a badge of rank, a form of what would later be called 'cultural capital'. A cultured person was a connoisseur, and connoisseurship helped define culture. A distinction developed between the fine arts, associated with high culture, and the decorative arts, still respected but associated with the lower-status craftsman rather than the higher-status artist. Previously, fine and decorative arts had not been distinguished. For the Ancient Greeks, both were equally *techne* – created products.

Discussions of taste led to discussions of standards, with various proposals of what made beauty and what defined good art. Harmony, balance, and a combination of unity and diversity were thought to be important. In painting, these discussions developed into discussions of different styles: Neoclassicism, Rococo, or Romantic. The field of art history developed, and experts learned to classify artworks and trace the historical development of styles.

All these discussions focused on classical and European art, even though non-European art became known in Europe in the seventeenth century, as trade with China developed. Chinese styles became ever more popular, giving rise during the eighteenth century to a fashion for so-called *chinoiserie*, European versions of Chinese products. Chinese styles also influenced European styles. Rococo is Chinese-influenced, as can be seen in the work of painters such as François Boucher, whose paintings were highly regarded in the middle of the eighteenth century. Actual Chinese art, however, remained outside European discussions: it was generally treated as decoration rather than fine art. Indian art, though familiar to some Europeans for almost as long as Chinese art, never became fashionable in the way that Chinese art did, and even at the end of the nineteenth century was not seen as fine art. Judged by naturalistic aesthetic standards, it did not excel. One English critic, Ernest Havell, however, argued in two pioneering works published in 1908 and 1911 that these were the wrong standards to apply: the intention of Indian artists was not to imitate nature but to convey ideas.[1] Havell referred to the Neoplatonic understanding of the forms and their representation. The key to understanding Indian art, he argued, was provided by the Vedas.

The nineteenth century brought with it an entirely new

issue: the industrial production of such decorative items as cloth, china, and wallpaper. Industrial production was problematic from two perspectives. The conditions in which industrial workers laboured and lived were poor, and the aesthetic quality of industrial products was also poor, however low the products' prices. Industrial production was also fast replacing artisanal production, so that techniques and practices that had developed over the centuries were being lost. This was an issue that John Ruskin addressed. Factory work dehumanized the worker, who was transformed from human being into machine, he thought. It also produced things that were perfect and uniform in their finish, and for that reason aesthetically inferior: 'The difference between the spirit of touch of the man who is inventing, and of the man who is obeying directions, is often all the difference between a great and a common work of art,' wrote Ruskin.[2] The worker who had been transformed into a human tool was merely obeying directions. The freedom to design as well as to make needed to be restored to the worker both for his own sake, and for the sake of that which was produced.

One of those who responded to Ruskin's call was the poet William Morris, with whose name the Arts and Crafts movement is closely associated. Morris, Marshall, Faulkner & Co., later simply Morris & Co., restored the unity of design and production and ignored the division between fine and decorative arts, with craftsmen producing stained glass, wallpaper, embroideries, tapestries, jewellery, and other such products from 1861 until 1940. Its products were very popular, and some of its most successful designs are still made today – though not by methods of which Morris would have approved. Morris also established the Kelmscott Press, which printed extremely fine editions, including of Chaucer and of some of Ruskin's work.

Early Traditionalist views

Guénon, as we have seen, had no real interest in art. Evola, though, was a talented painter – not first-rate, but a notable participant in the proto-surrealist Dada movement of the 1910s and 1920s. He expressed the default Traditionalist position on art, which echoed Hugh of St Victor: art had traditionally been connected to the metaphysical, and the separation of art from metaphysics was an aspect of the degeneration that was modernity. Even Cro-Magnon cave painting showed 'the inseparability of the naturalistic element from a magical and symbolical intention'; 'the emancipation of the purely "aesthetic", subjective, and human element' from the magical and symbolical was essentially modern.[3] The same was true of literature: traditional myth, saga, and epic dealt symbolically with the metaphysical, while modern literature merely dealt tediously with the 'sentimental, sexual, or social problems of insignificant individuals'.[4] In addition, Evola echoed Ruskin, proposing that art and the crafts had originally been one, including not just painters and masons but also weavers and even farmers. The medieval guilds, especially those connected with architecture and building, were initiatic (Evola here followed Guénon's idea of craft initiation). In contrast, modern work of all varieties is a 'contemporary slave system' in which people are 'condemned to perform shallow, impersonal, automatic jobs'.[5]

In his later book *Ride the Tiger*, Evola again discussed

the arts, and became the only Traditionalist ever to say anything at all favourable about modern art. He lamented the
'pure formalism of expressive perfection' of nineteenth-
century art, but generally saw avant-garde alternatives as
little better, since on the whole they 'give rise to nothing
constructive, permanent, or durable'. However, sometimes
their 'atmosphere of anarchic or abstract freedom may actually have a liberating value, as opposed to much of yesterday's bourgeois art'.[6] Evola did not, it seems, entirely
abandon his earliest Dadaist convictions. Some of the views
he developed in *Ride the Tiger* showed a greater interest in
the contemporary arts than might have been expected from
his initial condemnation of them, as when he discussed the
similarities between early Stravinsky and jazz.

COOMARASWAMY

Traditionalist views of art were developed most of all by
Ananda Coomaraswamy, who was already a well-established
museum curator and scholar when he encountered the work
of Guénon, just as Evola was already an established thinker
and political activist when he encountered Guénon's work.
Coomaraswamy had already developed views of his own, including perennialist and anti-modern views, independently of Traditionalist sources, which is one reason why his
thought later merged so easily with Guénon's Traditionalism.

Coomaraswamy was brought up in England by his English
mother after the death of his Sri Lankan Tamil father, the distinguished lawyer Sir Muthu Coomaraswamy, when he was
two. He trained at University College London as a mineral-
ogist, but after returning to his native Sri Lanka became more

interested in art, publishing a book on *Mediaeval Sinhalese Art* in 1908 with the Essex House Press, as the Kelmscott Press had been renamed after Morris's death. Morris and Ruskin were among the earliest and most important influences on Coomaraswamy. He then broadened his study beyond Sri Lankan Sinhalese art, and his monumental *History of Indian and Indonesian Art* was published in 1927, by which time Coomaraswamy had been appointed Keeper of Indian and Muhammadan Art at the Museum of Fine Arts in Boston, Massachusetts. The *History of Indian and Indonesian Art* established a foundational understanding of South Asian art that is still important today.

Coomaraswamy also wrote on progress and religion and developed views on both topics that were similar to those of the Traditionalists. As president of the Ceylon Social Reform Society in 1908 he lamented the impact of modernity on the Sri Lankan village. Once, 'to every man in this society a place was automatically assigned by a legal and religious sanction, and the exercise of his particular function was at once his duty and his pride'. This had produced cooperation and solidarity, a 'community of interest between men of different classes', all of which was being destroyed by so-called 'progress'.[7] 'Progress', especially land reform, was leading to social conflict, reduced productivity, and an increase in crime and drunkenness. Another early essay suggests universalism, and a universalist approach is found in his *Buddha and the Gospel of Buddhism*, which explains Buddhism in terms of Christian mysticism.[8] This may derive from Swami Vivekananda, the Hindu who presented Hinduism in universalist terms at the World's Parliament of Religions in Chicago in 1893, as Coomaraswamy knew and admired one of

Vivekananda's leading English followers, Margaret Noble (known also as Sister Nivedita).

Such views fitted well with Traditionalism when Coomaraswamy discovered the work of Guénon and his collaborators. In the same way that once Guénon had demonstrated the unity of traditional metaphysics, Schuon then argued for the transcendent unity of religion, Coomaraswamy argued for the transcendent unity of traditional art, including both non-Western art and pre-Renaissance Western art. He adopted the Traditionalist scheme that saw the Renaissance as marking decline rather than progress, though he did not emphasize the *kali-yuga*. He also merged the Traditionalist critique of modernity with a critique of both contemporary Western art and contemporary Western understandings of non-Western and pre-Renaissance art, and with a critique of industrial production that followed Ruskin.

Coomaraswamy's starting point was the same as Havell's and had something in common with Evola's: the Platonic understanding of beauty as reflecting the perfection of form, and the understanding of the function of art as being to reveal that form, not the whims of the artist. 'Art is an imitation of the nature of things, not of their appearances,' Coomaraswamy asserted.[9] He, too, rejected the distinction between the fine and applied arts, insisting that a carpenter or a farmer was as much an artist as a painter was. The 'art' lay in the skill of execution, not in the product. For this reason, Coomaraswamy rejected the very term 'aesthetic', which referred to subjective experience of the superficial, and was both sentimental and materialist, '*aisthesis* being sensation, and matter what can be sensed'.[10]

What mattered for Guénon was the intellectual in metaphysics, not the sentimental in religion, and what mattered for Coomaraswamy was the intellectual in art, not the sentimental in aesthetics.

Art reflected not only form but also symbolism, and thus metaphysics, though Coomaraswamy did not use this term – as much as possible, he avoided the Traditionalists' technical vocabulary, instead using equivalent terms that would already be familiar to most readers. And metaphysics, of course, was what really mattered, not the styles that so concerned art history, which were in fact 'the accident and by no means the essence of art'.[11] Rather than showing the development of styles in the standard fashion in an exhibition, wrote Coomaraswamy, he would rather

> put together an Egyptian representation of the Sundoor
> guarded by the Sun himself and the figure of the
> Pantokrator in the oculus of a Byzantine dome, and explain
> that these doors by which one breaks out of the universe
> are the same as the hole in the roof by which an American
> Indian enters or leaves his *hogan*, the same as the hole in
> the centre of a Chinese *pi*, the same as the luffer of the
> Siberian Shaman's *yurt* and the same as the foramen of the
> roof above the altar of Jupiter Terminus.[12]

He never actually did this at the Museum of Fine Arts, where by this time he had moved from his position as curator to a research fellowship, but his proposal of a radically different approach to curatorship was still remarkable, and has also had some impact.

Coomaraswamy's own metaphysics drew not just on

Advaita Vedanta but also on a wider reading of Hindu texts and of antique and medieval Western philosophy, which is one important way in which he differed from Havell, who had no comparable conception of tradition. Coomaraswamy's book on *The Transformation of Nature in Art*, probably the major work in his last, Traditionalist phase, took the German Neoplatonist mystic Meister Eckhart as the point of departure for its comparison of 'Asian' (Indian and Chinese) and 'Western' (medieval) art.[13] His references, then, were not the same as Guénon's, and the terms 'perennial', 'primordial', and 'esoteric' were only rarely used, but the overall conception was the same. His Traditionalism is most visible in one of his last works, *Why Exhibit Works of Art?*, later republished as *Christian and Oriental Philosophy of Art*. This collected various articles published between 1936 and 1941, some of which refer explicitly to the *philosophia perennis*.

For Coomaraswamy, the Renaissance was the point where Western art had gone into decline, moving away from its proper function of revealing forms and communicating metaphysics. Instead, what began to matter was the personality of the artist and the alleged originality of the work. Coomaraswamy illustrated this with reference to Christian art, which he saw as having moved from abstract symbolism (a cross) to the depiction of persons (a medieval crucifixion scene), though as 'a form and not a figuration', and thus still in keeping with art's real purpose. Then, with the Renaissance, 'the form is sentimentalised . . . the type is completely humanised, and where we began with the shape of humanity as an analogical representation of the idea of God, we end with the portrait of the artist's mistress posing as the Madonna and the representation of an all-too-human baby'.[14]

Contemporary abstract art was no better. Some compared it to traditional 'primitive' art, but in fact the resemblance was purely superficial, since, when contemporary abstract art used symbolism, it was not traditional symbolism. Individual artists made up their own 'personal symbolisms' based on 'private associations', with the result that 'every abstract artist must be individually "explained": the art is not communicative of ideas, but like the remainder of contemporary art, only serves to provoke reactions'.[15]

Just as contemporary art represented decline, so did contemporary art criticism, especially when it came to non-Western and pre-Renaissance art. Two approaches prevailed, felt Coomaraswamy, both equally misguided. One leaned on the narrative of progress, celebrating achievements in perspective and knowledge of anatomy, and seeing pre-Renaissance and non-Western art as inferior because it lacked these technical achievements. What this approach failed to appreciate was that, although perspective and anatomy were useful in portraying appearance, art was not actually about appearance – or should not be. Artists who had focused on truth and meaning rather than appearance were actually superior, not inferior. The other approach of contemporary art criticism, thought Coomaraswamy, was to focus on the aesthetic qualities of ancient and primitive art – on its appearance, not its meaning. Again, this missed the point. 'If we are disturbed by what we call the "vacancy" of a Buddha's expression, ought we not to bear in mind that he is thought of as the Eye in the World, the impassible spectator of things as they really are, and that it would have been impertinent to have given him features moulded by human curiosity or passion?'[16]

Contemporary understandings had also divided art from use, and art from production: 'The manufacture of "art" in studios coupled with an artless "manufacture" in factories represents a reduction of the standard of living to subhuman levels.'[17] Coomaraswamy also followed Ruskin's social criticism: 'There could hardly be found a stronger condemnation of the present social order than in the fact that the man at work is no longer doing what he likes best, but rather what he must, and in the general belief that a man can only be really happy when he "gets away" and is at play.'[18] Coomaraswamy thus connected art and life in a way that Havell had not.

Coomaraswamy's combination of Traditionalism with pre-existing understandings, most importantly those going back to Ruskin and before him to Plato, created a new way of seeing non-Western and medieval art. This was well received in a West that had grown tired of naturalistic art. Coomaraswamy and Havell are now seen as the founders of contemporary Western scholarship in Indian art. Coomaraswamy was a curator and researcher, not a practising artist, and therefore never attempted to put his views into practice. As we will see, his application of Traditionalism to art was also further developed and applied by other Traditionalists, notably Schuon and a Swiss collaborator and follower of Schuon, Titus Burckhardt, the son of the Neoclassical sculptor Carl Burckhardt (whose monumental works occupy several prominent sites in Basel). Coomaraswamy's project, then, was and remains successful.

Later Traditionalist views

Like Evola and Coomaraswamy, Frithjof Schuon also emphasized the relationship between true art and the transcendent,
but without visibly depending on Platonism. Confusingly,
he even used the term 'form' in its standard, non-Platonic
sense. The artistic 'form' (by which he meant a work of art),
he argued, 'symbolically, corresponds . . . to the Intellect',[19]
and such forms (works) 'are the work of human hands in
a secondary manner only; they originate first and foremost
from the same suprahuman source from which all tradition
originates'.[20]

Schuon introduced a clear distinction between 'sacred'
and 'profane' art, a distinction which corresponded roughly
to the distinction between the traditional and the modern,
although traditional art could sometimes be predominate-
ly profane, and modern art could sometimes attempt to be
sacred, usually with little success. While traditional sacred
art was 'determined, illuminated, and guided by spirituality', modern profane art 'calls only for a superficial copying
of Nature. Reaching the extreme limit of its own platitude,
naturalism inevitably engendered the monstrosities of sur-
realism.'[21] Modern attempts at sacred art were sometimes so
bad that the impact was actually anti-religious in its 'insipid
hypocrisy'. 'That which was meant to stimulate piety in the
believer . . . serves to confirm unbelievers in their impiety.'[22]
Schuon was here presumably thinking of the mass-produced
plaster figures of saints once popular in Catholic countries,
valued by some but ridiculed by others. Traditional sacred
art, in contrast, had been 'the most direct means of action' of

esotericism, as works of sacred art 'act as vehicles of the integral religious doctrine, and . . . thanks to their symbolism translate this doctrine into a language that is both immediate and universal'.[23] The universality of the symbolism of sacred art means that it can transmit both metaphysical truths to the spiritual elite and 'psychological attitudes that are accessible to all men'.[24] This is what makes sacred art so important.

As examples of sacred art, Schuon gave medieval cathedrals (which he saw as benefiting from craft initiation, following Guénon and Evola) and icons of the Virgin Mary. A Byzantine icon of the Virgin, Schuon argues, is 'closer to the truth of Mary' than a post-Renaissance Western European painting, as 'a naturalistic image . . . of necessity is always that of another woman'.[25] The point is the same as Coomaraswamy's, without bringing in the artist's mistress. The icon, in contrast, 'transmits the holiness or inner reality of the Virgin and hence the universal reality of which the Virgin herself is an expression: in suggesting both a contemplative experience and a metaphysical truth, the icon becomes a support of intellection, whereas a naturalistic image transmits . . . only the fact that Mary was a woman'.[26]

Schuon, unlike Evola and Coomaraswamy, did not entirely reject the term 'aesthetic', and saw those who thought that the aesthetic was unimportant, like some modernists, as products of the decadence of modernity. Rather, he moved aesthetic appreciation into a secondary position, for example explaining the apparent lack of 'aesthetic discernment' in Oriental peoples when faced with the products of Western modernity in terms of the difference between Western and non-Western artistic forms.

Schuon, unlike Coomaraswamy, was himself active as a painter. His paintings of the Virgin and of Native American scenes are valued by his followers as icons, but are little appreciated by others. It has been suggested that they are inspired, perhaps unconsciously, by Paul Gauguin. A comparison of Schuon's paintings with those of Gauguin makes the similarity clear, and also makes clear that Gauguin's work is very much the better, whatever one's aesthetics.

TITUS BURCKHARDT

The Traditionalist philosophy of art was further developed by Titus Burckhardt, who argued that the sacred art of all religions reflected and gave access to metaphysical truth. He showed how not only religion but also sacred art was a way of approaching esoteric metaphysics. 'The study of Islamic art, or any other sacred art, can lead . . . to a more or less profound understanding of the spiritual realities that lie at the root of a whole cosmic and human world,' he argued.[27] In this he was following Coomaraswamy, but making the point more explicitly, and more systematically.

Burckhardt gave a special place to Islamic art. It has been argued that he did for Islamic art what Coomaraswamy had done for Indian art, bringing it within the artistic canon as understood in the West. Coomaraswamy's impact was greater than Burckhardt's, though, partly because it was earlier – he was writing his main works in the 1920s, while Burckhardt's *Art of Islam: Language and Meaning* was not published until 1976, by which time many others had written on Islamic art.

Burckhardt's Traditionalist philosophy of art is to be

found most clearly expressed in his *Sacred Art in East and West: Its Principles and Methods*, first published in French in 1958.[28] In this work, he expanded on the established Traditionalist understanding of art, and then provided a systematic survey of Hindu, Christian, Islamic, Taoist, and Buddhist sacred art, emphasizing their shared cosmology and showing how, despite the way in which they all 'reflect the spiritual vision characteristic of a particular religion', they are all also, in the end, expressions of 'the fullness of Divine Truth and Grace'.[29] Just as each tradition has its own divine revelation but all have the same, single divine essence, so each tradition has its own sacred art. In contrast, 'modern individualism has produced, apart from a few works of genius which are nevertheless spiritually barren, all the ugliness – the endless and despairing ugliness – of the forms which permeate the "ordinary life" of our times'.[30]

In *Sacred Art in East and West*, Burckhardt's focus was on architecture: Hindu temples, Christian cathedrals, Islamic mosques. The Hindu temple is a sanctuary for the Divine Spirit, and the altar is a 'primordial inheritance'. The Hindu altar can be understood with the help of the rituals of the Oglala Lakota in North America – Burckhardt is here following Schuon's interests. The portal of a Christian cathedral is made up of a door and a niche, and the niche is universal, found also in the mosque. But while the focus of Christian worship is the Incarnate Word and the eucharistic sacrament, the focus of Islamic worship is outside the mosque, distant – the Kaaba, to which Muslims everywhere in the world turn to pray. 'A Muslim's awareness of the divine presence is based on the feeling of limitlessness; he rejects all objectification of the Divine, except that which presents itself to him in the form of limitless space.'[31] This fits with Islam's ancient connection with nomadism and the empty spaces of the desert. 'An acute sense of the fragility of the world, a conciseness of thought and action and a genius for rhythm are nomadic qualities,' wrote Burckhardt.[32] It is certainly true that a Muslim in prayer turns towards the Kaaba, and, while it is over a thousand years since a substantial proportion of Muslims were nomads, Burckhardt's proposal undeniably has poetic force. He also argued that Islamic art is characterized not only by the nomadic sense of rhythm but also by a 'geometrical genius, which . . . flows directly from the kind of speculation favoured by Islam, which is "abstract" and not "mythological"'.[33] Again, whether or not it is right to distance Islam from mythology (and there are plenty of stories in the Quran that might easily be understood as mythological), Burckhardt's idea has a certain poetic beauty, and does explain the prominent role that geometrical decoration has indeed played in Islamic art – or, if we accept the distinction, Islamic crafts.

Burckhardt resolved two problems with which earlier Traditionalists had struggled: the place in art of originality and genius, and the issue of the apparent quality of Renaissance art. The general tendency for Traditionalists before Burckhardt had been to dismiss appreciation of originality and genius as a modernist delusion, comparable to mistaken modern passions for progress and individuality. Burckhardt compromised on this, arguing that 'no work exists that is traditional . . . which does not give sensible expression to a certain creative joy of the soul'.[34] Creativity is back, then, if in a subordinate position. Similarly, the general tendency had been to dismiss Renaissance art altogether. The issue here is that it is really hard to look at the masterpieces of the Renaissance and conclude that they are entirely worthless. Burckhardt did not deny the genius of Renaissance painters and sculptors, conceding that 'like the bursting of a dam the Renaissance produced a cascade of creative forces'. These, however, ultimately lost their 'unity and force'.[35] This was inevitable, as 'Renaissance art is rationalistic – this is expressed in its use of perspective and in its architectural theory – [but] at the same time passional, its passion . . . amounting to a general affirmation of the ego'.[36] Artists can 'seek the Infinite in a relatively simple form' or 'seek the Infinite in the apparent richness of diversity and change, though it must lead in the end to dispersion and exhaustion'.[37]

In his *Art of Islam*, Burckhardt addressed a more general audience, as he was writing in connection with the World of Islam Festival, a high-profile series of exhibitions and events in London in 1976 that was mostly arranged by followers of Schuon and made possible by generous sponsorship, especially from the then newly rich United Arab Emirates. The *Art of Islam* is almost as much an introduction to Islam as it is to Islamic art, and much of the book is devoted to presenting and describing high points of Islamic architecture, calligraphy, arabesques, and even clothing. It draws on both standard art history and the conclusions of *Sacred Art in East and West*. On the one hand, Islamic art has many different styles, but, on the other hand, they are all a reflection of 'diversity in unity, or of unity in diversity'.[38]

In the end, tradition is beautiful and transcendent, and

Islam is traditional and beautiful. Modernity is ugly, and Islam is not troubled by modernity or ugliness, save when these have been introduced by the West. Once, even in the West, 'every artist who produced an object was called a "craftsman", and every discipline which demanded not only theoretical knowledge but also practical ability was an "art". This remains true of the Islamic world wherever – and such places are becoming increasingly rare – there has been no Western influence.'[39] Sometimes Burckhardt went a little further than might be thought justified, as when he insisted that 'the affinity between art and contemplation is strong enough, in many Islamic cities, for entry into a craft corporation to coincide with attachment to a spiritual affili-ation which goes back to the Prophet through 'Alī'.[40] It was true in the eighteenth century that many trade guilds were paired with Sufi orders, an arrangement reminiscent of Guénon's craft initiation, but by 1976 this had long ceased to be the case.

The *Art of Islam*, like the World of Islam Festival itself, in many ways achieved the objectives of its sponsors, present-ing Islamic civilization to the British and Western publics in terms that were very positive and also made sense – Islam was as much a cultural achievement as the Renaissance, if not more so. The project, then, succeeded on its own terms. As has since been pointed out, however, this presentation was also problematic, as it positioned the Muslim world firmly in the past. The photographs in *Art of Islam* are beautiful, but the Muslims who appear in them are riding donkeys, not driving cars. Islam and Islamic art both become timeless and, thus, essentialized, an understanding that contemporary

Muslims and scholars of Islam struggle against. Islam, in reality, is not timeless but living and changing, and is quite at home in the modern world, not a relic of the past.

Artistic Traditionalism today

After Burckhardt, the three major representatives of the Traditionalist philosophy of art became the Iranian-American architect Nader Ardalan, the English art scholar Keith Critchlow, and the English composer Sir John Tavener. They respectively brought architecture, Islamic geometric patterns, and music into Traditionalist artistic project.

ARDALAN'S ARCHITECTURE

In his *The Sense of Unity: The Sufi Tradition in Persian Architecture*, co-written with an Iranian-American Traditionalist, Laleh Bakhtiar, Nader Ardalan took the Traditionalist understanding of art to its furthest conclusion. It is not just traditional arts and crafts and architecture that give access to metaphysical truth, he argued, but all varieties of space, shape, surface, colour, and matter, especially in sacred and domestic architecture and in city planning, and also in curtains, calligraphy, woodwork, tilework, carpets, and even nature. The survey in *The Sense of Unity* is even more comprehensive than Burckhardt's *Art of Islam*, but deals with Persia and Iran, not the whole of Islam, and sometimes also with pre-Islamic Persia.

This survey, however, is incidental to Ardalan's main purpose, which is to construct a total system of meaning. 'It is through the qualitative significances of space, matter, and all perceived objects or phenomena that the objective knowledge and aesthetics of the traditional man develops. These things are independent of the individual and lie beyond his subjective appreciation or rejection.'[41] Ardalan, then, agrees with the medieval European understanding of sacred art teaching directly, but does not limit this to sacred art. It also applies to an ordinary house. 'Carpeted floors . . . provide the traditional man with his locus of physical repose. Seated in his essential space, this man is devoid of extraneous furniture and objects that might complicate his full appreciation of the potent, qualitative values of carpet, garden, and the positive space of room.'[42] The city is especially important: 'Within the ordered world view of the traditional society, man moves between his macrocosmic conception of the universe and his microcosmic view of himself. His concept of "city" lies midway between these two poles, incorporating the symbolic principles of both views.'[43] *The Sense of Unity* is more an exposition of Ardalan's total system than a detailed proof of its traditional authenticity, though he does quote from Ibn Arabi and other Sufis as appropriate. In fact, Ardalan's system is probably not soundly grounded in the historical sources. But it has fascinated many of his readers, especially in Iran.

As well as writing *The Sense of Unity*, Ardalan has also had a distinguished career as an architect, designing a number of major buildings in Iran, the Gulf, and America, including a striking office block in Tehran that later became the Ministry of Education, a Sheraton hotel in Kuwait, and a 37-floor condominium tower in New York City. To what extent these succeed in combining his system with the economic and structural requirements of contemporary building is open to debate.

CRITCHLOW'S ISLAMIC PATTERNS

Keith Critchlow, an Englishman who had worked on Platonic and Pythagorean geometry before encountering Tradition-alism, developed Burckhardt's observations rather as Ard-alan did, but in a more restrained fashion. He focused not on architecture but on geometrical patterns, developing his analyses in great detail in a number of works, notably his *Islamic Patterns: An Analytical and Cosmological Approach*, published in 1976, and his *The Hidden Geometry of Flowers: Living Rhythms, Form and Number*, published in 2011. Critch-low combined his extensive knowledge of geometry with Traditionalist metaphysics and cosmology, again applied especially to Islam. His key argument was that 'self-evident mathematical patterns with their esoteric philosophical values became the invisible foundation upon which the "art" was built . . . mathematics was integral to . . . art as it was a "universal" structure supporting the intuitive insights that characterise all true art'.[44] This gave art a particular function, as looking at it directly deepened one's spiritual understand-ing. The same was true of flowers, as 'what is evident in the geometry of the face of a flower can remind us of the geom-etry that underlies all existence. Studying the geometry of flowers is therefore a powerful way to reconnect us with the idea that we are all one.'[45]

Critchlow's book on *The Hidden Geometry of Flowers* is beautifully illustrated and aimed at a general audience, but his real work was on patterns, especially in *Islamic Patterns*, which devotes more space to graphical demonstrations and mathematics than to discussion. These demonstrations and calculations are practical more than theoretical. Critchlow put these and other Traditionalist understandings of art into practice, first in his courses as Professor of Islamic Art at the Royal College of Art in London and then, from the 1980s until his death in 2020, through what started as a programme in Visual Islamic and Traditional Arts (VITA) and subsequently became an independent educational institution, the Prince's School of Traditional Arts, part of a foundation run by the United Kingdom's Prince Charles before his accession to the throne as King Charles III. It continues to flourish, and is a successful Traditionalist project in the field of art.

TAVENER'S MUSIC

Sir John Tavener was already famous as a composer before discovering Traditionalism. His early composition *The Whale*, written in 1966, was received enthusiastically, and a recording was released by the Beatles' Apple Records label. Tavener later described *The Whale* as a cul-de-sac, and proceeded in very different directions after his conversion to the Orthodox Church and then his encounter with Traditionalism. The later Tavener draws directly on Schuon, to whom he often referred, and less directly on Coomaraswamy and Burckhardt. His starting point is, once again, the idea of the function of art being to reveal the perfection of form. Tavener understood music as the 'sound of God', as pre-existing, and saw the task of the composer – his own task – as being to recover that which already existed.

The later Tavener sought to find, or to compose, what he called the *musica perennis*, applying to music an approach similar to Schuon's approach to religion. At its core, music was one, felt Tavener, but its expressions were multiple, different in different traditions. These different traditions each had their own specificities, and could not just be mixed together. 'There can be no crude, facile syncretism in composing the *Musica Perennis* . . . I had to "imbibe" the ethos of other great traditions, and then by a mysterious alchemical process of change try to produce an inner unity out of the apparent multiplicity. One does not produce a cacophony of musical chants East and West, but rather looks for the unity beneath the outward forms.'[46]

Tavener's 'alchemical process' was, in some sense, creative: the composer could not merely repeat. To some extent, then, Tavener follows Burckhardt. 'We are forced to reinterpret, because the copying of past examples implies keeping something alive which is undergoing the process of dying. The term "survival" implies continuity of an "ethos", but the maintenance of an ethos does not presuppose the preservation of *eidos* [a form].'[47] A purely theoretical approach to art would not work: in order to really understand the problems of producing sacred art, one had to be a practising artist. Tavener also echoed Burckhardt on the issue of post-medieval art. Yes, this had produced 'the hellish realms of modernism', but it had also produced music that was sublime. 'Mozart was a child of the Enlightenment, but he confounds the theory that this age could not produce a paradisal music. Mozart was quite literally . . . "a ray of God" . . . I often hear his instruments in the quartets, as voices talking to each other in Paradise.'[48] Reality, then, does not always conform to theory, and there is no point in pretending that it does.

Tavener felt his task in composing the *musica perennis* was made easier by the *kali-yuga*, because it was so easy for a modern composer to hear the music of other traditions. Just as Schuon could do what had never been possible before and write with knowledge of all religious traditions, not just one, so a composer could now compose with knowledge of all musical (and religious) traditions, thought Tavener. This is what he tried to do. His *musica perennis* remained rooted in the Christian tradition, but also drew on other traditions, both in terms of musical styles and instruments – most frequently the large Tibetan temple bowl – and in theological terms. Tavener's monumental *The Veil of the Temple*, which premiered at the Temple Church in London in 2003, starts with a Sufi poem by Rumi, moves (over several hours) through psalms and Orthodox liturgy, and ends as 'Mary Magdalen, recognising the divinity of Christ, cries "*Ravouni*" (Master). She has realised the Self, or Atma, within her, which activates an explosion into the Hindu world, as the basses begin changing [*sic*] in Sanskrit "*Tat tvam asi*" (That I am). The *Upanishad Hymn* which follows introduces brass instruments and timpani as all the forces sing the opening of the *Isa Upanishad*: "Sink this universe in God".[49]

The Veil of the Temple was well received, and Tavener is certainly the greatest artist within the Traditionalist movement, but his most popular work is from his Orthodox rather than his Traditionalist period. His best-known composition is 'Song for Athene', which was played at the funeral of Princess Diana in 1997, and has since been heard by many millions. It draws on Orthodox models, but is purely Christian. His 'The Lamb', composed in 1982, is also very popular, and is a setting of the poem by William Blake. Blake's poem is part of the Western esoteric corpus, but Tavener's 'The Lamb' does not fit his own later understanding of the *musica perennis*. This does not undermine Tavener's Traditionalist theories of music, however. It perhaps just shows that his most popular works are his most accessible. The success of his project, then, is hard to judge.

Conclusion

The application of the Traditionalist philosophy to art meant the revival of the Platonic idea of the representation of the forms as both the essence of beauty and as the most important function of art, the combination of this idea with some of the perspectives of John Ruskin, and the application of Frithjof Schuon's perennialism to art criticism, to writing about art, to teaching art, and – in the case of Sir John Tavener – to composing great music.

The Traditionalist philosophy of art owes little to René Guénon, unlike the foundations and core projects of Traditionalism. The central point about the forms was made by Julius Evola, but the earliest important Traditionalist writings about art were by Ananda Coomaraswamy, whose contributions to Traditionalism's foundations and core projects were, conversely, of less importance. Coomaraswamy was already well known for his work on South Asian art before he became a Traditionalist. This made his later, Traditionalist work even more influential. The idea that South Asian art should be understood in terms of its symbolism and metaphysics became well established. His understanding of art in perennial terms rather than in terms of historical development was also influential.

Frithjof Schuon did not himself take the Traditionalist philosophy of art much further, but his followers did. Titus Burckhardt did not quite do for Islamic art what Coomaraswamy had done for South Asian art, but he did encourage an understanding of it in symbolic, metaphysical, and perennial (rather than historical) terms. He also extended the Traditionalist understanding beyond painting and sculpture to architecture and geometrical patterns. These understandings were taken further in the case of architecture and space by Nader Ardalan, perhaps more in his writings than in his own work, and in the case of geometrical patterns by Keith Critchlow, in both his writings and the teaching institution that he established.

Tavener was the most gifted Traditionalist artist, and his attempt to create the *musica perennis* was widely appreciated – and perhaps more successful than Schuon's attempt to create the *religio perennis*. Tavener also moderated some of the more difficult parts of the Traditionalist philosophy of art with a dose of realism. Although he maintained the Traditionalist insistence that art is ultimately about the transcendent, not about the creativity of the artist, he accepted that creativity did matter. Although he adhered to the Traditionalist historical narrative, he conceded that Mozart wrote great music. He maintained that in order to understand art, one also has to be a working artist.

CHAPTER 11
Gender

Traditionalism's second further project relates to gender. Gender is a major topic in humanity's earliest myths; it interested Aristotle, among other thinkers, and it is still much debated. First- and second-wave feminism have now given way to third and even fourth waves. The application of Traditionalism to questions of gender, however, mostly ignores the contemporary debate, which it dismisses as typically modern in its emphasis on equality and its denial of difference. Only the Traditionalist fellow-traveller Jordan Peterson has engaged directly with the contemporary debate. Given Traditionalist positions on modernity, equality, and hierarchy, the Traditionalist project was never going to be feminist when it came to gender. The Traditionalist project instead seeks to maximize and even utilize gender differences.

The Traditionalist gender project has focused on a number of related issues. One of these is the issue of self-realization for women, given that the varieties of self-realization discussed in an earlier chapter were mostly thought appropriate for men, not women. Julius Evola's path of the warrior was especially male. As well as the practical issue of self-realization, Evola and Frithjof Schuon also investigated what Evola called 'the metaphysics of sex', its nature and significance at a spiritual level, coming to very different conclusions. Finally, Evola – and only Evola – applied Traditionalism to sexuality, to the sexual act.

The use of the terms 'sex' and 'gender' is now fluid. A distinction was originally made between the biological, termed 'sex', and the psychological or social, termed 'gender', a distinction that is important both for some feminists and for some Traditionalists. In this use, sex is a physical reality that can be seen, while gender is a social construction that must be performed. The term 'gender', however, is tending to replace the term 'sex' when referring to the biological, while 'sex' is tending to refer more and more to the sexual act. This chapter follows the older usage, treating 'sex' as biological and 'gender' as social.

Earlier views

The distinction between male and female was fundamental in premodern human societies, some of which also had conceptions of a third sex and of transgenderism. At the most basic level, human languages normally distinguish past from present and future, singular from plural, and male from female, usually assigning gender even to inanimate objects. The distinction between male and female is also fundamental in early human mythologies. Gods and other supernatural beings usually had one or another sex, and behaved in ways that seemed appropriate to the related gender.

Early representations of female gods and earthly women are often no more negative than representations of male gods and earthly men, but the poet Hesiod, in whose work we find the earliest periodization in terms of Golden Age through to Iron Age, set the tone for many centuries of misogyny by assigning the cause of all evils to a woman, Pandora, and warning men against allowing themselves to be enslaved by women's beauty and cunning, which allowed women to consume the fruits of men's labour without contributing to it. In the Bible, a similarly negative role was assigned to Eve.

The one God of the Bible is not gendered in the way that earlier supernatural beings were. The God of the monotheistic religions is not a material being, and is thus generally understood as being beyond sex, which is a characteristic of material beings. Despite this, the non-sexed monotheistic God has until very recently always been referred to as 'He', and has in practice usually been conceived of as male

Sex interested Aristotle, who wrote at length on it, looking at different kinds of animal and plant and investigating such questions as how the sex of offspring is determined. His writings on these topics are closer to what we would now call biology than to what we would now call philosophy. He saw the female, from whom new life emerges, as similar to the earth, and the male, whose seed acts on the female as seeds do on the earth, as similar to the sun. The male is active, and the female is passive, in this respect and in others. Male seed is comparable to Platonic form, and its female counterpart is comparable to matter.

Sex in humans was never Aristotle's main topic, and, when it was discussed, he generally understood it in terms of what he observed in animals. Having noted that, with the exception of the bear and the leopard, the female animal was 'softer in disposition than the male . . . and more attentive to the nurture of the young' while the male was 'more spirited than the female, more savage, more simple and less cunning',[1] he concluded that human beings provided the perfect example of this general tendency. 'Woman is more compassionate than man, more easily moved to tears, at the same time is more jealous, more querulous, more apt to scold and to strike. She is, furthermore . . . more void of shame or self-respect, more false of speech, more deceptive, and of more retentive memory.'[2] In the association of certain negative qualities with women, Aristotle echoed Hesiod.

Positive rather than negative qualities were associated by early Christianity with one particular woman, the Virgin Mary. Devotion to her grew over the centuries. In the fifth century, she became the 'Mother of God', and by the nineteenth century the Catholic Church celebrated her as second only to Jesus among creation, in numerous images, prayers, feasts, and even apparitions. The Virgin Mary always remained human, however, though some Protestants accused the Catholics of assimilating her to the Divine, and others accused Christians of, in their devotion to the Virgin, resurrecting and rehabilitating pagan goddesses such as Isis. The significance of the Virgin Mary was more theological than social: her many virtues were examples for men as well as women. The model for human couples was still Adam and Eve, not God and Mary.

The model of the non-sexed but effectively male God that was challenged in Christianity by growing devotion to the Virgin Mary was also challenged in Judaism. Just as Sufism developed within Islam, a school of thought and practice known as Kabbalah ('reception' or 'tradition') developed within Judaism, first becoming visible in the twelfth century.

The Kabbalistic cosmology is close to the Neoplatonic cosmology, and some scholars see it as having Neoplatonic origins. A distinction was made between the God that humans can experience and Ein Sof ('without end'), a concept that is close to the One of Plotinus. As in the Neoplatonic model various emanations proceed from the One, in the Kabbalistic model ten *sefirot* (countings, singular *sefira*) proceed from Ein Sof. The *sefirot* can also be understood as aspects or manifestations of God. And they are gendered.

Most of the *sefirot* are male. Notably, the first *sefira*, Keter (the crown), which proceeds directly from Ein Sof, is male. But the third and tenth *sefirot* are female. The third *sefira* is Binah (understanding), the counterpart of the male Hokmah (wisdom), and the tenth is the Malkhut (kingdom), from which the sensible world emanates. The Malkhut is identified with the Shekhinah (dwelling), the divine presence on earth. Ultimately, then, the female Malkhut receives the male Keter, in a divine male–female union. For this reason, human sexual relations are sacred. They are parallel to, and affect, the divine male–female union.

Just as the significance of the Virgin Mary for Catholics was more theological than social, so the significance of the gendering of the *sefirot* was more theological or philosophical for the Kabbalists. Relations between actual men and women remained governed by the *halakha* (way), the Jewish equivalent of the Sharia, as they were for Jews who were not Kabbalists.

Pre-modern Jews, Christians, and Muslims, rather like Aristotle, generally saw the difference between the sexes as innate, and explained by biological function, and saw women as inferior to men. This perspective was widely accepted for many centuries, but was challenged by the English educator Mary Wollstonecraft, the key writer of what is now termed 'first-wave feminism'. Her *A Vindication of the Rights of Woman* was published in 1792 at the height of the French Revolution, during which discussion of the 'Rights of Man' led to discussion of the rights of women. Wollstonecraft argued for granting women civil and political rights, and – especially – for educating them to develop reason and virtue. She argued against men who 'try to secure the good conduct of women by attempting to keep them always in a state of childhood',[3] and against women who teach their daughters that 'a little knowledge of human weakness, justly termed cunning, softness of temper, outward obedience, and a scrupulous attention to a puerile kind of propriety, will obtain for them the protection of man; and should they be beautiful, everything else is needless'.[4] Her implicit argument is that the alleged inferiority of women, visible in feminine characteristics that correspond in part with those listed by Aristotle, is learned, not innate, and her explicit argument is that proper education can and should enable women 'to cherish a nobler ambition' than merely to attract a dependable man. Certain female characteristics might seem to justify granting rights to men but not women; but as these characteristics were acquired rather than innate, they might change, and so might the relationship between the sexes.

Not everyone agreed with early feminist positions, however. During the 1850s, the elderly German philosopher Arthur Schopenhauer entered the discussion, arguing against granting rights to women. Women, he felt, should never be allowed unfettered control of property. His essay 'On Women', which is now notorious, argued explicitly that the inferiority of women was innate, and explained this in quasi-evolutionary terms: 'Nature has equipped woman, as every other creature, with the weapons and tools she needs for securing her existence.'[5] 'Just as nature has endowed the lion with claws and jaws . . . and the cuttlefish with ink that clouds the water, so too nature has endowed woman with the art of dissimulation for her protection and defence.'[6] Schopenhauer, then, made much the same argument as Aristotle.

Schopenhauer also discussed sexuality. In his 'Metaphysics of the Love of the Sexes', he argued that the way in which love 'constantly lays claim to half the powers and thoughts of the younger portion of mankind, [and] is the ultimate goal of almost all human effort',[7] could be explained in terms of the central importance of love and sexuality in the continuation of humankind. He wrote:

> We contemplate the turmoil of life . . . its want and misery . . . its multifarious sorrows . . . In the midst of the tumult, we see the glances of two lovers meet longingly: yet why so secretly, fearfully, and stealthily? Because these lovers are the traitors who seek to perpetuate the whole want and drudgery, which would otherwise speedily reach an end; this they wish to frustrate, as others like them have frustrated it before.[8]

Schopenhauer also discussed homosexuality, which presented a problem for his argument from nature, since homosexuality does not obviously contribute to the continuation of humankind. In the final revised edition of an appendix to his

'Metaphysics of the Love of the Sexes' he proposed the ingenious, if scientifically untenable, theory that homosexuality served nature's purposes because the sperm of young men and of old men was weak. Avoiding the begetting of weak children by having old men have sex with young men thus served the good of the species as a whole.

Late nineteenth-century Vienna also saw interest in sexuality. The work of Freud, much of which dealt with sexuality and sex, is well known, was generally ignored by the Traditionalists, and will not be reviewed here. Less well remembered, but once widely read and discussed, is *Sex and Character: An Investigation of Fundamental Principles* by the young Viennese philosopher Otto Weininger, who shot himself at the age of 23, shortly after publishing his masterwork, which was a revised and extended version of his PhD thesis. Weininger agreed that female characteristics were innate rather than learned, but accepted the legal equality of the sexes without discussion. He broke new ground by rejecting the binary understanding which places men and women in opposition to each other, as if all men and all women were identical. In fact, 'there are any number of intermediate stages between the complete Man and the complete Woman',[9] he wrote. The analytical starting point is therefore not masculinity or femininity as with Wollstonecraft and Schopenhauer, but bisexuality, a concept Weininger borrowed from the German surgeon Wilhelm Fliess, as did Freud (though some dispute this). In Weininger's view, all humans are partly male and partly female. Men are normally more male than female, and women are normally more female than male.

Weininger drew various conclusions from this. One was

that the 'laws of sexual attraction' operated to match complementary proportions of maleness and femaleness, so that the resulting couple was as close as possible to half male and half female. Somewhat female men were thus attracted to somewhat male women, and so on. This, he further argued, explained homosexuality: an extremely female man or an extremely male women would be homosexual. Homosexuality was thus innate, not acquired, as most other theories proposed. Weininger did not explain why an extremely female man should be attracted to another man rather than to an extremely male woman, as his basic law would seem to suggest.

Another conclusion was that a further basis of analysis was 'a psychic type of Woman and of Man ... even though they are never reached by reality'.[10] Weininger sometimes labelled these ideal-types 'W' and 'M', to distinguish them from actual, living women and men. A final conclusion, somewhat running contrary to his main line of thought, was that 'all intermediate sexual forms notwithstanding, a human being is ultimately one of two things, either a man or a woman'.[11]

Weininger's book has remained controversial, combining as it does ideas that are seen as progressive with ideas that are seen as quite as misogynistic as those of Schopenhauer. The book also addressed 'the Woman Question' squarely, describing its position as 'anti-feminist'.[12] Women who favoured 'emancipation' and wanted to live like men, explained Weininger, were women who had an unusually high proportion of masculinity in their make-up. Talented and emancipated women were generally lesbians.

A further wave of discussion started in post-Second World War Paris with the publication of *The Second Sex* by the French philosopher Simone de Beauvoir, who occupies the same place in 'second-wave' feminism as Mary Wollstonecraft does in first-wave feminism. De Beauvoir, like Wollstonecraft, held that what matters was what was learned, not what was innate. 'One is not born, but rather becomes, woman. No biological, psychic, or economic destiny defines the figure that the human female takes on in society.'[13] This famous statement is the basis for the distinction that came to be generally made between sex, as physical, and gender, as acquired or learned.

For de Beauvoir, homosexuality is sometimes innate – a matter of physiology – and sometimes chosen. She disagreed with Weininger, who did not distinguish between sex and gender, and therefore maintained that a homosexual 'always shows an anatomical approximation to the opposite sex'. Weininger thought that homosexual men were always 'partly feminine in their external appearance and behaviour';[14] de Beauvoir conceded that physiology could be relevant, but this was far from the norm.

The distinction between sex and gender has since been questioned, notably by Judith Butler, who pointed out that physical sex is not inevitable, as the body is 'a passive medium that is signified by an inscription from a cultural source figured as "external" to that body'.[15] The body is male or female only once it is deemed to be male or female; sex, like gender, has to be 'performed'. Even so, the idea of gender as socially constructed – and thus as not innate – remains popular. Butler does not in fact question this; she rather extends it.

A slightly different question was raised by feminist theorists of the 1970s, who asked why women were subordinated to men in nearly all human societies, a phenomenon that they described as 'patriarchy'. This term had originally been used mostly by anthropologists to describe a system of male-headed households and patrilineal descent and inheritance, but 1970s theorists expanded it to denote the whole system of subordination and domination. The American feminist Kate Millett identified eight possible explanations of patriarchy in 1969, of which the most important were ideological and sociological: just as gender was acquired or learned, so were gender roles and status, especially through the family, 'patriarchy's chief institution', which ensured 'control and conformity', and through economics.[16] Even on the rare occasions that women could earn their own living, they were paid less than men.

Other feminist theorists emphasized capitalism, producing Marxist critiques. Some also suggested biological explanations, notably the Canadian-American feminist activist Shulamith Firestone, who argued in 1970 that the family was the site of patriarchy because it was the site of reproduction. 'That women throughout history before the advent of birth control were at the continual mercy of their biology . . . made them dependent on males . . . for physical survival,' she wrote, and the length of time taken by a human infant to become independent also made the family essential. But this need not always be the case. 'We are no longer just animals. And the Kingdom of Nature does not reign absolute . . . Humanity has begun to outgrow nature.' The biological basis of female oppression could and should be swept away, initially by socialism and changing 'the social institutions of childbearing and childrearing', and ultimately by 'artificial reproduction'. The objective should be that 'the sex distinction itself' be abolished, and 'genital differences between human beings would no longer matter'.[17]

To some extent, Firestone's call has been answered. Even if artificial reproduction remains a dream and childbearing itself has not changed fundamentally since 1970, the institutions of childrearing have changed in major ways in many countries, notably in Scandinavia, and both the importance of the family and the nature of the patriarchy in those countries have changed as a result. Understandings of patriarchy, however, generally focus more on the ideological than the sociological and economic explanations that Millett emphasized.

Traditionalist views

Guénon was not interested in questions of gender or sexuality. His cosmology is not gendered. He rarely discusses feminism, which, when he does mention it in passing, he sees as an instance of the modern egalitarianism that refuses to see differences in nature between one person and another, and results in woman being 'taken out of her normal role by being granted access to functions that ought to belong exclusively to men'.[18] The idea that certain functions belong to certain types of person is important for Guénon, but is far more often discussed in terms of caste than in terms of sex.

Guénon did, however, consider the question of initiation from the perspective of sex. In a short article on 'Feminine Initiation and Craft Initiations' that was published posthumously, he noted that a male initiation is no more suitable for a woman than a female initiation is for a man, given that men and women have different natures. This view fits with his view that different types of initiation were suitable for different natures, generally understood in terms of different castes and civilizations, which explains why there are so many different initiatic paths. He lamented the absence of surviving female initiatic paths in the contemporary West. There was 'Co-Masonry', a branch of Freemasonry which admits women, but this was not a 'regular, traditional organization' of the sort that is required, in Guénon's view, for effective initiation. He concluded that there is perhaps a possibility of reconstituting a Western craft initiation for women through Compagnonnage. There are, of course, female initiatic paths in the East, he wrote, notably among Sufis. In this respect, despite what Westerners think, 'Western women are in reality much more disadvantaged than they are in Eastern civilizations.'[19]

Guénon, then, saw paths to self-realization as gendered at a practical level. Traditional Freemasonry did not admit women, and Co-Masonry was not traditional. At a more abstract level, his discussions of metaphysics and self-realization were not gendered.

EVOLA ON SEX AND SEXUALITY

Evola, in contrast to Guénon, wrote at length about sex, gender, and sexuality. As well as considering female paths to self-realization, he considered the use of sexuality as a path to self-realization in itself, as well as the connection between gender and spirituality.

One of Evola's starting points was Johann Jakob Bachofen's portrayal of primitive matriarchy in *Mother Right*, which, as we have seen, also had an impact on Marxism. Another was Plotinus, and another was Weininger. From Bachofen, Evola took the idea of a transition from primitive matriarchy to a male-dominated civilization, which he saw as mature and heroic. From Plotinus he took the idea of the One as self-sufficient, to which he added the idea of the One as masculine, and – following Aristotle – as solar. Self-sufficiency, transcendence, and the state are thus masculine, and multiplicity – which is lunar – is feminine. The priestly, the sentimental, and the religious are lunar and feminine, as are society and 'pantheistic, orgiastic promiscuity'.[20] From Weininger, Evola took the idea that, whatever their bodily features, all people are a mixture of the masculine and the feminine. He combined this idea with the Greek myth (found in Plato's *Symposium*) of an earlier human race of androgynous or hermaphrodite beings that were both male and female, by whom the gods felt threatened. They therefore split these beings into two halves, one male and one female, and ever since male halves and female halves have been desperately seeking for each other. Or, in Evola's version of Weininger, have been seeking a half with a complementary mixture of male and female.

Evola echoed the distinction between sex and gender made by de Beauvoir (though he never cites her, and may not have read her), terming biological sex 'bodily sex' and metaphysical sex 'inner sex'. 'Bodily sex' is thus what de Beauvoir called 'sex', and 'inner sex' is close to 'gender', as it is not physical. For Evola, however, inner sex is not a social construction. Both bodily and inner sex are innate, and a mixture of the masculine and the feminine, following Weininger.

He writes that it is possible for the 'outer, artificial, acquired part' of sex to be de-gendered, in which case it will 'seem of little importance whether one is man or woman,

and such a fact will have less and less value in the determin-
ation of vocations, self-development, conduct of life, model
of occupations'.[21] This, he notes, is what is happening in
modernity, where the outer part of humanity is ever less connected to the essential part. What really matters, however, is
inner sex. Here Evola, like Weininger, distinguishes an ideal-
type of man and woman distinct from actual human men and
women, which he roots in myth by identifying them with the
Platonic forms, and which he calls 'absolute man' and 'absolute woman'.[22] Inner sex is not incidental: one is not human
first, and then either male or female. One is either man or
woman, and then, in that capacity, human. 'Before and be-
sides existing in the body, sex exists in the soul and, to a
certain extent, in the spirit itself.'[23] Given the transcendent
origins of sex in the Platonic forms of male and female,
homosexuality is 'a deviation, not from a conventional or
ethical point of view, but precisely from the standpoint of
the metaphysics of sex'.[24]

Since the form represents perfection, actual men and
women who are seeking perfection should aim at the form of
perfect masculinity or perfect femininity, as the case might
be. Rather than minimizing gender difference, as is generally
the objective for feminists, or explaining gender difference,
as is the objective for non-feminists such as Schopenhauer
and Weininger, Evola aimed to maximize gender difference.
The objective was 'to reduce in a woman all that is masculine and in a man everything that is feminine; and to strive
to implement the archetypes of the "absolute man" and of
the "absolute woman"'.[25] This, wrote Evola, was the opposite of what feminists were trying to do, as they failed to

recognize that 'a woman who is perfectly woman is superior to a man who is imperfectly man, just as a farmer who is faithful to his land and performs his work perfectly is superior to a king who cannot do his own work'.[26] Feminism is actually reducing perfection. 'Modern woman in wanting to be for herself has destroyed herself. The "personality" she so much yearned for is killing all semblance of female personality in her.'[27] This, however, is not the fault of women, but of men, who in modernity have ceased to be real, absolute, men. Equally, the solution lies with men, who must again become absolute men.

Striving to become absolute man or absolute woman is in itself a path to self-realization. The man who is following the path of the warrior is reducing that which is feminine in him, and striving to become absolute man. This is the path of active heroism. The corresponding path for the woman is to become absolute woman; this is the path of passive heroism, of devotion, giving oneself for another. This path, in Evola's view, takes two forms: that of the lover (Aphrodite), and that of the mother (Demeter). In either case, the woman is 'totally giving of herself and being entirely for another being . . . finding in this dedication the meaning of her own life, her own joy, and her own justification'.[28] These female paths have something of the ascetic about them, expressed in a different way.

A further path to self-realization lay through sexuality. For Evola, that men and women fall in love with each other was not, as it was for Schopenhauer, a degrading consequence of the need for reproduction, but rather a metaphysical impulse towards unity and transcendence. 'Sexual love is the most universal form of man's obscure search to eliminate duality for a short while, to existentially overcome the boundary between ego and non-ego, between self and not-self.'[29] There is the possibility of 'erotic experience leading to a displacement of the boundaries of the ego and to the emergence of profound modes of consciousness'.[30] Sexuality may allow someone to go 'beyond the life of an ego enclosed within the limits of the empirical . . . Only that which goes beyond such a life . . . and displaces the centre outside of itself . . . can, perhaps, open the way to a higher region.'[31]

Evola did not, however, idealize the union of male and female. He rather envisaged a 'metaphysical "war of the sexes"', in which women seek to seduce, possess, and transform men, and men seek to possess women, or rather the absolute woman that is contained in each individual woman. Much classical myth does, in fact, fit this perspective. In the case of men, seeking possession includes rape, and from the male perspective 'a specific element of sadism . . . exists in almost every coitus', as the man tries to break through an individual woman to reach absolute woman.[32] Evola fails, as his critics have pointed out, to indicate that he finds rape in any way problematic. The metaphysical war of the sexes extends to sexuality as a path to self-realization. The elimination of duality might happen in one of two ways. The risk is that the male principle (which is one, and self-subsistent) gives in to desire, which is a variety of 'fall', and 'a danger for those who are in search of the supernatural',[33] as the male thus becomes possessed by the female. Alternatively, instead of the female transmitting instability to the male, the male can transmit stability to the female. This produces a positive synthesis.

In his major post-war work on gender and sex, *The Meta-physics of Sex*, Evola discussed sexual rituals as found in a variety of different traditions. What they generally had in common was much careful preparation, and then a result in which the male partner withheld ejaculation, consigning the energies thereby released to transcendent ends. There is almost no discussion of what such practices might mean for a woman, beyond the repeated observation that it is generally safer to work with a woman who does not understand sexual ritual practices, since otherwise she might divert them to her own ends. Sexual rituals, it seems, may benefit the man, while the woman is incidental.

Evola is the only Traditionalist to write at length about sexuality. His understanding of sex has something in common with Guénon's, but his understanding of sexuality is unique. It is Traditionalist in that it draws on ancient myth, as does Evola's understanding of self-realization. A basis for his idea of a metaphysical war of the sexes can, indeed, be found in those sources, but the development of the idea is purely Evola. It makes the general Traditionalist rejection of feminism seem liberal and progressive by comparison. Nothing comparable is found elsewhere in either the foundations or the applications of Traditionalism. Evola's sexual project was, in the end, his own.

SCHUON AND THE FEMALE SOPHIA

Frithjof Schuon took gender one stage further, seeing the transcendent itself as gendered, as the Kabbalists did, and in some ways following Aristotle. Schuon, like Guénon and Evola, saw different paths to self-realization as either male or female. Unlike Evola, however, he saw the male and the female as complementary, not opposed. His understanding of gender was thus almost the opposite of Evola's.

Schuon explicitly rejected the Greek myth of an earlier human race of androgynous beings. Sundered half-beings are not, actually, looking for the opposite sex, he held. 'The opposite sex is only a symbol: the true centre is hidden within ourselves, in the heart-intellect. The creature recognizes something of the lost centre in his partner; the love that results from this is like a distant shadow of the love of God.'[34] Here Schuon is close to a major strain in Islamic theology, which sees the human spirit as ungendered, following a Platonic logic according to which the universal spirit is also ungendered. Gender, in this view, is constructed: not socially, but physically. Individual bodies are male or female, even if the spirits that dwell in them are not. For Schuon, although 'the metaphysical, cosmological, psychological and physiological subordination [in effect, inferiority] of woman is apparent enough', women and men were equal 'in respect of sanctity, but not in respect of spiritual functions'.[35]

In respect of spiritual functions, at the level of self-realization, Schuon saw the male and the female as complementary, not just as alternatives. Like Evola, he identified two gendered paths: a way of knowledge that is 'virile' and a way of love that is 'feminine'.[36] Schuon's virile way of knowledge matched Evola's path of the warrior, and his way of love was identical to Evola's female path. But he then put the two paths together: 'love needs a complement of intelligence or discernment . . . whereas intellectual activity needs a complement of beauty in the soul and secondarily in the visible environment'.[37] Similarly, 'strength, a warrior quality, includes a mode or complement that is static or passive, and this is sobriety, love of poverty and of fasting and incorruptibility, all of which are pacific or non-aggressive qualities'.[38] Schuon's warrior, then, had female characteristics, unlike Evola's warrior, who must strive to be absolutely male.

At the metaphysical level, Schuon saw the divine Logos as having both male and female elements, both of which were important, rather as did the Kabbalists. Much of his later writing was very occupied with the Virgin Mary, who he thought epitomized the feminine and the universal. 'The Virgin Mother embodies supra-formal Wisdom; it is from her milk that all the Prophets have drunk; in this respect she is greater than the Child, who here represents formal wisdom, hence a particular revelation,'[39] wrote Schuon. As usual, he is using the word 'formal' to mean 'in a particular form', not in the Platonic sense. On another occasion, he explicitly describes the Virgin Mary as 'the nonformal and primordial essence' in relation to the child Jesus.[40] The Virgin Mary represents primordial esoteric unity; Jesus represents exoteric form. In this sense, the Virgin Mary becomes one with the eternal Sophia or wisdom. And, though Schuon does not make this identification himself, the Virgin Mary approaches the Kabbalistic understanding of the Shekhina.

Given Schuon's conviction that exoteric religion reflects the esoteric and that the important things that exist in one religion therefore also exist, in one form or another, in other religions, he sought an equivalent to the Virgin Mary in Islam. While Virgin and child were distinct and complementary in Christianity, he saw them as combined in Islam.

The Prophet Muhammad, he held, was '"virgin" or "illiterate" insofar as he is inspired only by God and receives nothing from men, and he is "Mother" by reason of his power of intercession with God'.[41] That the Prophet was illiterate is important in Islamic theology, as it supports the contention that the Quran is a divine revelation, not something that was written by Muhammad. It is not usual, however, to describe the Prophet as 'virgin' in this context. Similarly, it is agreed that the Prophet intercedes with God on behalf of individual humans. Again, intercession is not understood in terms of motherhood in mainstream Islamic theology.

At a metaphysical level, then, the hierarchy of male and female is almost reversed. Although Schuon considered the psychological and physiological inferiority of women to be self-evident, he also thought that woman 'incarnates esoterism by reason of certain aspects of her nature and function; esoteric truth, the *haqiqa*, is felt as a feminine reality, and the same is true of *barakah*'.[42] The *haqiqa* is here supra-formal wisdom, and *barakah* is the Islamic term for divine grace and blessings. The implications of this in terms of social organization, however, were those that feminists condemn. Schuon defended classic Islamic gender practices, on the basis that:

> Islam makes a sharp separation between the world of man
> and that of woman, between the community as a whole and
> the family which is its kernel, between the street and the
> home, just as it sharply separates society and the individual
> or exoterism and esoterism. The home, and the woman
> who is its incarnation, are regarded as having an inviolable,
> and hence sacred, character.[43]

Schuon's understandings of gender were applied to ideas about music by his follower Sir John Tavener, who thought that good music required both masculine and feminine elements, and saw his own task as including 'reinstating the sacred, feminine principle back into art', given that 'the feminine is something which is largely absent from our times. It's got distorted, contorted by feminism.'[44]

PETERSON ON PATRIARCHY

During the first quarter of the twenty-first century, Jordan Peterson became an extremely prominent commentator on matters of gender. Like other Traditionalists, and following directly from Mircea Eliade, he was interested in metaphysical gender. He understood the unknown, nature, and chaos as productive of the new and thus as metaphysically feminine; he saw order as masculine. He did not break new ground in this respect, however. Where he has broken new ground is with his views on patriarchy, to which he has applied his political project of defending traditional hierarchies of competency against postmodern leftist understandings of power as inherently exploitative.

Peterson's central argument is that the relationships between women and men that are commonly regarded as patriarchal social constructs and therefore as exploitative are in fact determined by biological differences and benefit everyone. He is, then, unknowingly following Firestone, but without making her argument that 'we are no longer just animals'. For Peterson, it seems, the Kingdom of Nature still reigns absolute – because the differences between the genders are simply too deeply ingrained to change.

Human biology – the difficulty of childbirth and the resources needed to bring a human infant to independence –
means that 'women become more vulnerable when they have
children', writes Peterson. 'They need someone competent
to support mother and child when that becomes necessary.
It's a perfectly rational compensatory act, although it may
also have a biological basis. Why would a woman who de-
cides to take responsibility for one or more infants want an
adult to look after as well?'[45] What is called patriarchy, then,
is not a system for exploiting women, but a way in which
men and women long ago learned to cooperate to the mutual
benefit of both, and of their children.

One consequence of human biology, writes Peterson, is
that men and women are fundamentally different in many
ways, as can be seen by looking at children. Boys 'are more
disobedient – negatively – or more independent – positively –
than girls . . . They are less agreeable (agreeableness being a
personality trait associated with compassion, empathy and
avoidance of conflict) and less susceptible to anxiety and
depression . . . Boys' interests tilt towards things; girls' interests tilt towards people.'[46] This, claims Peterson, is what
really causes different outcomes in the labour market, not
discrimination.

The negative consequences of attempts to remedy patriarchy are felt by both sexes, as they reduce the supply of
suitable husbands for women, and risk damaging the proper
functioning of society for everyone. But the most negative consequences are felt by men, in Peterson's view, as they are taught
from school onwards that they should behave more like girls.
Their achievements are regarded with suspicion, and they are

encouraged to be less assertive and aggressive – even though 'aggression underlies the drive to be outstanding, to be unstoppable, to compete, to win – to be actively virtuous, at least along one dimension'.[47]

As well as arguing that so-called patriarchy is actually good for all concerned, Peterson has also taken aim at contemporary understandings of gender and sexual orientation, which he also sees as radical leftist inventions. It was a post about a transgender actor that led to his being banned from Twitter. Gender identity was one of the main topics of his first major video, 'Professor against Political Correctness', in which he argued that gender was primarily binary 'because there's two forms of biological sex', and that the proposition that 'a person's gender identity is fundamentally different from and not related to their sexual orientation' is untrue, since 'if you ran a correlation analysis between gender identity and sexual orientation the correlation is going to be something like 0.95, which indicates an almost perfect correlation for the vast majority of people. Gender identity and sexual orientation are the same thing.'[48]

Peterson has conceded that what he says about gender makes a lot of people angry. He has suggested that this is because contemporary liberal understandings of gender are 'at the heart of the radical leftist doctrine' of social constructivism.[49] There may be some truth in this. Disagreements about gender may sometimes be bitter not only because they are so personal, but also because of their implications for other important issues.

Aristasia

The Traditionalist understanding of gender was further developed, and in some ways completely reversed, by a Traditionalist who wrote under the pen-name 'Alice Lucy Trent', and who was a member of a feminine community called Aristasia. The origins of this community are obscure, but it developed from a small group called the Silver Sisterhood that moved to Burtonport, a remote fishing village in County Donegal, Ireland, in 1982, led by an English woman who self-identified as 'Sister Breca'. The Silver Sisterhood rejected modernity, used candles rather than electricity, dressed in late Victorian style, and worshipped a female God. Some regarded it as a new religious movement, but it also had elements of performance art about it, and its members were happy to perform for television cameras. Aristasia was a successor community to the Silver Sisterhood, established in London in the 1990s by the same woman, now calling herself 'Miss Martindale'.

Aristasia developed a chronology close to the Traditionalist historical narrative which emphasized the 1960s as 'the Eclipse', the start of an even worse phase of modernity. Refuge from contemporary, post-Eclipse modernity ('the Pit') could be found in any previous era, and the Victorian styles of the Silver Sisterhood were replaced by Aristasia with styles from the 1920s to the 1950s. Electricity was allowed, and Miss Martindale drove a 1950s car. The point, explained Miss Martindale to a British television team, was not to recreate any specific historical era, but simply that dress, furniture, and behaviour should be from before the Eclipse. Aristasia's alternative reality was populated only by women, who were divided into two sexes: blondes and brunettes. Many Aristasians were lesbians. In 1998, Aristasia went online, and flourished there for some twenty years as an elaborate and often rather light-hearted alternative reality.

It is not clear whether Sister Breca/Miss Martindale was a Traditionalist, or whether Alice Lucy Trent was an alias for her or for someone else, or perhaps for a group of people. What is clear is that in 1997 Trent published a book that combined the Aristasian system with Traditionalism, *The Feminine Universe: An Exposition of the Ancient Wisdom from the Primordial Feminine Perspective*. Trent built on the standard foundations of Traditionalism – perennialism, history, and the critique of modernity – but ignored their core projects. She was not interested in self-realization, save briefly as an alternative way of escaping the Pit for a small minority; nor was she interested in religion or politics, save in a final invitation for female readers of *The Feminine Universe* to escape from the Pit's 'image-world' by joining 'the Aristasian image-sphere'.[50] Instead, she focused on history and gender.

Trent agreed with Evola and Bachofen that human history started with matriarchy, though she did not cite either of them; however, she then differed from both in arguing that the shift from matriarchy to patriarchy was an aspect of modernity. Trent conceded that it was unclear whether or not matriarchy had ever actually included rule by females; what mattered was that the chief deities had been female, and that the feminine was 'recognised as the highest principle both on earth and in the higher realms'.[51] The human archetype was female, not male; the male was an imperfect female. Female qualities were not, as many falsely supposed,

created by 'social conditioning'; they were innate, and valuable. Trent named 'serenity, peace and contemplation' as
female characteristics, in contrast to Wollstonecraft's 'cunning, softness of temper, outward obedience, and a scrupulous attention to a puerile kind of propriety'. In a more
fundamental sense, the archetypal feminine means beauty,
quality, and harmony.

In late modernity, all this is lost. Late modernity means
'the eclipse of femininity itself – the banishment of the feminine principle from the earth'.[52] Trent agreed with Guénon
that one consequence of modernity was that the abnormal
was seen as normal. This meant that male characteristics and
values were seen as normal not only by society as a whole,
but even by women, who sought to replace their natural
femininity with an imitation of maleness. Feminism was not
the liberation of women but their enslavement: 'the ultimate triumph of patriarchy'. 'Women are trained to think like
men, talk like men, act like men and dress like men, to have
the same ambitions and . . . preoccupations.'[53] This is what
a few women, perhaps, can escape – for example, by joining
the Aristasian image-sphere. Modernity enters the individual
consciousness through its image-world, 'the things it sees,
the things it believes to exist, the things it thinks about –
these are the world to that consciousness'.[54] Aristasia's alternative reality, seen in this way, was partly light-hearted
fantasy, but also partly very serious.

Aristasia is one of the more unusual projects of the later
twentieth and early twenty-first centuries. It is not really a
Traditionalist project, but it is in sympathy with the Traditionalist understandings of Trent in *The Feminine Universe*.

It is partly in agreement with the Traditionalists whom Trent cites, but in the end comes to very different conclusions, as it establishes the superiority of the female, not the centrality of the male.

Conclusion

The application of the Traditionalist philosophy to questions of gender, then, is anti-feminist in that it emphasizes differences between the sexes rather than equality, and understands gender characteristics as innate, not as acquired. Traditionalists invariably reject feminism as an aspect of modernity. Their understandings of gender, however, are generally based not on a response to feminist theory, but rather on more fundamental positions. Julius Evola is one exception in that he incorporates the views of Otto Weininger, which were part of an earlier discussion that is otherwise ignored. Jordan Peterson, who responds directly to feminist positions, is another exception.

As was the case with the application of Traditionalism to art, the starting point is not the views of René Guénon, who was not particularly interested in gender. The starting point is Julius Evola, and the next major Traditionalist to consider gender was Frithjof Schuon. Alice Trent then came to her own conclusions. Evola, Schuon, and Trent, in fact, all came to different conclusions. For Evola, the transcendent was male; for Schuon, it had both male and female aspects; for Trent, it was female. For Evola, Weininger's understanding of gender as non-binary matched the Greek myth of an earlier race of androgynous beings, a myth that Schuon rejected, seeing the human spirit as non-gendered. Trent saw it as gendered, and female. The Traditionalist project with regard to gender, then, is very diverse.

As well as applying Traditionalism to gender, Evola also applied gender to Traditionalism. While Guénon did not see self-realization as gendered except in terms of the practical issue of initiation, Evola not only saw distinct paths for men and women but even saw gender as an element of those paths. The warrior should strive to be more perfectly male, and the female lover or mother should strive to be more perfectly female. Sexuality was also a path to self-realization, as sexual union might eliminate duality, and sexual rituals might carry one towards the transcendent. Evola's vision of relations between the sexes was not one of complementarity, however, but rather of a metaphysical war of the sexes in which neither rape nor sadism was condemned.

Schuon's gendered metaphysics assigned the esoteric to the female, to the Virgin Mary as the personification of eternal Sophia and primordial wisdom. The representatives of the exoteric religious forms, Jesus and Muhammad, were male, but Jesus depended on the Virgin, and Muhammad contained the Virgin and the Mother within himself. At the level of self-realization, there were distinct paths for men and women, as for Evola, but the male path needed female elements, and the female path needed male elements. Although Schuon's understanding of gender might seem much more positive from a feminist perspective, one of its conclusions was still that the woman is the incarnation of the home, hardly a feminist position.

Peterson subscribed to Traditionalist understandings of metaphysical gender, and broke new ground with his insistence that patriarchy was neither a social construct nor exploitative, but rather traditional and natural and to the benefit of all. In so doing, he annoyed more people than any Traditionalist before him.

Trent's understanding of gender deplored feminism, but was simultaneously pro-feminine. It is notable that Trent is the only female theorist of Traditionalism mentioned in this book, and the only female Traditionalist of importance. Her version of Traditionalism is little known among other Traditionalists, and is perhaps too radical in its reversal of the male and female to be easily compatible with other versions.

Nature

The third further area to which Traditionalism was applied was nature. Two of the earliest major voices in the promotion of organic agriculture and sustainable development, Lord Northbourne in the 1940s and E. F. Schumacher in the 1970s, both became Traditionalists, but neither based his environmentalist arguments on Traditionalism. In 1966, however, the Iranian-American philosopher Seyyed Hossein Nasr used Traditionalism to argue for environmental protection, establishing himself as a prominent proponent of environmentalism based in religion, and as the first major proponent of Islamic environmentalism, as Nasr himself is Muslim, even if his arguments are not especially Islamic. His conclusions have been widely accepted and were promoted in the United Kingdom by a very high-profile environmentalist activist, the then Prince Charles, who not only gave countless speeches promoting environmentalism but in 2010 also published a widely read book that took Nasr's work one stage further.

Agriculture has been linked to the transcendent since very ancient times, and harvest festivals are still celebrated, even though understandings of the origins of rain, drought, and blight have changed considerably since the period when they were ascribed to the will of the gods. Objections to polluting wells and to similar behaviour that causes harm to others are also very ancient, and medieval English law classed these together as 'nuisances'(harms), a category that also included excessive smoke, smells, and noise. Contemporary environmentalism, however, is of more recent origin, really emerging only in the 1960s and 1970s, with roots in the nineteenth century. Nasr was a pioneer, not just as the first major proponent of Islamic environmentalism, but as one of the first proponents of environmentalism based on any religious perspective.

Earlier views

Although environmentalism is a relatively recent phenomenon, it has earlier roots. One of its origins is the Romantic movement, which strengthened awareness of nature and of nature's connection with the spiritual and the transcendent. Another origin is the Industrial Revolution itself, which created pollution beyond the wildest imaginings of a medieval Inspector of Nuisances, and led to the growth of areas of cheap urban housing and to related environmental problems.

Concern with the consequences of industrialization emerged slowly. In 1864, the American politician and diplomat George Perkins Marsh published *Man and Nature; or Physical Geography as Modified by Human Action*, aiming to 'point out the dangers of imprudence and the necessity of caution in all operations which, on a large scale, interfere with the spontaneous arrangements of the organic or the inorganic world'.[1] Marsh drew on technical and scientific literature in many languages to discuss the dangers associated with large-scale agriculture, forestry, and management of waters and sands. A similar scientific perspective was also taken by other writers and associations, and in some cases provided the basis for government legislation. There was always a moral overtone, as private damage to nature provides a perfect example of the dilemma known as 'the tragedy of the commons': although it may be in everyone's collective interest not to overgraze common land, it is also in everyone's individual interest not to be the person who moves their animals elsewhere, so common land often ends up overgrazed, to the detriment of everyone. One of the primary functions of human morality, it is often argued, is to deal with this dilemma. It may be in my private interest to do something that will harm everyone else, but if I am being moral, I will refrain from that action, and everyone will benefit. I will also benefit from other people's moral behaviour.

A primarily scientific framing combined with definite moral overtones continued through the twentieth century, as modern environmentalism became established during the 1970s and 1980s. The American marine biologist Rachel Carson published her *Silent Spring*, showing the damage done by indiscriminate use of pesticides, especially DDT, in 1962. The US Environmental Protection Agency was established in 1970, and Greenpeace in 1971. Awareness of the challenges posed by global warming then grew during the 1980s. Discussions since then have been mostly about science, morality, and practicalities. Some of these discussions have been particularly difficult in relation to development. It is all very well for rich countries, which have already industrialized at considerable cost to the environment in the past, to insist on environmental protection now, but what of countries that have not yet industrialized? This is also a moral question.

Until the 1980s, little attention was paid to the role of the transcendent. Exceptions to this included the work of two American Protestant theologians. H. Richard Niebuhr started constructing a system of environmental ethics in the 1930s, and Joseph Sittler called in 1954 for a 'Theology for Earth', regretting that 'today, man is no longer related to nature in God's intended way . . . That, fundamentally, is why he plunders what he ought to tend.'[2] These, however, were unusual positions, and attracted little attention at the time. More attention was paid to the argument made by the American historian Lynn White in a lecture in December 1966, as environmentalism was beginning to take off, that the roots of the ecological crisis were to be found not only in the Industrial Revolution but also in Christianity itself, which assigned domination over nature to man, and saw man as distinct from, and superior to, nature. White, then, saw religion, or at least Christianity, as contributing to the ecological crisis.

ORGANIC AGRICULTURE AND BUDDHIST ECONOMICS

Another exception to the general rule that little attention was paid to the transcendent was the Anthroposophical Society, where the idea of organic agriculture originated. This idea has transformed food production in recent decades, and goes back to Rudolf Steiner, an Austrian philosopher who led the German branch of the Theosophical Society and then, after a breach with the Society's international leadership, established his own Anthroposophical Society, based in Switzerland. Steiner, like the Theosophists, saw multiple layers of existence between the purely physical and the transcendent, of which the three lowest were the physical, the ethereal, and the astral. This understanding was the basis both of the Waldorf school system, which Steiner started shortly after the end of the First World War, and of a series of lectures on agriculture that he gave in 1924, which were later developed into what became known in German as *biodynamische Land-wirtschaft* ('bio-dynamic agriculture') and in English as 'organic agriculture', the name given to it by an English farmer and landowner, Lord Northbourne, in 1940.

Just as the Waldorf system combined progressive peda-gogical and Anthroposophical ideas in a way that produced an appealing result that is not obviously Anthroposophical, so organic agriculture combined practical agricultural tech-niques with Anthroposophical ideas. Chemical fertilizers, which were first developed during the First World War, were condemned for failing to enrich the soil in the way that nat-ural ones do. In Steiner's view, natural manure carries with it astral and ethereal content that chemical fertilizers lack. The horn of a cow is a natural conduit for the astral and ether-eal, and thus manure will be improved by burying it together with a cow horn.[3] Most organic farmers today do not bury cow horns with their manure, and the book by Northbourne that launched the term 'organic' in English, *Look to the Land*, mentions neither cow horns nor the astral and ethereal, but some Anthroposophists do still bury cow horns. Whether or not organic farmers know it, the basic idea of organic farm-ing derives from a particular view of the transcendent as well as from science.

Northbourne's *Look to the Land* took a position in another discussion, one in which Steiner did not engage: that of inter-national trade and finance. Marxists had long argued that this was essentially exploitative, and Northbourne agreed, adding a further element to the discussion. In order to pay the interest on its debts to a creditor country, a debtor country has to produce something, probably through 'exhaustive farming', which despoils its land, and also damages the agriculture of the creditor country, which cannot compete with the low prices of imported food. 'It is not noticed that "development" has destroyed the one inalienable and potentially inexhaustible source of wealth of both [debtor and creditor countries]: till, perhaps, too late.'[4]

Northbourne's warning of 1940 was repeated in 1973 by E. F. Schumacher, a German-British economist who started to question standard development economics while working in Burma (now Myanmar) in the 1950s. Schumacher launched the idea of 'intermediate technology' in the 1960s, and in 1970 became president of the Soil Association, a British group dedicated to the promotion of organic farming. In 1966, even before Lynn White's famous lecture blaming Christianity, Schumacher published an essay on 'Buddhist Economics' in which he argued against the focus of 'modern economics' on production rather than on the worker. In contrast, an economics based on Buddhism, a religion that Burma claimed to respect, would place the worker before the product, since 'the Buddhist sees the essence of civilisation not in a multiplication of wants but in the purification of human character'.[5] Here Schumacher cited an early work of Ananda Coomaraswamy, *Art and Swadeshi*, from 1910 (Swadeshi was an Indian movement for nationalist self-sufficiency). 'Creative activity' matters more than consumption, maintained Schumacher, and people matter more than goods. John Ruskin was not cited, but might well have been, as this is where the views of Coomaraswamy on this point originated. 'Production from local resources for local needs is the most rational way of economic life,' continued Schumacher, and 'non-renewable goods must be used only . . . with the greatest care and the most meticulous concern for conservation'.[6] This essay was reprinted and developed in Schumacher's *Small is Beautiful: A Study of Economics as if People Mattered*, published in 1973. This book had a tremendous impact on public opinion worldwide, and argued convincingly that current models of development were not sustainable, and that people mattered more. Local production and the village economy were good models to follow.

The concept of sustainable development is now as widespread and as influential as the concepts of organic agriculture and environmental protection. The concepts of sustainable development and of organic agriculture, then, are both grounded not only in science but also in other considerations: Anthroposophy for organic agriculture, and Buddhism, Coomaraswamy, and (behind the scenes) Ruskin for sustainable development.

Traditionalism played no role in Lord Northbourne's *Look to the Land*, and only a minor role in Schumacher's *Small is Beautiful*. Both Northbourne and Schumacher, however, later became Traditionalists, finding in Traditionalism the complement to views they had already developed. Both wrote books on Traditionalism, but neither went far in applying Traditionalism to the question of nature. Environmentalism led them to Traditionalism, not Traditionalism to environmentalism.

Early Traditionalist views

Guénon had no particular views on nature, but he was often critical of what is now called 'development'. The contrast between West and East was central to his thought, and, in this context, he often lamented the impact of the West on the East, which was leading Easterners to adopt a modern Western mentality, and then to distort Eastern traditions to match modernity. Guénon thought that talk of economic development was generally a cover for Western economic exploitation of Eastern countries. Although Easterners had little interest in economic competition with the West, thought Guénon, their desire to free themselves from Western domination might lead to their embracing such competition.[7] Development, then, was a negative factor.

Coomaraswamy, like Guénon, was little interested in nature in its own right, but was interested throughout his life in questions of development. Schumacher's 'Buddhist Economics' cited *Art and Swadeshi* once, but might have cited it much more often: Coomaraswamy's book of 1910 and Schumacher's essay of 1966 are in substantial agreement. Coomaraswamy's views in 1910, however, cannot be described as Traditionalist, since he had not then encountered Traditionalism, and, when he did encounter it, his views on development were little changed by it.

Although Evola did not always regard 'world conquest by white Europe' as a bad thing[8] – it was, after all, heroic and virile – he endorsed Guénon's and Coomaraswamy's views on development. 'It is better to renounce the allure of improving general social and economic conditions and to adopt a regime of austerity than to become enslaved to foreign interests or to become caught up in world processes of reckless economic hegemony,[9] he wrote. He also anticipated by forty years Lynn White's argument that Christian dualism had a negative impact on the environment. One of the consequences of the Christian distinction between the supernatural and the natural was 'the deconsecration of nature'. 'Nature ceased to be something living. The magical and symbolical perception of nature that formed the basis of priestly sciences was rejected and branded as "pagan".'[10] Before Christianity, in Evola's view, things had been different. In the traditional world, he argued, nature was lived as though it were a great, sacred, animated body, 'the visible expression of the invisible'. Knowledge about nature derived from inspiration, intuition, and visions, and was transmitted by initiation, as 'living mysteries'.[11] 'Between man and his land, between blood and soil, there existed an intimate relationship of a living and psychic character',[12] which was why, in many traditions, ownership of land was reserved for the nobility. Land itself is in some way sacred.

Schuon loosely followed Coomaraswamy on development, adding a concern with sustainability that is not found among earlier Traditionalists. While the old hand loom had been 'a kind of revelation and a symbol which by its intelligibility allows the soul to breathe . . . a mechanised loom is suffocating for the man who serves it'.[13] Mechanization not only suffocated those it had enslaved, but also used up natural resources. The first point goes back to Ruskin, but the second point is new. Machines 'feed insatiably on materials . . . instead of being set in motion by man alone or by some natural force such as wind or water; in order to keep them "alive" man is forced to resort to a wholesale stripping of the earth'.[14] Schuon also associated nature with the primordial. 'Everything legitimate is connected with nature on the one hand and with the sacred on the other,' he wrote.[15] Nature, however, was not a topic on which Schuon wrote at any length.

Nasr's philosophy of nature

The real Traditionalist philosophy of nature was developed relatively late, by Seyyed Hossein Nasr, who in 1966 was invited to deliver four lectures at the University of Chicago in a series addressing the dangers posed to peace by science, a hot topic in the aftermath of the invention of the atomic bomb. That same year, E. F. Schumacher would publish his essay 'Buddhist Economics' and Lynn White would deliver his lecture on the negative impact of Christianity. Nasr spoke not on the dangers science posed to peace but on the dangers it posed to nature, applying the Traditionalist analysis of modernity and Schuon's understanding of the transcendent unity of religions. He avoided the confrontational and polemic tones that are found in Guénon and Evola, and to some extent in Schuon. He was an insider in terms of Western scholarship and intellectual life, not an outsider. Almost thirty years later, in 1994, he delivered another major series of lectures on nature, this time at the University of Birmingham in England, 'Religion and the Order of Nature'. The 1994 lectures, especially, display an impressive breadth and depth of scholarship. Both series of lectures were published, and together established Nasr's position as the leading Muslim thinker on the topics of nature and the environment.

Nasr's basic argument in 1966 was that the 'disequilibrium

between man and nature that threatens all man's apparent victory over nature' was the result of the 'alienation of man from nature', itself a result of modernity's loss of traditional metaphysical knowledge, the 'secularization of the cosmos'.[16] To this he added in 1994 a greater sense of urgency, 'as man succeeds in destroying so much of the order of nature and even threatens cosmic chaos'.[17] In 1994, Nasr blamed the alienation of humanity from nature not on the loss of metaphysical knowledge but on the loss of religion, a more mainstream formulation, and expanded his argument to include people's relationships with their own bodies.

Nasr's first lecture in 1966, on 'The Problem', applied the Traditionalist narrative of decline and the critique of modernity to the history of science to demonstrate that the real problem was the desacralization of nature. It started by listing the problems caused by this, a list that was very much of the 1960s: 'over-population, the lack of "breathing space", the coagulation and congestion of city life, the exhaustion of natural resources of all kinds, the destruction of natural beauty, the marring of the living environment by means of the machine and its products, the abnormal rise in mental illnesses'.[18] The central focus was not, however, on these problems, but on what Nasr saw as their cause: desacralization. Quite how desacralization leads to overpopulation and congestion was not demonstrated, but it makes sense that the destruction of natural beauty can result, at least in part, from lack of appreciation of, and respect for, that beauty. In 1994, Nasr no longer needed to list environmental problems, as they were by then very well known, but he did refer in his final lecture to how humanity 'has not only caused the disappearance of numerous plant and animal species and endangered many others, but has nearly caused humans themselves to become an endangered species'.[19]

In 1966, Nasr's second lecture, on 'The Intellectual and Historical Causes', proposed a Traditionalist reading of 'the history of science' as the history of decline from tradition to modernity, showing how Western civilization inherited Greek materialism and Christianity 'reacted . . . by emphasizing the boundary between the supernatural and the natural and by making the distinction between the natural and supernatural so strict as to come near to depriving nature of the inner spirit that breathes through all things'.[20] Things then declined further with the triumph of rationalism and rationalistic science after the Renaissance and especially during the seventeenth century, and, although the Romantic movement rediscovered 'the beauty of virgin nature, it could not affect the current of science nor add a new dimension within science itself'.[21] The same argument was made in 1994, at greater length and in greater detail, especially in regard to the history of philosophy, attaching less blame to Christianity and more to Descartes, and recognizing the positions taken by earlier Christian theologians and philosophers and also by contemporary Christian theologians such as Niebuhr. The analysis was also broadened slightly, recognizing the role played by human greed, which was itself unleashed by individualism and rationalism.

The third lecture in 1966, on 'Some Metaphysical Principles Pertaining to Nature', argued that traditional metaphysics showed 'a devotion to nature and a comprehension of its metaphysical significance'.[22] It started by defining metaphysics as 'the science of the Real, of the origin and end of things, of the Absolute' and as a science that 'can only be attained through intellectual intuition and not simply through ratiocination'.[23] It then proceeded through various quotations, from the *Tao Te Ching* and the Hindu tradition to Islam, asserting that 'in Islam as in China observation of nature and even experimentation stood for the most part on the side of the gnostic and mystical element of the tradition'.[24] What Nasr showed, then, was not that nature was treated in any particular fashion – and indeed this was not an issue in this period – but that nature was understood within a wider metaphysical framework. This discussion ended with Native Americans and medieval Christians. In 1994, the survey was longer and more detailed, dealing with almost all religions, not just a selection. It made a fundamental division between 'primal' religions such as shamanism and the Native American tradition, in which 'nature is not only a symbol of spiritual realities but *is* those realities',[25] Iranian and Abrahamic religions, in which the Divine Order and the order of nature are separate, and the order of nature may (or may not) be understood as reflecting the Divine Order, and Hinduism, which lies between the two. The 'primal' religions 'have been for millennia the guardians of the natural environment with an ear finely tuned to the message of the Earth',[26] a view which is not exclusive to Nasr. It might, of course, be asked whether the peoples in question were actually in a technical position to make much impact on nature, for good or for evil.

In 1966, the fourth and final lecture, on 'Certain Applications to the Contemporary Situation', showed the various benefits that would result, both for nature and for science, from adopting an approach based on traditional metaphysics that 'could also aid in the re-discovery of virgin nature by removing the strangulating hold that rationalism has placed upon man's vision of nature'.[27] In 1994, the solution was instead to be found in 'religion in its traditional forms as the repositories of the Sacred and the means of access to it'.[28] Solutions only at the practical level would not be enough, and philosophical approaches to nature were also insufficient. 'One must question what power save external brute force can bring about control over the passionate elements within the souls of human beings so that they will not demand so much materially from the world of nature. There might be a few philosophers for whom such a power might be reason, but for the vast majority of human beings it cannot but be religion.'[29]

The major new topic discussed in 1994 was the human body, to which an entire lecture was devoted. Nasr observed that the last aspect of the physical world to be desacralized was the body, and that this had also been the first aspect of the physical world to be resacralized. That purely mechanistic understandings of the body were no longer widely accepted, he argued, could be seen in both the interest in 'alternative forms of medicine based on the holistic view of the human being that embraces body, soul, as well as Spirit' and in 'the enormous questions posed by bioengineering and related problems of bioethics'.[30] Attempts to rediscover the sacrality of the body, however, needed to follow the tradition and 'spiritual techniques dealing with the body', rather than getting lost in 'the glorification of sports and athletics' and 'the desacralization of sexuality peddled ever more commercially'.[31] Ultimately, 'the recovery of the religious view of nature must turn to the central issue of the body where the spiritual, psychic, and physical elements combine in a unity, the whole of which is of necessity of significance to religion'.[32]

Nasr's argument in both 1966 and 1994 was essentially Traditionalist. It was implicitly perennialist in that he discussed multiple religious traditions, doctrines, and mythologies as one single unit, following Schuon's idea of the transcendent unity of religions. It used the Traditionalist narrative of decline since the Renaissance. It also used the Traditionalist critique of modernity, though this was restricted to the relationship between people and nature, rather than applied to modernity as a whole. Finally, the remedy proposed was Traditionalist: the recovery of traditional metaphysics, following Guénon, later replaced by the recovery of the sacred through religion, following Schuon.

Nasr's application of Traditionalism to nature was one of the most widely influential applications of Traditionalism. The application of Traditionalism to self-realization, politics, and gender by Evola was welcomed only by a few. The application of Traditionalism to religion and art by Schuon and his followers was more widely accepted, but still remained somewhat marginal. Nasr's application of Traditionalism to nature became as mainstream as Tavener's music. It was one of Traditionalism's most successful projects.

Later developments

Although Nasr himself is Muslim, his application of Traditionalism to nature was perennialist more than Islamic. A fully Islamic version of Traditionalist environmentalism was developed by a Jordanian Traditionalist, Prince Ghazi bin

Muhammad, working together with a British Traditionalist, Reza Shah-Kazemi. In 2010 they published a long essay, *The Holy Qur'an and the Environment*, in a bilingual Arabic/English edition.[33] This proceeds in the fashion of classic Islamic scholarship, basing its argument on extensive quotations from the Quran, which are then interpreted to make what is, essentially, Nasr's basic argument. The interpretations are always plausible, though sometimes departing from general understandings, as when the word 'corruption', which is used often in the Quran and generally understood as referring to human sinfulness, is read as referring to environmental degradation.

In the United Kingdom, another prince, Prince Charles, also further developed Nasr's thought. Before his accession to the throne as Charles III in 2022, Prince Charles was better known in the United Kingdom for his campaigning than for his philosophy, but in 2010 he published *Harmony: A New Way of Looking at Our World*.[34] In this book, he argued for a revolution to solve 'the many environmental and social problems that now loom large on our horizon' that required both 'right action' and 'right thinking'.[35] The action required was of the sort that he himself had already been taking for some time in his capacity as landowner, in areas such as organic agriculture, local production for local consumption, improved urban planning, and reforestation. The problem with initiatives such as these, however, was that they remained 'alternative', which was not enough. For them to become mainstream, which he argued was what was needed, thinking had to change. People needed to learn to see their relationship with nature in terms of what the prince called 'traditional philosophy'. Nasr is not credited, but what follows is very much his argument from

1966, though with occasional differences. Prince Charles, for example, dated modernity not from the Renaissance but from the triumph of Enlightenment humanism.

Prince Charles also developed Nasr's argument. He not only argued, as Nasr had, that nature had traditionally been understood within a wider metaphysical framework, but went on to state that nature actually demonstrates and inhabits that framework. The patterns of sacred geometry, he argues (following Critchlow), are also found in nature and (following Titus Burckhardt) in sacred architecture. 'The ratios and proportions that define the way natural organisms grow and unfold are the same as those that underpin the structure of the most famous ancient buildings.'[36] The patterns of sacred geometry that are found in the temples of India 'are models of the universe'.[37]

Prince Charles also went further than Nasr in that he discussed practical solutions at length. What all these had in common was that they were the opposite of modern approaches: organic agriculture instead of chemical agriculture, architecture that embodies sacred geometry rather than buildings that 'seem deliberately to summon up chaos rather than conjure up harmony',[38] and so on. These solutions are not purely reactive, however. Organic agriculture should make use of modern knowledge and techniques. In general, we should 'restore in a contemporary way the best parts of the abandoned and ancient understanding of harmony'.[39] The solution is not to return to a lost Golden Age; indeed, there never has been a Golden Age. In the past, 'life was harsh and short. Disease, starvation or invasion could wipe out entire societies.'[40] As, indeed, they often did.

Prince Charles, then, went further than almost any other Traditionalist in recognizing that there may, actually, be some good things about modernity. He also brought together Nasr's application of Traditionalism to nature with Burckhardt's and Critchlow's application of Traditionalism to art, and added to these extensive practical discussions. Sir John Tavener, who was a friend of Prince Charles, maintained that in order to understand art, one had to be a working artist. Prince Charles was a working environmentalist. After his accession to the throne in 2022, he announced that he would in future not be able to give so much of his time and energies to the charities and issues on which he had focused as Prince of Wales, which many read as a message that he would in future carefully avoid controversy, and which led some of those who knew of his Traditionalism to expect it to become less visible. Some light-hearted comments on social media, however, expressed hope that his Traditionalism meant that he would permanently dissolve the British parliament, following the examples of kings Charles I and Charles II. In fact, there were never any signs that Prince Charles in any way supported Traditionalism's political project.

Conclusion

The application of the Traditionalist philosophy to nature, then, is one of Traditionalism's most successful projects. Traditionalism fits comfortably with organic agriculture as promoted by Lord Northbourne, and sustainable development as promoted by E. F. Schumacher. René Guénon, Ananda Coomaraswamy, and Julius Evola all opposed development, which they saw as imposing modernity on tradition and also as inspired by imperialism. Evola anticipated the analysis later made popular by Lynn White that environmental damage could be blamed on the alienation from nature produced by Christian dualism. Frithjof Schuon added a concern with sustainability.

Most important was Seyyed Hossein Nasr, who blamed the alienation of man from nature not on Christian dualism but on the loss of traditional metaphysical knowledge and of religion. He applied the Traditionalist narrative of decline to demonstrate this, and proposed a solution in the reconstitution of certain forms of the tradition, especially as found in what he called 'primal' religions, which were in effect primordial. This analysis was promoted by Prince Charles, with some modifications and additions.

The success of Nasr's analysis owes something to the fact that he was an insider in terms of Western scholarship and intellectual life, unlike most other Traditionalists. His tone was always measured rather than polemical, and his scholarship was impressive and beyond criticism. The success of his analysis also owes something to its apparently limited ambition. Nasr was not trying to explain and critique all of modernity, but only one aspect of it. And that aspect, nature, was one that many people were growing increasingly concerned about, and also one that many people already associated with the transcendent.

CHAPTER 13

Dialogue

The final area to which the Traditionalist philosophy has been applied is interfaith dialogue, first in principle by Seyyed Hossein Nasr, and then in practice by Traditionalist Muslims in Bosnia and Jordan. The Jordanian approach has had a worldwide impact. Traditionalism's interfaith dialogue projects have been especially important because they have been seen as Islamic initiatives in a field that has generally been dominated by Christian institutions.

Like environmentalism, interfaith dialogue is a recent development. Inter-religious debates have taken place from time to time for many centuries, but mostly in a polemical framework, where the objective was to convince followers of another religion to convert to one's own, to dissuade followers of one's own religion from converting to another, or to justify measures taken against followers of another religion. Such debates are based on monist, exclusivist understandings of religious truth: our religion is true; yours is false.

Debates between Christians, Jews, and Muslims have been especially frequent, given that the followers of these religions have often lived close to one another. The three religions understand each other in different ways, for chronological reasons. Judaism's scriptures do not refer to Christianity, while Christianity's core scriptures and doctrines do refer to Judaism. Jesus is often critical of Jewish practices and especially the Pharisees, and in the Gospel of St John 13:34–5 gives a 'new commandment' that has been generally understood by Christians as bringing a 'New Covenant' that abrogates the commandments that are central to Judaism. Most Christian theology has until very recently held that Jews should become Christian. Similarly, while Christianity's scriptures do not refer to Islam, Islam's core scriptures and doctrines do refer to both Judaism and Christianity, which are often criticized in the Quran as misinterpretations of God's earlier revelations. The Prophet Muhammad is described in Quran 33:40 as 'the seal of the prophets', and this has been generally understood by Muslims as meaning that Islam abrogates both Judaism and Christianity. While Islamic theology has held that Jews and Christians should become Muslim, it has also held that they are entitled to continue to practise their own religions in peace if they so wish.

Universalist, theological, and inter-communal dialogue

New approaches to the issue of religious variety were developed during the nineteenth century, as we have seen. The Chicago Parliament of Religions in 1893, which was based on a universalist view of relations between religions, was in fact one of the earliest instances of what is now termed interfaith dialogue, where the objective is not to convert or vilify the other, but to find common ground. Another early example, also in the United States, was the National Conference of Jews and Christians, established in 1927 to work against

Christian anti-Semitism and to end Protestant attempts to convert Jews to Christianity. The objective here was different. It was not universalist, but rather inter-communal. The main objective was to reduce tensions between Jewish and Protestant communities. These remain the two main motivations for interfaith dialogue today: universalism, often associated with theological dialogue, and improving inter-communal relations. Theological dialogue is primarily intellectual and is often conducted at a personal level between individual theologians. Inter-communal dialogue is generally conducted in an institutional setting, involving individuals in their capacities as communal leaders. It may be aimed at avoiding or reducing conflict, or at what is now called 'peace-building', which includes overcoming traumas caused by past conflicts. Inter-communal dialogue often includes an element of theological dialogue, but theological agreement is not its main point. Its main point is avoiding or reducing conflict.

CHRISTIAN INITIATIVES

Institutional initiatives initially focused mostly on Christian ecumenism and proliferated after the end of the Second World War, especially in the 1960s and 1970s. The World Council of Churches, founded in 1948, brought together many Protestant and Orthodox Churches, though not the Catholic Church. The Catholic Church then established a Secretariat for Promoting Christian Unity in 1960, which established relations with the World Council of Churches. These bodies were 'ecumenical' in the sense that they aimed, at least in principle, at reuniting all the various Churches into which the original Christian community had split over the centuries. Their concern was thus both theological and inter-communal, based on a specifically Christian universalism.

Christian initiatives aimed at other religions followed. In 1964, the Catholic Church established a Secretariat for Non-Christians, and issued *Nostra aetate*, the Declaration on the Relation of the [Catholic] Church with Non-Christian Religions, in 1965. The concern was primarily inter-communal; what was finally published as *Nostra aetate* had started life as a draft 'Decree on the Jews', motivated by concerns about anti-Semitism. Exchanges of official visits between the Secretariat for Non-Christians and Egypt's Supreme Council for Islamic Affairs started in 1970. In 1969, the World Council of Churches started occasional dialogue sessions with Muslim theologians, and established a subunit for Dialogue with People of Living Faiths and Ideologies in 1971. In 1973, a Center for the Study of Islam and Christian–Muslim Relations was established by American Protestants at the Hartford Seminary, and a similar centre was established in the UK in 1976 under Protestant auspices in Birmingham.

As well as institutional initiatives, there have also been individual theological initiatives. During the mid-twentieth century, Louis Massignon, a French scholar of Islam and part-time Catholic theologian, and then Kenneth Cragg, an Anglican bishop and part-time scholar of Islam, did their best to make Islamic theology acceptable to Christians, arguing for understanding Islam as an Abrahamic religion and Muhammad as a prophet comparable to the biblical prophets. They were not exactly engaging in interfaith dialogue in the contemporary sense, however, since they were only addressing Christians, and did not attempt to make Christian theology acceptable to Muslims. It has been argued that reducing Muhammad to a lesser type of prophet is not very useful so far as Muslims are concerned, since the status of the Prophet Muhammad as the seal of the prophets is of central importance in Islam.

A different approach was taken in 1989 by the Anglo-American Evangelical religious philosopher John Hick, whose *An Interpretation of Religion: Human Responses to the Transcendent* approached the perennialist position in proposing that transcendent reality – 'the real' – was one, even if different religions understood it differently. He also argued that no religion was better than any other, as all had strengths and weaknesses. Unlike the positions of Massignon and Cragg, Hick's approach addresses followers of all religions equally, not just Christians. It differs from the Traditionalists' position in that it places unity in the transcendent itself, not in the esoteric metaphysical core of the religions, where the Traditionalists find it. It resembles the old argument that if there is only one God, someone who is trying to worship a tree as a god is actually worshipping the one God.

Hick's position, which was taken as a classic formulation of a truly pluralist position, has been criticized, for example by the American Baptist theologian S. Mark Heim, who argued that Hick had no real justification for his conviction that transcendent reality is one. Christians, Jews and Muslims actually have somewhat different gods. Religions are actually unique, not universal. Heim's conclusion was that we 'are not competitors for the same thing. We are seekers after various things.'[1]

MUSLIM INITIATIVES

Until recently there were almost no comparable theological initiatives by Muslims, and Muslim institutions often did no more than respond to Christian approaches. One rare exception is Abdul-Hadi, the Swedish-French Sufi who inspired Guénon in 1910, who for some years at the start of the twentieth century edited an Egyptian journal that addressed Christians in Italian and Muslims in Arabic. It defended and explained Islam to its Italian readers, using the word 'Islamophobia' in print for the first time. In Arabic, however, it defended and explained not Christianity but Italian foreign policy – the journal was paid for by the Italian government. Other exceptions include the Tunisian historian Mohamed Talbi, who published a book on Islam and dialogue in 1970. Until very recently, there were no institutional initiatives comparable to the Catholic Church's Secretariat for Non-Christians or the Hartford Seminary's Center for the Study of Islam and Christian–Muslim Relations, however.

There are two explanations for this relative lack of Islamic initiatives. One is that Christians, whose core scriptures do not refer to Islam, have much more scope for interpretation than Muslims, whose core scriptures do refer to Christianity. It is easier for a Christian theologian to propose a novel understanding of Islam than it is for a Muslim theologian to propose a novel understanding of Christianity. The other is that Muslim theologians spent most of the nineteenth century on the defensive against European culture and imperialism, and sometimes also against Christian missionaries. It is thus easier for Christian theologians to make concessions from a position of strength than for Muslim theologians to make concessions from a position of weakness.

THE RETURN OF RELIGIOUS CONFLICT

In the 1960s and 1970s, interfaith dialogue seemed important to Christians mostly as a way of righting ancient wrongs, and Islam seemed to most Westerners to be of little importance in a world divided by the Cold War. The Iranian revolution changed this, relaunching Western understandings of Islam as a threat. Then, in 1991 and 1992, religious warfare returned to Europe as Yugoslavia collapsed and Catholic Croats fought Orthodox Serbs, and then Serbs and Croats both fought Muslims in Bosnia. The Yugoslav wars were one reason why the American political scientist Samuel P. Huntington proposed, in 1993, that a 'Clash of Civilizations' would replace the clash of ideologies that had characterized the Cold War. Huntington's civilizational blocks were defined mostly in religious terms. In 2001, when al-Qaeda attacked America on 9/11 in the name of Islam, Huntington seemed to have been proved right. One response was a renewed emphasis on interfaith dialogue.

Many scholars question the extent to which conflicts like those in Yugoslavia and that unleashed by 9/11 are actually 'religious' in the first place. One view is that differences of religion are simply identity markers, like differences of language. Religious difference no more causes conflict than linguistic difference does. Scholars also point out that while it may sometimes seem that religious groups have been in conflict since for ever, this is never actually the case. Protestants and Catholics in Ireland may have been fighting each other since

Cromwell, for example, but they have not been fighting consistently. Conflicts do not remain constant; they get better and they get worse. Something else must be going on. And that something else is conflicts of interest, combined with the activities of people or small groups who find it serves their purposes to exacerbate conflict. The scholarly consensus, then, is that religious difference is part of the problem, not the cause of the problem. Given this, interfaith dialogue can be part of the solution, if not the whole of the solution.

Traditionalist views

Guénon expressed hope for Traditionalism as the basis for an unusual form of interfaith dialogue long before the idea had been developed or the term coined. In the conclusion to his *Introduction to the Study of the Hindu Doctrines*, he hoped that his explanation of Eastern and traditional doctrines might assist 'the doubtless long drawn out but none the less effective preparation for an intellectual understanding between East and West'.[2] 'Intellectual' here means something like 'spiritual', as it always does for Guénon. Guénon hoped for such an understanding, however, not as an end in itself, but in connection with two of his three scenarios for the future of the West. If the West was not to fall into barbarism and disappear, it might be assimilated by the East, in which case there would be a need for a small Western elite that could communicate with the East. Alternatively, if the West were to reconstitute itself, there would be a similar need for a small Western elite that understood traditional doctrines.

Evola did not share Guénon's views, as he did not hope for the assimilation of the West by the East, nor its reconstitution on an Eastern basis. He probably never encountered contemporary forms of interfaith dialogue, since these did not develop until he was an old man. Schuon, in contrast, did encounter the early development of interfaith dialogue, and, although he never wrote on this topic, the World of Islam Festival in which his followers played such an important part might be understood as a form of dialogue, given that it aimed to present Islam to Westerners in terms that might appeal to them, rather as Massignon and Cragg had.

NASR AND INTERFAITH THEORY

The first Traditionalist to write at length on interfaith dialogue was Seyyed Hossein Nasr. In the first lecture in the series he delivered at the University of Birmingham in 1994, described in the previous chapter, Nasr presented four approaches to the multiplicity of religions, arguing against three of them and in favour of the Traditionalist understanding of the transcendent unity of religions. Two approaches obviously led nowhere: the contention that only one's own religion is true, and the conclusion that all religions are equally false, a conclusion that the multiplicity of religions might seem to support. Another approach that had been the basis of much interfaith dialogue was 'the sentimental embracing of all religions within a unity that some envisage as a least common denominator among religions and which they hope to achieve at the expense of casting aside sacred doctrines and forms of a particular religion that do not seem to accord on the formal plane with those of another religion'. This approach, he noted, was 'damaging to the very forms of that reality with which there is the need to create accord'.[3]

Nasr is here using the term 'form' to refer to the exoteric, as Schuon did. At the exoteric level, religions contradict each other. In the short term, these contradictions can indeed be resolved by dismissing the doctrines in question, but in the long term, not much is left of any of the religions involved. Only the Traditionalist understanding of the transcendent unity of religions leaves the religions concerned intact.

In 1998, Nasr published an article on 'Islamic-Christian Dialogue: Problems and Obstacles to be Pondered and Overcome' in *The Muslim World*, a journal published by the Hartford Seminary, where the Center for the Study of Islam and Christian–Muslim Relations had been established. He started by noting that even though 'Islamic-Christian dialogue has turned from a rivulet into a roaring river, from an occasional conference to numerous meetings, oral and written exchanges and round table discussions', 'many major theological problems have not received a proper solution', since 'on the formal level it is simply not possible to reach an accord'.[4] By 'formal', Nasr again means 'exoteric'. At this level, insoluble issues included the incarnation, the trinity, salvation, and sacred law (Sharia). What was needed was to accept that this was the case and to instead work at the metaphysical and esoteric level. This had in fact already been done by the Traditionalists, but 'a chasm separates the fruit of such efforts from the ordinary dialogues carried out by many scholars and theologians of both sides who are either impervious to such writings or are opposed to the esoteric dimension of their own tradition'.[5]

Nasr also drew on Traditionalism to point out that everyone had been ignoring a 'silent third partner' in Muslim–Christian dialogue: modernity. Christians, as Westerners, wondered why Islam could not modernize, while Muslim partners in dialogue often did not fully understand this, and 'in carrying out debates with Christian theologians think and act as if they were facing St. Bonaventure, St. Thomas or Nicholas of Cusa' (all great medieval Christian theologians). They were, in fact, facing modern Westerners. 'In order to remove this obstacle in dialogue, it is essential to take full cognizance of the third apparently "silent partner" and to realize that in fact this partner, although its voice seems to go unrecognized, is far from being silent and in fact wields pervasive influence.'[6] The issues that Westerners have with Islam are indeed often with aspects of Islam that seem incompatible with modern Western values such as equality, not with aspects of Islam that seem incompatible with classic Christian doctrine.

MAHMUTĆEHAJIĆ AND
THE INTERNATIONAL FORUM BOSNIA

The approach recommended by Nasr was taken by a Muslim Bosnian Traditionalist, Rusmir Mahmutćehajić, a former professor of electrical engineering who had served as Bosnian minister for energy, mining, and industry during the first years of the Bosnian war, in which capacity he was responsible for arming the Bosnian army. He served under Bosnian President Alija Izetbegović, but disagreed with Izetbegović's vision of Bosnia's past and future, and as a result resigned from his government in 1993. After the end of the Bosnian war, he established a dialogue institution, the International Forum Bosnia, in 1997.

Mahmutćehajić applied Traditionalism and Nasr's

interfaith theory to Bosnia's specific and rather complex circumstances. The Socialist Republic of Bosnia and Herzegovina had been one of the constituent republics of the Socialist Federal Republic of Yugoslavia, and was unusually diverse, with Muslims, Serbs, and Croats, none of whom constituted a majority. As Yugoslavia collapsed, some favoured the partition of the territory of the Socialist Republic of Bosnia and Herzegovina between the newly independent countries of Serbia and Croatia, with a small, residual territory to be left for the Muslims. In the event, Serb, Croat, and Muslim forces all established control over parts of the former republic during a war characterized by ethnic cleansing and numerous atrocities, which ended with the US-sponsored Washington Agreement of 1994 and the Dayton Agreement of 1995. These agreements combined Croat-held and Muslim-held territories into a Federation of Bosnia and Herzegovina, which was then combined with the Serb-held territories into a new state, called Bosnia and Herzegovina. The hope was that over time institutional and economic unification would bring the Croat, Muslim, and Serbian populations and territories together.

In a series of essays and books written mostly after the end of the war, Mahmutćehajić applied the Traditionalist philosophy to this situation. First, he established a historical narrative that blamed post-war disunity on modernity and contrasted it with traditional unity. He identified peaceful coexistence as the traditional norm in Bosnia, which he saw as characterized by 'unity in diversity'. He then explained the growth of the ethnic nationalism that had destroyed this unity in diversity in terms of modernity. Finally, he called for the re-establishment of unity in diversity through recognition of the transcendent unity of religions, arguing that the institutional and economic measures agreed at Dayton were not, on their own, sufficient to restore Bosnia.

Mahmutćehajić painted a picture of a Bosnia where, 'for a period of over five centuries, both churches and mosques existed side by side, each on the same firm footing'.[7] The churches were both Catholic and Orthodox, and 'the members of the three peoples that constitute the Bosnian-Herzegovinan nation lived intermingled throughout the region, living proof of unity in diversity'.[8] The explanation of this unity in diversity was the transcendent unity of religions: 'The Bosnian-Herzegovinan model of tolerance and inter-religious relationships can be interpreted as accepting that all religion should enable the reunion of all human beings with their single transcendent origin', and 'Bosnian history . . . can be understood as a belief that the three main religious routes can and should be seen in relationship to Unity, to their common origin'.[9]

This picture of former interfaith tolerance coincides with historical reality, but the explanation might be challenged. Bosnia came under Ottoman control during the mid-fifteenth century, and as a result was administered under the Ottoman *millet* (denomination) system, which granted toleration and a degree of autonomy to Christian groups, though churches were not exactly on the same footing as mosques, at least in the towns, since mosques were often subsidized and endowed by the state, while churches were not. A form of tolerance, then, certainly resulted from the *millet* system, whether or not Bosnians or their Ottoman rulers accepted that all religions should enable reunion with people's transcendent origin.

In Mahmutćehajić's narrative, the model of unity in diversity was destroyed by modernity. Modernity brought secularization, which in turn led to ethno-nationalism, and the transformation of religious discourse and institutions into the tools of the nationalist political elite. This is, again, compatible with general understandings of the history of the Balkan provinces of the Ottoman Empire during the nineteenth century. In the case of Bosnia, Mahmutćehajić blames not only the ideology of secular ethno-nationalism, but also the political elites that acted on and encouraged it: the Croatian and Serb leaderships above all, but also the Bosnian president, Izetbegović, whom he accused – with some justification – of also being a secular nationalist.

Mahmutćehajić's analysis also suggests the way forward:

> The destructive frenzy of exclusivity is surely the worst advertisement for those interpretations of faith that are used to justify the frenzy. To suggest that separation of communities according to religion is the solution is to claim that religion promotes hatred more successfully than it promotes tolerance. The only constructive answer is to initiate dialogue between all members of Bosnia's unity in diversity. This dialogue is most urgently needed between those who justify their exclusivity on the basis of holy teachings, since these are the ones who give the strongest support to the evil elites, ideologies, and organizations and the perpetrators of crimes that they generate.[10]

Dialogue was also urgently needed because institutions and economics could not on their own re-establish tolerance between Bosnia's different religions. Even if rational self-interest explained most of human behaviour, it did not explain all of it. Culture, which is irrational, is also always important, and culture depends on religion. Further dialogue was not only needed in Bosnia: with globalization shrinking the world, Europe as a whole was becoming a large Bosnia, and what happened in Bosnia might also happen elsewhere. Beyond Europe, most states were, like Bosnia, multi-ethnic. The basis of dialogue, of course, must be the acceptance of the transcendent unity of religions: 'The multitude of religious manifestations can return to unity only by way of their esoteric roots',[11] as other approaches stress the differences between religious forms.

Mahmutćehajić's efforts to promote dialogue were based around his International Forum Bosnia, which he directed together with a (Catholic) Croatian Franciscan theologian and an (Orthodox) Serbian political scientist who had been a Yugoslav diplomat. The forum arranged lectures and conferences, sponsored research, held an annual summer camp, and published a bilingual journal in Bosnian and English. As time passed, however, the Forum became less active, and it is not clear how much it actually achieved. At an economic and political level, Bosnia and Herzegovina has made some progress towards unity, but at a social, cultural, and religious level, little progress has been made. This suggests that Mahmutćehajić was right that rational self-interest, institutions, and economics could not on their own re-establish tolerance. Convincing Bosnians of the transcendent unity of religions, however, has not proved easy. That Mahmutćehajić had little success in this project was perhaps because pre-modern interfaith tolerance in Bosnia had owed most to the Ottoman *millet* system, not to traditional tolerance.

PRINCE GHAZI AND A COMMON WORD

Another institution that has to some extent applied a Traditionalist approach to dialogue is the Royal Aal al-Bayt Institute for Islamic Thought, a Jordanian institution. This has produced one of the most widely discussed dialogue documents of recent years, *A Common Word Between Us and You*, addressed by Muslim theologians to Christian leaders, as well as another document, *Common Ground*, dealing with Islam and Buddhism. *A Common Word* was drafted by a Jordanian Traditionalist, Prince Ghazi bin Muhammad, the director of the Royal Aal al-Bayt Institute, with the help of Nasr and of several Arab Muslim theologians who were not Traditionists but who were still firmly opposed to Islamic modernism, including Ali Goma'a, the Grand Mufti of Egypt. Given that Prince Ghazi was the first cousin of King Abdullah II, whose confidence he enjoyed, *A Common Word* received the full support of the Jordanian state and was signed in 2007 by 138 Muslim theologians and dignitaries, including the muftis and grand muftis of Bosnia, Dubai, Egypt, Russia, and Syria, as well as Mahmutćehajić and a number of Western Traditionalist Muslims. Positive responses to it were issued by Christian leaders, including the Pope and the Archbishop of Canterbury.

The starting point of *A Common Word* is the position recommended by Nasr in his 1998 article, that 'Islam and Christianity are obviously different religions – and . . . there is no minimising some of their formal differences'. *A Common Word* did not, however, seek agreement on an esoteric or metaphysical plane, which would undoubtedly have been too much for some of its signatories, but rather at the alternative level that Nasr later described as 'what is most essential in our worldviews'.[12] In the words of Ali Goma'a, the document was 'an attempt to create an essential common ground deeply rooted in the shared Abrahamic tradition in order to put an end to the misgivings between us that act as stumbling blocks in the way of respecting one another'.[13] The 'essential' elements of the Abrahamic tradition on which it focused were love of God and love of one's neighbour. The importance of these 'two commandments' for both religions was then demonstrated through parallel quotations from the Bible and the Quran.

The theology of A *Common Word* was original, as love of God and love of one's neighbour are not normally given as much prominence in Islam as they are in Christianity. Although A *Common Word* is not a Traditionalist document, it still owes something to Traditionalism in the way in which it distinguished the essential from the formal to focus on the essential, echoing the Traditionalist distinction between the esoteric and the exoteric, and also in its method of reading sacred texts and myth from different traditions as one.

Common Ground, which deals with Islam and Buddhism, was published in 2010 and was less widely received than A *Common Word*, and was more explicitly Traditionalist. It was addressed by Prince Ghazi to the Dalai Lama, who wrote a foreword to the book in which it was published, and was drafted by Reza Shah-Kazemi, the British Traditionalist who worked with Prince Ghazi on Islamizing Nasr's Traditionalist environmentalism. Rather than making a distinction between the formal and the essential, it made a distinction between formal doctrine and 'spiritual wisdom (*ma'rifa*)', which 'pertains to the subtleties of the heart, to inward con-templative states, to mystical experience'.[14] This wisdom also 'pertains to the domain of ultimate principles . . . It does not contradict the formal dogmas of Islam, but rather constitutes their dimension of inner mystical depth.'[15] Shah-Kazemi's 'spiritual wisdom', then, is esoteric, not just essential. *Ma'rifa* is a term often used in Arabic to describe esoteric knowledge. On this basis, Shah-Kazemi argued that Islam and Buddhism recognize the same ultimate reality, and that the ethical values of both traditions are rooted in a quest for the absolute. He established common ground between several crucial concepts in Islam and Buddhism, such as *samad* and *dharma* (both terms of multiple significances), and *fanā'* (absorption in unity) and non-duality. *Common Ground* is, in many ways, closer to an individual theological initiative than to institutional dialogue, which is perhaps why it is more explicitly Traditionalist.

The Royal Aal al-Bayt Institute and Prince Ghazi were also responsible for a range of further dialogue initiatives, including consultations with various Christian Churches, persuading the UN to launch an annual 'World Interfaith Harmony Week', and restoring and protecting Christian sites in Jordan, including what Prince Ghazi claimed as the site of the baptism of Jesus by John the Baptist (there are also two alternative sites on the Israeli side of the River Jordan).

The Royal Aal al-Bayt Institute for Islamic Thought and *A Common Word* have been more successful than Mahmutćehajić and the International Forum Bosnia. This is partly because they have been backed by the government of Jordan and represent a 'moderate Islam' that is attractive to Muslim states that seek improved relations with the West. It is also because

A Common Word was less ambitious than Mahmutćehajić, aiming at agreement between religions not at an esoteric level, but only at the level of 'an essential common ground'. The Royal Aal al-Bayt Institute for Islamic Thought is not a Traditionalist institution but is a successful one, and *A Common Word* was not a Traditionalist text but was likewise successful. Both, however, draw on Traditionalism.

Conclusion

The application of the Traditionalist philosophy to interfaith dialogue is a recent development that owes most to the work of Seyyed Hossein Nasr. The Traditionalist idea of the transcendent unity of religions provides an excellent basis for interfaith dialogue at the theological level, and theological dialogue can contribute to the success of inter-communal dialogue, and thus to improved inter-communal relations.

René Guénon saw his Traditionalism as a basis for understanding between East and West following the imminent collapse of the West. Julius Evola probably never encountered interfaith dialogue and had no views on it. Frithjof Schuon never wrote on it, but arguably contributed to it through his followers' participation in the World of Islam Festival.

Nasr was the first Traditionalist to apply the idea of the transcendent unity of religions to interfaith dialogue, pointing out that this solved the problem of disagreements between exoteric religions while leaving those religions intact, which the more popular approach of ignoring disagreements did not. He also pointed out that dialogue between Muslims and Christians generally ignored the issue of modernity, so that Muslim participants failed to recognize that they were in dialogue with modernity at least as much as they were in dialogue with Christianity.

Two attempts were made to implement Nasr's ideas. One, by Rusmir Mahmutćehajić, applied them to the specific circumstances of post-war Bosnia, blaming the conflict on modernity, and seeking a return to traditional tolerance based in an appreciation of transcendent unity. That that traditional tolerance had actually resulted more from the Ottoman political system than anything else may explain his limited success. That Prince Ghazi had more success with *A Common Word* also has something to do with politics: he had the support of the Jordanian state, and garnered the interest of other Muslim states in improved relations with the West. This does not mean, however, that the theological dialogue promoted by Traditionalists has not also supported inter-communal dialogue. Theological dialogue, in the view of many, is also a good thing in its own right.

PART IV

Post-Traditionalism

CHAPTER 14

The Radical Right

The philosophy of Traditionalism was applied to politics by Julius Evola, first in the context of the Fascist period, and then in the post-war context. Today's political context is very different, and Traditionalism has been applied in this context in new ways, generally selectively. Traditionalist perennialism has often been abandoned. What has proved most useful for today's radical right is the Traditionalist critique of modernity and the pair of traditional and modern that Aleksandr Dugin has called 'Traditionalism as language' and 'a methodological and ontological paradigm'. These partial applications of Traditionalism are something different from the projects discussed in previous chapters, and are best understood as post-Traditionalism. Post-Traditionalism is the exception to the rule that all Traditionalists are perennialists.

Today's radical right is a loose milieu rather than an organized movement, and draws on a variety of streams of thought, some of which have nothing to do with Traditionalism or have even been condemned by it. In America, for example, there is an important stream of 'white supremacism', a form of racism that is incompatible with the views of René Guénon, who minimized the significance of race, and with the views of Evola, who insisted that race was spiritual more than biological. Two major streams in the contemporary radical right, however, do incorporate Traditionalism. The oldest of these is the French 'New Right', which is the origin of the ideology of the Identitarian movement, now a growing force across Europe. The more recent stream, which also draws on the French New Right, is associated with an influential Russian post-Traditionalist, Aleksandr Dugin.

The post-Traditionalism of the radical right is quite different from that of the Traditionalist fellow-traveller Jordan Peterson, with which it is contemporary, and which also benefits from some of the same recent developments, such as the growing importance of social media. Peterson has not abandoned Traditionalist perennialism, and does not use either the Traditionalist critique of modernity or the pair of traditional and modern. This is why Peterson was discussed in earlier chapters, and is not discussed in this chapter.

The French New Right

The single most influential thinker of the post-war radical right in France, and perhaps anywhere, is Alain de Benoist, who was among the founders of GRECE, a 'Groupement de recherche et d'études pour la civilisation européenne' (Research and Study Group for European Civilization) that was established in 1968 to serve as a think tank for the right. Over the years since then, GRECE has engaged a variety of radical theorists, and published several journals and many books, including the writings of de Benoist himself, who became the leading figure in GRECE. The milieu around GRECE came to be known as the 'New Right'. It is sometimes described as neofascist, as in some ways it seems to echo fascism, but this is an oversimplification.

De Benoist's relationship with Traditionalism is complex. He has denied that it is a significant influence on his thought, perhaps to avoid any association with the occultist milieu out of which René Guénon's Traditionalism originally grew, but one GRECE journal, *Elements*, has run several articles about Traditionalism, and it is clear that Traditionalism is among the sources on which de Benoist draws. Traditionalism is very visible in the short 'Manifeste pour une renaissance européenne Renaissance', published in 1999, that de Benoist wrote with Charles Champetier, the editor of *Elements*.

This manifesto was organized in three parts: 'predicaments', 'foundations', and 'positions'. The central predicament with which it opens is the crisis of modernity, described very much in Traditionalist terms. Modernity is characterized by individualization, massification, desacralization, rationalization, and universalization. Only the last of these, 'a planetary expansion of a model of society postulated implicitly as the only rational possibility',[1] is not standard in Traditionalist accounts of modernity. The seeds of modernity are to be found in liberalism and Christianity – de Benoist agrees with Evola (and Nietzsche) in this respect. Modernity 'attempts by every available means to uproot individuals from their individual communities', especially through the market economy.[2] Freedom and equality are promised, but not provided. 'The ideology of progress . . . is in a deep crisis.'[3] 'Modernity has given birth to the most empty civilization mankind has ever known',[4] and is coming to an end. It 'will not be transcended by returning to the past, but by means of certain pre-modern values in a decisively post-modern dimension'.[5] 'Pre-modern values' are not quite the same as the primordial tradition. Values are exoteric, not esoteric.

If de Benoist's understanding of the crisis of modernity is close to the Traditionalist analysis, the 'foundations' of his response to it are less Traditionalist, and do not include perennialism. De Benoist's point of departure is that people are first and foremost animals, subject to 'human limitations', and that 'what lies beyond these limitations may be called God, the cosmos, nothingness, or Being . . . [but] is by definition unthinkable'.[6] This is the opposite of the position of Guénon, who spent much of his life trying to recover primordial metaphysics in order to understand that which de Benoist sees as unthinkable.

De Benoist is not, however, a materialist. He maintains that man creates meaning 'by adhering to what is greater than himself', and that a 'return of the sacred' is needed, and 'will be accomplished by returning to some founding myths'.[7] They are only myths, however, even if important myths. Among them is the paganism of European antiquity, which is 'always alive in hearts and minds precisely because it does not belong to yesterday, but is eternal'[8] – de Benoist is himself a pagan, as was Evola. Paganism is a means to an end, however, not a way to self-realization. Being a pagan for de Benoist is about responding to Nietzsche's critique of Christianity and 'looking behind religion and . . . seeking for . . . the inner world it reflects'.[9] Paganism allows the resacralization of the world. A form of sacred tradition is placed in opposition to desacralized modernity, as it is in Traditionalism, and that sacred tradition is pre-Christian, but it is neither primordial nor universal.

Following the recognition that people are fundamentally animals, the second foundation of de Benoist's response is the recognition that people live in communities, each with its own distinct culture. This has nothing to do with Traditionalism, and in some ways even contradicts it. Traditionalist thought recognizes that there are different cultures, but does so as the counterpoint of the more important point that exoteric difference hides esoteric agreement. De Benoist is not interested in esoteric agreement. He stresses that differences between cultures must be respected, and that 'the idea of an absolute, universal, and eternal law . . . is the basis of all totalitarianisms'.[10] The modern tendency towards the elimination of difference must therefore be resisted, and 'the true wealth of the world is first and foremost the diversity of its cultures and peoples'.[11] Traditionalism has never celebrated diversity in this way.

In the third part of the manifesto, the positions that de Benoist advocates have even less to do with Traditionalism. They are resistance to globalization, homogenization, racism, immigration, sexism, and 'the New Class'. By sexism, de Benoist means universalist views that deny the difference between men and women. Feminism is thus understood as universalist and sexist. By the New Class, he means 'the world-wide domination of a ruling class . . . [that] provides the manpower for the media, large national and multinational firms, and international organizations. This New Class produces and reproduces everywhere the same type of person: cold-blooded specialists, rationality detached from day to day realities' and from any local culture.[12]

Guénon never used the term 'homogenization', but he condemned the way in which, in modernity, the ideal of equality and the practice of uniform education try to make every individual as similar as possible to every other individual. Traditionalists, too, condemn the denial of difference. Traditionalism, however, has never expressed views on immigration or the New Class, which in de Benoist's conception has nothing to do with the regression of castes or the Shudras.

De Benoist's objection to immigration is rooted in his objection to homogenization, and is that immigrants are uprooted from their own culture for economic reasons that are no fault of their own, and that 'host populations . . . are confronted, against their will, with sometimes brutal modifications in their human and urban environments'.[13] Future immigration should therefore be restricted, and the 'ethnocultural identity' of immigrants already present in France should 'be acknowledged and recognised in the public sphere . . . [through] a communitarian model which would spare individuals from being cut off from their cultural roots'.[14] This 'communitarian model' is the basis of a position that has become known as 'ethnopluralism'. Some critics see ethnopluralism as old-fashioned racism in disguise, and in practice many who espouse ethnopluralism may well be racists at heart, but for de Benoist ethnopluralism is not about race, and does not involve the questions of superiority and inferiority that are central to racism. For de Benoist, racism should be opposed because of the 'right to difference', and because it can only be argued that any one race is superior to another on a universalist basis. On a local basis, every people is always superior according to its own standards.

De Benoist, then, is not a Traditionalist. Some of his most important positions have nothing to do with Traditionalism. With the exception of his dismissal of perennialism, however, none are actually incompatible with Traditionalism, and some are very close to Traditionalism. It has therefore been easy for Traditionalism to merge with New Right thought.

Aleksandr Dugin

Many of de Benoist's positions were combined with Traditionalism by Aleksandr Dugin, a Russian who passed from being a Soviet dissident in his youth to becoming a well-known public philosopher and media figure. Dugin is the youngest of the Traditionalists discussed in this book, born in Moscow in 1962. As a student, he joined a circle of dissident poets, novelists, and thinkers, where he discovered Traditionalism. After the collapse of the Soviet Union he made contact with de Benoist. New Right ideas then joined Traditionalism in his writings, and he moved towards a post-Traditionalist position. He now stresses the need to avoid merely repeating Guénon's discourse. What is most valuable, he has argued, is 'Traditionalism as language', the pair of tradition and modernity. This is the basis of much of his political thought.

Ever since an editor at *Foreign Affairs* described Dugin as 'Putin's Brain' in a headline in 2014, to which *Breitbart* quickly added the even catchier 'Putin's Rasputin', there has been much speculation in the West about his influence on President Putin.[15] In fact, Dugin has never been one of Putin's close advisers, and there is no evidence that he has ever had any influence on day-to-day decision making. His views on geopolitics, however, fit well with Putin's own, and either Putin or someone close to him has approved of Dugin, as otherwise he would never have had the access to the Russian media that he has enjoyed. The 2022 Russian invasion of Ukraine had many causes, and was not just a result of Dugin's geopolitics.

TRADITIONALISM AS LANGUAGE

Dugin may have accepted Guénon's accounts of traditional Eastern metaphysics in his youth, but he later concluded that Traditionalism and tradition were not the same thing. Guénon did not speak for any one tradition, he concluded, but rather for traditions as a whole, which was in fact something that could only be done in modernity. Traditionalism, therefore, is actually not traditional at all, but rather 'radically new'. What matters most is not Guénon's account of tradition, which is in some ways problematic, but the pair of tradition and modernity, which provides a language for analysis, just as Marx's pair of capital and labour once did. 'The definition of "modernity" in Guénon's teachings,' Dugin has argued, 'is the identification of a certain paradigmatic proto-mechanism that determines how our world works.'[16]

'Traditionalism as language' was the title of the first chapter in Dugin's book *The Philosophy of Traditionalism*, in which he argued that Traditionalism should be used and developed, not simply maintained. He sarcastically dismissed authors who 'are engaged in the repetition of Guénon's discourse . . . with very slight deviations and who regard this occupation as a kind of intellectual hobby' comparable to stamp collecting.[17] What was needed was a sort of 'post-Guénonianism', the 'deep assimilation of Guénon's Traditionalism as a fundamental language . . . a methodological and ontological paradigm'.

Dugin's post-Guénonianism led in two directions. One was backwards, towards tradition, which was not actually as easy as it looked, as individual traditions tend to differ from 'the pure paradigm' of Traditionalism, often being more modern than they appear. The other direction was forward, to interrogate modernity, which also differs from the pure paradigm.

Looking backwards in regard to practice, Dugin argued that, in a Russian context, tradition was to be found in the Russian Orthodox Church. An early book of his, *The Metaphysics of the Gospel*, demonstrated at length the exoteric and esoteric validity of Orthodoxy in strict Guénonian terms.[18] Dugin especially recommended the Old Believers, a section of the Russian Orthodox Church that had rejected a seventeenth-century ecclesiastical reform and had maintained a distinct, and somewhat esoteric, identity and practice. Dugin and his closest followers belong to an Old Believer denomination that is recognized by the Orthodox Patriarchy.

Dugin remains a perennialist, however, though more in the line of academic perennialism than in the standard Traditionalist line. He understands 'the sacred' as defined by Rudolf Otto, Mircea Eliade, and Carl Gustav Jung as one, and as the basis on which superstructures of what he calls 'theology', 'the rational (philosophical) shaping of the basic impulse of the sacred', are built.[19] Human understandings of the sacred can be found outside the structures of theology, but not often. Generally, understandings are found in religious form, 'woven into complicated models of myths and symbols'. But all are, equally, attempts to grasp the same sacred.

Dugin then combined Guénon with other sources such as the French philosopher (and follower of Jung) Gilbert Durand, identifying three basic types of theology. One was 'a radical absolutization of the Other', the basis of the 'façade of monotheism' in 'such large-scale religious phenomena as Christianity or Islam'.[20] This first type of theology corresponds, in effect, to Guénon's category of 'religion'. The second type 'recognizes the relative equivalence of the Other', and the third 'is built on the paradox of the parallel recognition of the transcendence of the Other . . . and the denial of this transcendence', as in Advaita Vedanta and Neoplatonism. Both the second and third types are found, within large-scale religions, 'in the field of esotericism and mysticism'.[21]

Looking forward, the main task was resistance to global modernity, or rather global postmodernity. Dugin, then, is close to de Benoist in understanding modernity in terms of globalism, but closer to Guénon in his metaphysical commitment.

Dugin also proposed a response to the problem that recent non-Traditionalist scholarship on the origins of Traditionalism, including some work by the present author, has revealed Guénon's non-traditional sources, some of which were discussed in earlier chapters. While Guénon had identified the Renaissance as the point of decline leading to modernity, non-Traditionalist scholars have pointed to the Renaissance as the origin of one of Guénon's most important theoretical bases, perennialism. Dugin responded that, for 'Traditionalism as language', it did not really matter where perennialism came from. Secondly, even if perennialism did come from the Renaissance just as modernity did, and even if the Renaissance was about the revival of Greek thought, as Guénon had argued, Greek thought was not only rationalist. Plato was heir to earlier traditions in a golden chain, and his secret doctrine was a sort of illumination.

Neoplatonism combined Plato with other traditions to produce something that was itself a form of perennialism: 'Neoplatonism conceived itself to be a universal tradition on the basis of which one could interpret all existing religions and philosophical systems.'[22] And, for good measure, Renaissance Neoplatonism was partly of Byzantine origin, providing a link to Orthodoxy.

GEOPOLITICS AND NEO-EURASIANISM

Dugin became well known in Russia in 1997, when his *The Foundations of Geopolitics: The Geopolitical Future of Russia* became a bestseller.[23] This book was the Russian equivalent of Samuel Huntington's *Clash of Civilizations*, attempting to predict the shape of future conflict. Traditionalism is mentioned only towards the end of the book, but on one occasion Dugin describes geopolitics as an 'application of the spatial language of tradition',[24] and the book can certainly be read as the translation of Traditionalism into spatial terms.

In *The Foundations of Geopolitics*, Dugin followed the early twentieth-century German political theorist Carl Schmitt in emphasizing 'large spaces' rather than the civilizations that were emphasized by Hegel and Huntington, and drew on the work of several interwar theorists to stress the fundamental opposition between an 'Atlantic' world that included the USA and a 'Eurasian' world that included Russia. Dugin, then, transformed Guénon's pair of West and East. His West remains the home of modernity, and is placed in the Atlantic world. The East remains the opposite of modernity, but is no longer Guénon's colonial East of Islam and Hinduism; it becomes Russia and Eurasia. Russia and Eurasia are thus the champions of other areas that are resisting Western modernity, including Guénon's East.

The Foundations of Geopolitics gives most space to Schmitt and similar thinkers, including a group of Russian émigré intellectuals who had promoted what they called 'Eurasianism' during the 1920s, emphasizing the fundamental differences between the Slavs and the West. For centuries, there have been two main approaches to the difficult question of Russia's relationship with Western Europe, that of the Westernizers who see Russia as European and favour Westernization, and that of the Slavophiles who see Russia and the Slavs as quite distinct from Western Europe and resist Westernization. The Eurasianism of the 1920s grew out of the Slavophile position.

Dugin later conceded that Russia and Eurasia are in some ways modern as well as traditional, but only in some ways. Something of pre-modernity always survives in modernity, he maintained, and 'Soviet or Chinese communism contains more elements of the language of Tradition (expressed, however, paradoxically and contradictorily) than does modern Protestant theology'.[25] Dugin, like Guénon, sees Protestantism as distinctively modern. The survival of tradition – of the archaic – in modernity was especially visible in Russia, he maintained. Russia ended in a condition that he called 'archeomodern'. Russia had never actually been truly modern. Communism was never really modern. 'In Russia, they took a rational Marxist model of disenchanting the world, with the proof that there is no God, and turned it into the instrument of a new enchantment.'[26] This does not mean, however, that Soviet society was actually traditional. 'Where have you seen such a traditional society, in a state of permanent delirium? Traditional society has its own order, routine . . . It certainly has moral and ethical standards, rational prohibitions and explanations.' Soviet society did not. 'The typical figure of the Soviet period is an alcoholic worker. But this is not a member of a traditional society.'[27] After the Soviet period, the Yeltsin administration was the latest attempt of the Westernizers to modernize Russia, and it had failed, running up against archeomodernity. What was true of Russia was true of many other non-Western societies, as archeomodernity was especially likely to result when a society was modernized from the outside, either by a colonial power or by voluntarily imported but alien models. Again, then, it is the West against the rest, with Eurasia leading the rest.

Not only did Dugin develop the foundational Traditionalist understanding of modernity to fit the circumstances of Russia in the early twenty-first century, but he also developed this foundational understanding to accommodate ways in which Western modernity has changed since the death of Guénon. Although something of pre-modernity always survives in modernity, he maintained, very little of pre-modernity has survived in the West, which is now more postmodern than modern. 'Liberal discourse, consistently conquering (and displacing) first nationalist, then communist ideologies, is gradually approaching the pure model of the language of modernity.'[28] The pure modernity found in America, and increasingly in Western Europe, is postmodernity, revealed by 'the philosophy of suspicion'. This philosophy notes that modernity was not, actually, rationalist and scientific. It had been thought that modernity started with the Cartesian

human 'subject', the rational individual. But the philosophers of suspicion said to themselves: 'Friends, we fundamentally underestimated the irreflexive side of the [human]
subject . . . This side is so powerful that it often subjugates
reason, makes it an expression of hidden and unconscious
forces and regularities, so that, quite often, what we consider
to be a rational explanation or rational system is an expression or distortion of a basis carefully hidden from the light of
reflection.'[29] The project of postmodernity is thus the elimination of hidden and unconscious forces, the final elimination
of tradition. This is an unusual view of Foucault and the other
Western theorists of postmodernity.

Following on the success of *The Foundations of Geopolitics*, Dugin set up an International Eurasian Movement and a
Eurasian Youth Union to promote a 'Neo-Eurasianism' that
combines the Eurasianism of the 1920s, the New Right, and
Traditionalism. The Eurasian Movement has been tolerated
and sometimes supported by the Putin administration.

THE FOURTH POLITICAL THEORY

Dugin's neo-Eurasianism could and did attract support within
Russia, and also among those outside Russia who rejected the
'unipolar world' that seemed to have emerged after the collapse of the Soviet Union left America as the sole remaining
superpower. It still attracts support among those who remain
suspicious of American power. Neo-Eurasianism was less attractive in the West, however. An American might well prefer
tradition to modernity, and might even agree with Dugin that
multipolarity is preferable to unipolarity, but could hardly
be expected to prefer Russia to America. What Dugin called

The Fourth Political Theory, the title of a book he published in 2009, had wider appeal. It is ultimately inspired by his Traditionalism, but draws mostly on other sources.

In *The Fourth Political Theory*, Dugin argued that three political theories had dominated modernity: first liberalism, then communism, and finally fascism. These political theories had failed in reverse order, with fascism vanishing first, followed by communism, leaving only liberalism. Neither the second (communist) nor third (fascist) political theory could defeat liberalism, so what was needed was a fourth political theory. This theory could reuse what was of value in the second and third theories. What it must absolutely avoid was the racism that had destroyed Nazism. Nazi racism had proved disastrous in practice, leading to the Nazi attack on the Soviet Union and many millions of dead, but it was also wrong in principle, since no people was inherently superior to any other people, save by its own standards – which of course allowed every people to see itself as superior to all other peoples. What the fourth political theory might take from fascism was the fascist devotion to the ethnos, the community, in contrast to liberalism's emphasis on the individual. Equally, the fourth political theory should avoid communism's historical materialism. What it might usefully take from communism was its analysis of bourgeois liberalism. Something could even be taken from liberalism: the ideal of freedom, though not of individualist freedom. What should be taken from liberalism was 'the freedom given by ethnocentrism . . . the freedom of culture and the freedom of society'.[30]

The Fourth Political Theory was an analysis, not a programme for action, and Dugin was careful not to propose any programme, beyond pointing to Eurasianism, Traditionalism, and (outside Russia) Islamism, and in some contexts China. He ended up, then, with a clear political programme for foreign policy – which coincided with his neo-Eurasianism and with Putin's foreign policy – but no clear programme for domestic policy, which both simplified his task and minimized the risk of any conflict with the Kremlin. *The Fourth Political Theory* is the least Traditionalist of Dugin's theories.

Other applications of Traditionalism

De Benoist's positions include three that have been central to the political platforms of the 'populist' or 'nationalist' parties that have been so successful in Europe during the first decades of the twenty-first century: opposition to globalization, immigration, and globalized 'liberal' elites, the New Class. The standard nationalist position echoes de Benoist in wishing to restrict immigration, but does not accept separate 'ethnocultural identity', instead insisting on assimilation, often called 'integration'. It also often echoes de Benoist's acceptance of gender differences and consequent opposition to what he calls 'sexism'. The standard nationalist position, however, does not normally oppose racism.

De Benoist's most widely shared positions, however, are his least Traditionalist ones, and Traditionalism has made only occasional appearances in mainstream politics in recent years. De Benoist and Dugin are both influential in the contemporary radical right, however, notably in America, as are the writings of Evola. A radical-right publisher, Arktos, has translated much of the work of all three writers into English, making it globally available. While the contemporary radical right as a whole is not Traditionalist, Traditionalism is often referenced, especially among members of the Identitarian movement, now Europe's most important radical-right movement.

TRADITIONALISM IN THE POLITICAL MAINSTREAM

Traditionalism's first appearance in mainstream politics was in Hungary, where Evola was praised as 'one of the greatest thinkers of the twentieth century' by Gábor Vona, the politician who founded Jobbik, 'The Movement for a Better Hungary', which in 2018 became the second-largest party in the Hungarian parliament. In 2012, Vona felt that the right ran the risk of defining itself purely in terms of what it stood against, the left. Something more coherent was required, and this was provided by Evola. In a foreword to a Hungarian translation of a selection of Evola's writings published as *A Handbook for Right-Wing Youth*, Vona wrote that 'the potential of the "Right" to offer its own explanations and influence the war of concepts is a lot slimmer than that of the Leftist monopoly on opinion'. Leftist ideas sometimes even filled the vacuum on the right, and 'those who conduct their political thinking and activities without any real intellectual base and centre will . . . become nothing more than the playthings of powers unknown and imperceptible to them'. Given this, 'the aim should be pure Rightism, which stands upon the intellectual base of the universal Tradition. And this needs to be seriously absorbed. The real Right should not be engaging in spontaneous and uncontrolled action. Its genuine strategy must be preceded by thorough intellectual maturation.'[31]

A stronger endorsement of the political applications of

Traditionalism can hardly be imagined, but Vona was primarily a politician, not a philosopher, and his own views have showed the flexibility that is required in practical politics. His enthusiasm for Evola in 2012 probably derived from his adviser Tibor Baranyi, who for a while directed a Traditionalist training school under Jobbik's auspices, the King Attila Academy. This was closed as part of the strategy of moderation that enabled Jobbik's parliamentary success in 2014, when it became the third-largest party in the Hungarian parliament, with 20 per cent of the national vote. Jobbik's manifesto for the 2018 elections, the last for which Vona was responsible, promised sustainable long-term growth and an end to corruption, not the end of modernity, and showed no signs of Traditionalist influence or inspiration. Traditionalism, it seems, is not suited to being a mass ideology.

In the United States, Traditionalism served as an inspiration for an activist who played an important role in mainstream politics, Steve Bannon, the campaign manager of President Trump in 2016 and a presidential adviser for the first half of 2017. Bannon was an activist rather than a writer, but discussed his understanding of Traditionalism with a researcher, Benjamin Teitelbaum.[32] A Catholic rather than a perennialist, what Bannon took from Traditionalism was, once again, the critique of modernity combined with an emphasis on immanence and transcendence. He rejected the idea that the traditional hierarchy of castes could ever be reestablished in a world where the modern representatives of the higher castes no longer fulfilled their functions. Bannon agreed with de Benoist about the New Class, though his reference was closer to home: Christopher Lasch, author of *The*

Revolt of the Elites and the Betrayal of Democracy, a conservative American historian who also criticized the New Class. For Bannon, the only caste that retained any authenticity was the working class, and that was the class that he wanted above all to save from economic oppression. Once this had been achieved, transcendence might become an option. And, in order to achieve this, the modern world order had first to be disrupted – which was the function that Bannon had hoped that Trump would fulfil.

Bannon also discussed with Teitelbaum his opposition to globalization, the economic consequence of current modernity, on which subject his views had more in common with the New Right than with Traditionalism. On the one side lies China, the engine of economic globalization: 'What we have now is a system where slaves in China are manufacturing goods for the unemployed in the West.'[33] On the other lies a world of nations and borders, with or without walls.

Bannon rejected Dugin's geopolitical paradigm, arguing during a meeting with him that America did not represent modernity, and that the American working class was suffering from modernity and globalization just as much as anyone else. 'Modernity has advanced further with us,' Bannon recalled telling Dugin, 'like with Scandinavia. But our roots still exist, and they can be revived, and they are being revived. That's what you're seeing today with the Trump movement. That is America rising up against its overlords.'[34]

Bannon is not a Traditionalist, but adopted certain aspects of Traditionalism. Without reading Dugin on Traditionalism as language, he came to much the same conclusions: that what was most valuable in Traditionalism was the critique of modernity and the pair of traditional and modern. His example shows how Traditionalism can play a supporting role in mainstream politics, if never a leading role. Jobbik did enjoy parliamentary success in Hungary, but only after its strategy of moderation had almost eliminated its earlier Traditionalism.

THE IDENTITARIAN MOVEMENT

De Benoist's idea of ethnopluralism, the communitarian model that protects the ethnocultural identity of immigrants and of host populations, was further developed by a one-time collaborator of his, Guillaume Faye, and has since inspired the Identitarian movement, which is now an important part of the radical right in Europe. One of its key texts is a short and sharp primer, *Generation Identity*, by Markus Willinger,[35] which does not reference Traditionalist ideas. Some Identitarians, however, see Traditionalism as an ally.

The loose group that self-identifies as 'radical traditionalists' keeps the Traditionalist critique of modernity and calls for 'resacralization' while following a version of Faye's ethnopluralist vision and criticizing Traditionalism's universalism. Michael O'Meara welcomed 'traditionalists associated with Guénonian perennialism' into a common front against modernity along with 'radical traditionalism, neo-paganism, revolutionary conservatism, anti-modernism, and ethnonationalism'.[36] He rejected Guénonian perennialism, however, on the grounds that there is no single timeless truth. Different peoples have their own traditions. Radical traditionalists 'privilege the European heritage',[37] as Evola did. His 'heroic Way of Action inspires all who identify with his "Revolt against the Modern World"'.[38] Guénon, however, betrayed the European tradition as 'a Muslim apostate'.[39]

A less critical approach was taken by the Dutch Identitarian Alexander Wolfheze, who shared Dugin's understanding of postmodernity and the need for post-Guénonianism. He echoed Dugin in appreciating the 'hermeneutical functionality' of the pair of traditional and modern, and the Traditionalist critique of modernity. He also blamed the crisis of modernity on the 'breach of contract between the Western peoples and their ruling elites',[40] de Benoist's 'New Class', lampooned by Wolfheze as 'faceless *homo aeroporticus*'. Wolfheze argued that the crisis of modernity could be solved by taking 'the moral high ground' from *homo aeroporticus*, and then by political, economic, and cultural changes,[41] and a mixture of repatriation and segregation of immigrants. However, 'the toppling of . . . the neo-liberal regime . . . can only take place after an inner transformation',[42] which requires a Traditionalist analysis. 'A Traditionalist perspective,' argues Wolfheze, 'teaches that the existential threats of climate change, transhumanism, ethnomorphosis and social atavism are the logical end results of the dynamic cultural-historical mechanism of Modernity.' 'From a Traditionalist perspective meta-historical meaning follows directly from the degree to which macro-cosmic transcendental ideals are, or are not, reflected in micro-cosmic immanent reality.'[43] Wolfheze's language is very different from Guénon's, but his 'macro-cosmic transcendental ideals' play the same role as Guénon's primordial metaphysics did in relation to modernity, now called 'micro-cosmic immanent reality'.

TRADITIONALISM AS SYMBOL

The English translation of *A Handbook for Right-Wing Youth*, retaining Vona's foreword, was welcomed by a reviewer on AltRight.com, the website of an American group run by Richard B. Spencer, who combines classic white supremacism and anti-Semitism with some elements of the thought of the European New Right. The reviewer, Martel Mosley, noted that Evola's principles 'will clearly sit well with many', and that the alt-right embraced 'many different, perhaps mutually exclusive currents of thought', united only by their desire to 'achieve the removal of cultural Marxism and other ills from the Western space'. Thus 'a core ideology and set of principles needs to be clearly defined and agreed upon' to avoid the risk of fragmentation and infighting.[44] Mosley did not, however, propose Traditionalism as a core ideology, but – like O'Meara – as one among many strands of thought with which 'anybody who self-identifies as right-leaning' should be familiar.

This is the function that Traditionalism now fulfils for much of the radical right: one among many currents of thought that do, at least, provide an alternative to pure anti-leftism. One prominent American Traditionalist of the radical right, John Morgan, however, has lamented that Evola is 'someone more often referenced than actually read'.[45] There is some truth in this, to judge from far-right websites like 4chan, where Evola and the *kali-yuga* are sometimes referenced for their symbolic value, though they are also mentioned in contexts that suggest people have actually been reading Evola. This is also true of much of the 'neofolk' and related music scenes that are associated with the radical right, where Evola and Traditionalist themes are often referenced. Ten neofolk bands were included in a compilation CD dedicated to Evola, issued by the German label Eis und Licht, including a hymn to Odin by the American neofolk group Blood Axis. Elsewhere, the Italian post-industrial group Ain Soph released an album entitled *Kshatriya*, with the title track featuring the lyrics:

> Loyalty is stronger than fire
> Get up, rise again
> Create a shape and an order
> Standing among the ruins
> Choose the harder way
> Forge our courage
> Reborn in the blood
> Strong in our honour
> Kshatriya.[46]

This is certainly a version of Evola's application of Traditionalism to self-realization and politics, but a very abbreviated one.

One participant in this music scene, Joshua Buckley, believes that 'the majority of participants in these subcultures are largely attracted by music and fashion, and that any ideological component is strictly secondary – even in the case of explicitly political subcultures . . . When ideological positions are expressed, there may be little concern that these positions are consistent or coherent, and one must always question the extent to which they reflect real convictions. More often than not, they may be motivated by considerations of style.' This is not always the case, however. Buckley himself co-edits an occasional journal entitled *Tyr* (after the Germanic god) with Michael Moynihan, founder of the Blood Axis group mentioned above. *Tyr* describes itself as a 'radical traditionalist' journal, and publishes serious articles on all forms of Traditionalism, including some by de Benoist, and the article by O'Meara cited in the previous section.

Traditionalism and Evola, then, are read carefully by some in the music scene, but have also sometimes become symbols more than philosophy. On the one hand, it is tempting to dismiss symbols as unimportant. On the other hand, much research on the radical right in the age of social media emphasizes the growing practical significance of the visual and symbolic.

Conclusion

Traditionalism has been applied selectively in today's political context, especially by Alain de Benoist and Aleksandr Dugin. De Benoist's relationship with Traditionalism is complex, but some of his ideas seem to draw on Traditionalist thought. His analysis of the crisis of modernity matches that of the Traditionalists, and his response to it includes a 'return of the sacred'. He places no value on primordial metaphysics, however, and denies that the transcendent is knowable. Instead, he proposes resacralization on the basis of myth, almost in instrumental fashion.

De Benoist's 'positions', his programme, are resistance to globalization, homogenization, racism, immigration, sexism, and 'the New Class', and the promotion of ethnopluralism. Some of these have become mainstream positions among the nationalist political parties that have recently been doing so well, and ethnopluralism (along with its unusual understanding of racism) has become the basis of the Identitarian movement. These positions owe almost nothing to Traditionalism, however.

Dugin also drew more on the Traditionalist critique of modernity than on primordial metaphysics, turning to the Russian Orthodox Church rather than Sufism. He saw the pair of tradition and modernity as the most important aspect of Traditionalism, calling this 'a fundamental language . . . a methodological and ontological paradigm'. This is the basis of his neo-Eurasianism, which translates the pair into spatial terms, identifying tradition with Eurasia and modernity with America and the Atlantic world. Eurasia is not pure tradition, but is partly traditional in its archeomodernism. Dugin's formulation of an alternative to neo-Eurasianism in *The Fourth Political Theory*, however, is not Traditionalist, though it endorses Traditionalism as one possible way forward.

Traditionalism has made two appearances in the political mainstream. In an unusual and short-lived development, it was adopted by Jobbik in Hungary as a way to avoid the ideology of the right becoming no more than a negation of the ideology of the left, but was then abandoned when Jobbik moderated in order to achieve parliamentary success. In America, Traditionalism inspired Steve Bannon, who came independently to much the same conclusion as Dugin: that what mattered most was the pair of tradition and modernity. Just as Dugin preferred the Orthodox Church to primordial metaphysics, Bannon preferred the Catholic Church.

Traditionalism is welcomed as an ally by some Identitarians, the major group that is based on de Benoist's ethnopluralism. For the 'radical traditionalists', Evola is an inspiration. The European tradition is a necessary basis for resacralization, but there is no perennial truth, and Guénon betrayed the European tradition. Alexander Wolfheze of the Dutch Identitarian movement agrees with Dugin in rejecting Traditionalism as 'esoteric discourse', and welcomes 'Traditionalism as language', which he calls 'hermeneutical functionality', especially the critique of modernity.

Finally, Traditionalism and Evola became a symbol for the US radical right and the neofolk music scene. This may be more about style than ideology, but style is also important.

PART V

Concluding

CHAPTER 15
Conclusion

This book set out to make Traditionalism and its project for restoring sacred order better understood. Traditionalism can be difficult to follow, especially in some of its metaphysical details, but its broader lines are clear enough, and on particular topics they often fall within the range of familiar discussions. Traditionalism is, among other things, a series of contributions to ongoing and often ancient debates.

This book looked first at Traditionalism's foundations: perennialism, its view of history as decline, its critique of modernity, and its perspectives on how and when thought can change society. None of these are really new. As was said in the Introduction, what is new and powerful about Traditionalism is what its different elements add up to. Above all, it is the combination of perennialism with the Traditionalist critique of modernity that has made Traditionalism so powerful.

All Traditionalists are perennialists, but not all perennialists are Traditionalists. Perennialism has been around since at least the fifteenth century, initially as a response to the problem of religious diversity. It is similar to the universalism that finds multiple truths of comparable value, but differs from it in that it proposes one single truth, found in different places. The Theosophical Society was perennialist, but eclectic to the point of resembling what the American sociologist Marcello Truzzi called 'a wastebasket'.

Traditionalist perennialism is more selective, and avoids the wastebasket problem. It claims that its understanding of the sacred primordial tradition is derived only from authentic sources, and that it has found real esoteric doctrine. René Guénon's sources for what he called primordial metaphysics were mostly Vedanta, supported by oral transmission from Sufism. He contrasted his primordial metaphysics with exoteric religion, which he condemned as merely sentimental. Julius Evola, in contrast, drew more widely on myth of all kinds, and Mircea Eliade drew on archaic symbol, myth, and rite, especially shamanism. Frithjof Schuon drew on religion, despite Guénon's condemnation of religion as merely sentimental. Traditionalist perennialism, then, is a version of something that is quite widespread, and has had an appeal under several different circumstances, but is more carefully constructed than has often been the case.

The Traditionalist view of history builds on classic mythical narratives and the more recent tripartite periodization of ancient, medieval, and modern. It is a form of universal history, a genre that starts with Enlightenment optimism and becomes more pessimistic. Universal history seeks to explain the rise and fall of civilizations, as does Traditionalism. The Traditionalist understanding of history sees the fundamental dynamic as being one of decline from a Golden Age, and identifies modernity in Hindu terms as the *kali-yuga*. Traditionalism reverses the progressive tripartite narrative, seeing the Renaissance as the start of modern decline. Guénon, Evola, and Schuon all had slightly different versions of the Traditionalist historical narrative, and Seyyed Hossein Nasr reconciled it with mainstream scholarly understandings, while keeping the essential dynamic of decline. Historical narratives of decline are found as often as narratives of progress, and in the recent period have been more frequent. The Traditionalist narrative is unusual for incorporating the *kali-yuga*, and also for avoiding explanations in terms of race and civilization. It is also unusual for accepting the primordial tradition as the counterpart of modernity.

The third foundation of the Traditionalist philosophy is its critique of modernity. This rejects the optimistic view of modernity as a triumph of rationality and individual autonomy, and builds on a long tradition in Western thought that includes – in different ways – Karl Marx, John Ruskin, Friedrich Nietzsche, and Hannah Arendt. The Traditionalist critique combines the Traditionalist view of history with perennialism, seeing modernity as the *kali-yuga* and the negation of the primordial tradition. As tradition is the norm, modernity is fundamentally abnormal. Modernity is characterized by the worship of false idols, notably material and moral progress, and science. These are all illusions, as is the promise of equality, which actually leads only to enforced uniformity – the opposite of individuality.

The opposition between sacred tradition and abnormal modernity is what makes Traditionalism so powerful as a philosophy, in the view of both Julius Evola in the 1960s and of Aleksandr Dugin today. The Traditionalist critique of modernity is where its perennialism and its historical narrative come together and where Traditionalism becomes new and powerful.

A final foundation of Traditionalism is a particular view of the relationship between thought and society. The great mass ideologies of the twentieth century all addressed society as a whole, hoping to change it directly. Guénon thought that it was impossible to challenge the *kali-yuga* and change society in this way. At the most, a small elite that understood tradition might be able to have an impact indirectly. This is why Traditionalism has never been a mass ideology. Evola believed, for a while, that a revolt against modernity was possible, but then concluded that this was not the case. Schuon was, if anything, more pessimistic than Guénon.

The four foundations of the Traditionalist philosophy were immediately applied by Guénon and other Traditionalists to three core projects: self-realization, religion, and politics. While Guénon and the other Traditionalists were in general agreement concerning the foundations of Traditionalism, there was less agreement about their application. Guénon understood self-realization in terms of his reading of the primordial tradition, following an essentially Neoplatonic scheme, though he never recognized this. For those who had the necessary personal capacity, he recommended initiation into a valid esoteric tradition within the framework of a traditional orthodox exotericism, and himself chose Sufism within the framework of Islam. Evola agreed in principle, but concluded that no valid esoteric traditions survived, and turned therefore to the paths of the ascetic and the warrior. Of these, it was the path of the warrior that was most developed. Schuon followed Guénon in practice, running a Sufi order of his own, but in his writings minimized Guénon's distinction between the esoteric and the exoteric, so that religion became close to being a path to self-realization. Nasr also emphasized Sufism, and recognized that Guénon's scheme was in fact Neoplatonic.

The application of the foundations of Traditionalism to religion was mostly the work of Schuon, who took Guénon's understandings in a very different direction that ended by almost contradicting him. Guénon had insisted on the clear distinction between the esoteric and the exoteric that is fundamental to Traditionalist perennialism, and granted only a subsidiary role to exoteric religion. Evola followed Nietzsche in assigning religion in general, and Christianity in particular, a very negative role. Schuon, in contrast, rehabilitated religion, seeing it as an expression of the esoteric, and developed the idea of the 'transcendent unity of religions'. This allowed Traditionalism to play a significant role within the religious world, notably through the work of two prominent American scholars, Seyyed Hossein Nasr and Huston Smith.

Just as Schuon applied the foundations of the Traditionalist philosophy to religion, so Evola applied them to politics. Guénon was not politically active, but stressed the importance of spiritual authority as the proper basis for temporal power, combining this with an application of Hindu caste theory to European history. Democracy thus appeared as the triumph of the lowest caste, the Shudras, and modern society as the victim of the loss of hierarchy, so that particular roles were filled mostly by people who were not suited for them. Nothing, however, could be done about this, as it was a reflection of a larger problem, the *kali-yuga*. Evola broadly agreed with Guénon's analysis, though he combined the spiritual and the temporal, but disagreed that nothing could be done. He thought that a revolt from the depths might free people from modernity, and that Italian Fascism and German Nazism might together achieve this revolt. Evola was never exactly a Fascist or a Nazi, but he broadly favoured both systems, with certain reservations, especially concerning the Nazi understanding of race. After the collapse of Fascism and Nazism, he concluded that no revolt against modernity could succeed, but that one might protect oneself from modernity by 'riding the tiger', and that political activity was still possible, if only as a version of the path of action. Evola's political project is one of the things that has made Traditionalism important, in different ways in different periods, and is what makes Traditionalism most important today.

Self-realization, religion, and politics were the core areas to which the Traditionalist philosophy was applied. Traditionalism was also applied, however, to a number of further areas in which Guénon himself had little or no interest. The earliest were art, where Ananda Coomaraswamy developed views that were taken further by Schuon and his followers, and gender, where Evola and then Schuon developed views. Traditionalism was then also applied to areas that had barely existed in Guénon's time: nature, where Nasr developed influential theories, and interfaith dialogue, where understandings that originated with Nasr were applied in practice by other Traditionalists.

Art has long been associated with metaphysics and religion. Coomaraswamy, who was already well established as a leading specialist in Indian art when he encountered Traditionalism, had developed views that owed much to Plato and to John Ruskin. He combined these with Traditionalism to argue for the superiority of pre-modern and non-Western art, which he held served a sacred function. Schuon also stressed the importance of sacred art, and a number of his followers developed these views in particular directions. Titus Burckhardt investigated the metaphysics of Islamic art, and addressed the world, with the assistance of other Traditionalists, during the 1976 World of Islam Festival. Nader Ardalan applied these ideas to architecture, Keith Critchlow applied them to geometry and disseminated them through the Prince's School of Traditional Arts, and Sir John Tavener applied them to music, with considerable success.

The application of Traditionalism to questions of gender is unusual among its further projects because it led to no real consequence comparable to the music of Sir John Tavener or to actual interfaith dialogue. In some ways, it is an appendix to the application of Traditionalism to questions of self-realization, but it is not a core project. Guénon briefly considered questions of female initiation, but had no further interest in questions of gender. It was Evola who developed a Traditionalist understanding of gender. He understood it from a primarily metaphysical perspective, going far beyond those who maintained, against the arguments of feminists, that gender is innate. Feminists regard gender as acquired or even as performed. Evola saw gender as metaphysical, self-realization as gendered, and sexuality as a path to self-realization. He did not, however, see relations between male and female as cooperative, but rather as part of a metaphysical war of the sexes. Schuon took a very different view, agreeing that gender was metaphysical, but seeing male and female as complementary.

The application of Traditionalism to nature was more similar to its application to art than to its application to gender. Although the association of the natural with the sacred is very ancient, concern with the impact of humanity on nature is of more recent origin. Early proponents of organic agriculture and of sustainable development both found that Traditionalism fitted well with their arguments, but did not actually apply Traditionalism to them. This was what Nasr did, at the very beginning of the modern environmentalist movement. He presented the environmental crisis as an aspect of modernity, and used the Traditionalist historical narrative and critique of modernity in order to explain it. He further suggested the Traditionalist remedy of resacralization as a remedy for the environmental crisis. These views were adopted and to some extent implemented by the then Prince Charles, before his accession to the throne as Charles III.

Like environmentalism, interfaith dialogue is a relatively recent phenomenon. The initiative for interfaith dialogue came at first almost entirely from Christian groups and organizations, and Nasr was one of the first Muslims to write on the topic. He applied Schuon's theory of the transcendent unity of religions, arguing against universalist approaches to dialogue that attempted to resolve differences between religions by glossing over or ignoring central points of doctrine. Focusing on esoteric unity meant that exoteric religion could remain intact. Nasr also argued that dialogue was needed not only between Muslims and Christians, but also between Islam and modernity. Muslims should recognize that their partner in dialogue was often modernity, not Christianity. Nasr's lead was followed in practice by Rusmir

Mahmutćehajić in Bosnia, and by Prince Ghazi bin Muhammad in Jordan. Mahmutćehajić developed a detailed Traditionalist approach to dialogue adjusted to the Bosnian
context, while Prince Ghazi applied Traditionalism lightly to
A Common Word Between Us and You, which became one of
the most successful dialogue initiatives of the period since
9/11, partly because it was supported by the Jordanian state.

In addition to these core projects and various further projects, there have also been partial applications that are best
understood as post-Traditionalism. These post-Traditionalist
applications have been primarily political. They appear implicitly in some of the work of Alain de Benoist, and explicitly in the work of Aleksandr Dugin. They are then echoed
across the contemporary radical right, especially among some
Identitarians, and are found also in parts of the music scene,
and as symbolic references in radical chat forums. What distinguishes post-Traditionalism from Traditionalism proper is
that the perennialism that was Traditionalism's first foundation has been abandoned. Modernity is still placed in opposition to a tradition that is sacred, but the sacrality is no longer
primordial or universal. For Benoist, it consists of European
myth, which is seen as specific to Europe. For Dugin, it is Russian Orthodoxy, though, for those who do not have an Orthodox background, it may also be Islam or other religions. For
some Identitarians, Guénon is not an inspiration but rather
someone who betrayed European civilization.

Traditionalism, then, has taken its distinctive combination of perennialism, historical narrative, and critique of
modernity a long way, and in many directions. Combined
with Guénon's views on self-realization, the foundations of

Traditionalism have inspired many Westerners and some non-Westerners to seek the transcendent through Sufism and other comparable traditions, often leading others at least part of the way with them, and writing and broadcasting about their experiences. Schuon's version has had a similar impact, often at a less esoteric level, and often within Christian denominations. Combined with Evola's rather different views on self-realization, the foundations of Traditionalism have inspired many to follow the path of the warrior, often a political warrior, and sometimes a terrorist.

Combined with Schuon's transcendent unity of religion, Traditionalism has contributed to art, music, theology, and interfaith dialogue. It has been adjusted by Nasr to help protect the environment. Few other philosophies have found so many applications. There are Traditionalist monks, Sufis, theologians, artists, and political activists. Of these, only the political activists seem really problematic. Some people are uncomfortable with monks, Sufis, and theologians who present their Traditionalist-determined understandings of truth as truth, not as Traditionalism, so that the unwary may suppose that these understandings come from a major religion, not a philosophy of relatively recent origin. On the whole, however, most people who are not atheists can respect the applications of Traditionalism in these areas. Political activism on the radical right, however, is a different matter. The political theories of the neo-Eurasianists and the Identitarians may be theoretically and philosophically interesting as well as obviously problematic, but real-life events to which they contribute can be catastrophic. Dugin did not cause Russia's twenty-first-century invasion of Ukraine on his own, but neo-Eurasianism certainly contributed to it, and the resulting war has caused death and destruction on a massive scale. What might happen if, with the help of Identitarianism, real inter-ethnic conflict developed between Western Europe's Muslim and non-Muslim populations does not bear imagining.

Select Bibliography of Traditionalist Works

Date in brackets is date of first publication.

Ardalan, Nader, and Laleh Bakhtiar (1973). *The Sense of Unity: The Sufi Tradition in Persian Architecture*. Chicago: University of Chicago Press; current edition Chicago: Kazi, 2000.

Burckhardt, Titus (1958). *Sacred Art in East and West: Its Principles and Methods*. Originally published as *Principes et méthodes de l'art sacré*, Lyon: P. Derain; translated London: Perennial Books, 1967; current edition Louisville, KY: Fons Vitae, 2002.

Burckhardt, Titus (1976). *Art of Islam: Language and Meaning*. London: World of Islam Festival; current edition Bloomington, IN: World Wisdom, 2009.

Charles, Prince, Tony Juniper, and Ian Skelly (2010). *Harmony: A New Way of Looking at Our World*. London: Blue Door.

Coomaraswamy, Ananda (1934). *The Transformation of Nature in Art*. Cambridge, MA: Harvard University Press; current edition Kettering, OH: Angelico Press, 2016.

Coomaraswamy, Ananda (1941). *Christian and Oriental Philosophy of Art*. First published as 'Why Exhibit Works of Art?' in *The Journal of Aesthetics and Art Criticism*, volume 1: 27–41; republished under current title New York: Dover Publications, 1956; current edition New Delhi: Munshiram Manoharlal Publishers, 1994.

Critchlow, Keith (1976). *Islamic Patterns: An Analytical and Cosmological Approach*. London: Thames and Hudson.

Critchlow, Keith (2011). *The Hidden Geometry of Flowers: Living Rhythms, Form and Number*. Edinburgh: Floris Books.

Dugin, Aleksandr (1996). *Метафизика Благой Вести: Православный эзотеризм* [The Metaphysics of the Gospel: Orthodox Esotericism]. Moscow: Arktogeya.

Dugin, Aleksandr (1997). *Основы геополитики: геополитическое будущее России* [The Foundations of Geopolitics: The Geopolitical Future of Russia]. Moscow: Arktogeya.

Dugin, Aleksandr (2002). *Философия Традиционализма* [The Philosophy of Traditionalism]. Moscow: Arktogeya.

Dugin, Aleksandr (2009). *The Fourth Political Theory*. Originally published as *Четвертая политическая теория*, St Petersburg: Amfora; translated London: Arktos, 2012.

Dugin, Aleksandr (2013). *В поисках темного Логоса. Философско-богословские очерки* [In Search of the Dark Logos. Philosophical and Theological Essays]. Moscow: Akademicheskiy Proyekt. The chapter 'Traditionalism as a Theory: Sophia, Plato and the Event' (originally published as 'Традиционализм как теория: София, Платон и событие'), translated Eurasianist Internet Archive, 2019, at https:// eurasianist-archive.com/2019/06/13/traditionalism-as-a-theory-sophia-plato-and-the-event-alexander-dugin/.

Eliade, Mircea (1949). *Cosmos and History: The Myth of the Eternal Return*. Originally published as *Le mythe de l'éternel retour: archétypes et répétition*, Paris: Gallimard; translated Princeton: Princeton University Press, 1954; current edition Princeton: Princeton University Press, 2018.

Eliade, Mircea (1957). *The Sacred and the Profane: The Nature of Religion*. Originally written as *Le sacré et le profane* and published as *Das Heilige und das Profane: vom Wesen des Religiösen*, Hamburg: Rowohlt; translated from the French original New York: Harcourt, Brace and World, 1959; current edition San Diego: Harcourt Brace Jovanovich, 1987.

Evola, Julius (1928). *Pagan Imperialism*. Originally published as *Imperialismo pagano: il fascismo dinanzi al pericolo euro-cristiano*, Rome: Atanòr; translated NP: Gornahoor Press, 2017.

Evola, Julius (1931). *The Hermetic Tradition: In its Symbols. Doctrine, and 'Royal Art'*. Originally published as *La tradizione ermetica*, Bari: Laterza; translated Rochester, VT: Inner Traditions International, 1995.

Evola, Julius (1932). *The Mask and Face of Contemporary Spiritualism*. Originally published as *Maschera e volto dello spiritualismo contemporaneo*, Turin: Bocca; translated NP: Arktos Media, 2018.

Evola, Julius, *Revolt against the Modern World* (1934). Originally published as *Rivolta contro il mondo moderno*, Milan: Hoepli; translated Rochester, VT: Inner Traditions International, 1995.

Evola, Julius (1953). *Men among the Ruins: Postwar Reflections of a Radical Traditionalist*. Originally published as *Gli uomini e le rovine*,

Rome: Edizioni dell'Ascia; translated Rochester, VT: Inner Traditions International, 2002.

Evola, Julius, and the UR Group (1955). *Realizations of the Absolute Individual*, vol. 3 of *Introduction to Magic*. Originally published as *Introduzione alla magia quale scienza dell'Io*, Turin: Bocca; revised edition Rome: Edizioni Mediterranee 1971; translated Rochester, VT: Inner Traditions, 2021.

Evola, Julius (1958). *The Metaphysics of Sex*. Originally published as *Metafisica del sesso*, Rome: Atanòr; translated New York: Inner Traditions International, 1983.

Evola, Julius (1961). *Ride the Tiger*. Originally published as *Cavalcare la tigre*, Milan: Vanni Scheiwiller; translated Rochester, VT: Inner Traditions International, 2003.

Evola, Julius (1963). *The Path of Cinnabar*. Originally published as *Il cammino del cinabro*, Milan: Vanni Scheiwiller; translated London: Integral Tradition Publishing, 2009.

Evola, Julius (1964). *Fascism Viewed from the Right*. Originally published as *Il fascismo. Saggio di una analisi critica dal punto di vista della destra*, Rome: Volpe; translated London: Arktos Media, 2013.

Guénon, René (1921). *Introduction to the Study of the Hindu Doctrines*. Originally published as *Introduction générale à l'étude des doctrines hindoues*, Paris: Guy Trédaniel; translated London: Luzac & Co., 1945; current edition Hillsdale, NY: Sophia Perennis, 2004.

Guénon, René (1924). *East and West*. Originally published as *Orient et Occident*, Paris: Payot, translated London: Luzac & Co., 1941; current edition Ghent, NY: Sophia Perennis, 2004.

Guénon, René (1925). *Man and His Becoming according to the Vedanta*. Originally published as *L'Homme et son devenir selon le Vêdânta*, Paris: Bossard; translated London: Luzac, 1945; current edition Hillsdale, NY: Sophia Perennis, 2001.

Guénon, René (1927). *The Crisis of the Modern World*. Originally published as *La Crise du monde moderne*, Paris: Bossard; translated London: Luzac & Co., 1942; current edition Hillsdale, NY: Sophia Perennis, 2001.

Guénon, René (1927). *Lord of the World*. Originally published as *Le Roi du monde*, Paris: Ch. Bosse; translated Moorcote, North Yorkshire: Coombe Springs Press, 1983; current edition Hillsdale, NY: Sophia Perennis, 2004.

Guénon, René (1929). *Spiritual Authority and Temporal Power*. Originally published as *Autorité spirituelle et pouvoir temporel*, Paris: Vrin; translated Ghent, NY: Sophia Perennis, 2001.

Guénon, René (1931). *The Symbolism of the Cross*. Originally published as *Le Symbolisme de la Croix*, Paris: Véga; translated London: Luzac, 1958; current edition Ghent, NY: Sophia Perennis et Universalis, 1996.

Guénon, René (1945). *The Reign of Quantity and the Signs of the Times*. Originally published as *Le Règne de la Quantité et les Signes des Temps*, Paris: Gallimard; translated London: Luzac & Co., 1953; current edition Hillsdale, NY: Sophia Perennis, 2004.

Guénon, René (1946), *Perspectives on Initiation*. Originally published as *Aperçus sur l'Initiation*, Paris: Éditions Traditionnelles; translated Ghent, NY: Sophia Perennis, 2001.

Guénon, René (1952). *Initiation and Spiritual Realization*. Posthumous collection originally published as *Initiation et Réalisation spirituelle*, Paris: Éditions Traditionnelles; translated Ghent, NY: Sophia Perennis, 2001.

Guénon, René (1964). *Studies in Freemasonry and the Compagnonnage*. Posthumous collection originally published as *Études sur la Franc-maçonnerie et le Compagnonnage*, Paris: Éditions Traditionnelles; translated Hillsdale, NY: Sophia Perennis, 2004.

Mahmutćehajić, Rusmir (1998). *The Denial of Bosnia*. Originally published as *Kriva politika: Čitanje historije i povjerenje u Bosni*, Tuzla: Radio Kameleon; translated University Park: The Pennsylvania State University Press, 2000.

Mahmutćehajić, Rusmir (2000). *Sarajevo Essays: Politics, Ideology, and Tradition*. Originally published as *Sarajevski eseji: Politika, ideologija, tradicija*, Zagreb: Durieux; translated Albany: State University of New York Press, 2003.

Morgan, John (2018). 'What Would Evola Do?', *Counter-Currents*, 19 May 2018, https://counter-currents.com/2018/05/what-would-evola-do-2/.

Nasr, Seyyed Hossein (1968). *Man and Nature: The Spiritual Crisis of Modern Man*. London: Allen and Unwin; current edition London: Unwin Paperbacks, 1990.

Nasr, Seyyed Hossein (1996). *Religion & the Order of Nature*. New York: Oxford University Press.

Nasr, Seyyed Hossein (1998). 'Islamic-Christian Dialogue: Problems and Obstacles to be Pondered and Overcome', *The Muslim World* 88, no. 3–4 (October): 218–37.

O'Meara, Michael (2007). 'The Primordial and the Perennial: Tradition in the Thought of Martin Heidegger and Julius Evola', *Tyr* 3: 67–88.

Peterson, Jordan B. (1999). *Maps of Meaning: The Architecture of Belief*. New York: Routledge.

Peterson, Jordan B. (2018). *12 Rules for Life: An Antidote to Chaos*. Toronto: Random House Canada.

Schuon, Frithjof (1948). *The Transcendent Unity of Religions*. Originally published as *De l'Unité transcendante des religions*, Paris: Gallimard; translated London: Faber & Faber, 1953; current edition Wheaton, IL: Quest Books, 1993.

Schuon, Frithjof, *Gnosis: Divine Wisdom* (1957). Originally published as *Sentiers de Gnose*, Paris: La Colombe; translated London: John Murray, 1959; current edition Bloomington, IN: World Wisdom, 2006.

Schuon, Frithjof (1959). *Language of the Self*. Originally published Madras: Ganesh & Co.; current edition Bloomington, IN: World Wisdom Books, 1999.

Schuon, Frithjof (1961). *Understanding Islam*. First published as *Comprendre l'Islam*, Paris: Gallimard. Translated London: Allen & Unwin, 1963; current edition Bloomington, IN: World Wisdom, 1998.

Schuon, Frithjof (1965). *Light on the Ancient Worlds*. Originally published London: Perennial Books; new translation from the French original Bloomington, IN: World Wisdom, 2006.

Schuon, Frithjof (1980). *Sufism: Veil and Quintessence*. Originally published as *Le soufisme: voile et quintessence*, Paris: Dervy-Livres; translated Bloomington, IN: World Wisdom Books, 2006.

Schuon, Frithjof (1981). *Christianity/Islam: Perspectives on Esoteric Ecumenism*. Originally published as *Christianisme/Islam: Visions d'œcuménisme ésotérique*, Milan: Archè; translated Bloomington, IN: World Wisdom Books, 1985; current edition Bloomington, IN: World Wisdom, 2008.

Smith, Huston (1965). *The World's Religions*. Originally published as *The Religions of Man*, New York: Harper & Row; current edition New York: HarperOne, 2009.

Smith, Huston (1987). 'Is There a Perennial Philosophy?', *Journal of the American Academy of Religion* 55: 553–66.

Tavener, John (1999). *The Music of Silence: A Composer's Testament*. London: Faber and Faber.

Tavener, John (2005). 'The Veil of the Temple'. In Live Recording Concert Booklet, *The Veil of the Temple*, RCA.

Tavener, John (2005). 'Towards the *Musica Perennis*'. In *Every Man an Artist: Readings in the Traditional Philosophy of Art*, edited by Brian Keeble, Bloomington, IN: World Wisdom, pp. 222–30.

Wolfheze, Alexander (2018). 'The Identitarian Revolution: Dutch Preliminaries', Geopolitika.ru, 7 August, https://www.geopolitica.ru/en/article/identitarian-revolution-dutch-preliminaries.

Wolfheze, Alexander (2019). 'The Light of Traditionalism', *Arktos Journal* 4 (November), https://arktos.com/2019/11/04/the-light-of-traditionalism/.

Notes

CHAPTER 1: TRADITIONALISM AND THE TRADITIONALISTS

1. Paul Chacornac, *La vie simple de René Guénon* (Paris: Éditions traditionnelles, 1958). The English translation is *The Simple Life of René Guénon* (Hillsdale, NY: Sophia Perennis, 2004).
2. Mark Sedgwick, *Against the Modern World: Traditionalism and the Secret Intellectual History of the Twentieth Century* (New York: Oxford University Press, 2003).
3. Aleksander Dugin, *Основы геополитики: геополитическое будущее России* (Moscow: Arktogeya, 1997). Several subsequent editions.
4. Julius Evola, *Imperialismo pagano: il fascismo dinanzi al pericolo euro-cristiano* (Rome: Atanòr, 1928).
5. Frithjof Schuon, *De l'Unité transcendante des religions* (Paris: Gallimard, 1948).

CHAPTER 2: HISTORICAL PERENNIALISM

1. Isaiah Berlin, 'The Counter-Enlightenment', in *Against the Current: Essays in the History of Ideas* (1979; Princeton: Princeton University Press, 2013), pp. 1–32.
2. Berlin, 'Counter-Enlightenment', p. 11.
3. Berlin, 'Counter-Enlightenment', p. 13.
4. Jacob and Wilhelm Grimm, *Kinder- und Haus-Märchen* (Berlin: Realschulbuchhandlung, 1812), translated as *The Original Folk and Fairy Tales of the Brothers Grimm: The Complete First Edition*, trans. Jack Zipes (Princeton: Princeton University Press, 2014).

5. James Frazer, Preface to the Second Edition of *The Golden Bough* (1900), reprinted in Frazer, *The Magic Art and the Evolution of Kings* (London: Macmillan and Co., 1920), pp. xvii–xxvii, at pp. xxv–xxvi.

6. C. G. Jung, 'Instinct and the Unconscious', *British Journal of Psychology* 10 (1919): 15–23, at p. 23.

7. Jung, 'Instinct and the Unconscious'.

8. Ralph Cudworth, *The True Intellectual System of the Universe* (1678; New York: Andover, 1837), vol. 1, p. 420.

9. John Toland, *Clidophorus* (London, 1720), pp. 65–66.

10. Swami Vivekananda, 'Response to Welcome', *The Complete Works of the Swami Vivekananda* (Almora, India: Prabuddha Bharata Press, 1900), vol. 1, pp. 1–2, at p. 2.

11. Alfred Sinnett, *Esoteric Buddhism* (London: Trübner & Co., 1883).

12. Aldous Huxley, *The Perennial Philosophy* (New York: Harper and Brothers, 1945).

13. Marcello Truzzi, 'Definition and Dimensions of the Occult: Towards a Sociological Perspective', *Journal of Popular Culture* 5:3 (1971): 635–46, at 637.

14. William James, *The Varieties of Religious Experience: A Study in Human Nature* (London: Longmans, Green and Co., 1902), p. 425.

15. James, *The Varieties of Religious Experience*, p. 400.

16. James, *The Varieties of Religious Experience*, p. 425.

17. Rudolf Otto, *Das Heilige. Über das Irrationale in der Idee des Göttlichen und sein Verhältnis zum Rationalen* (Breslau: Trewendt und Granier, 1917).

18. Rudolf Otto, *West-östliche Mystik: Vergleich und Unterscheidung zur Wesensdeutung* (Gotha: Leopold Klotz, 1926).

19. Huston Smith, *The Religions of Man* (New York: Harper & Row, 1965), p. 4.

CHAPTER 3: TRADITIONALIST PERENNIALISM

1. Aleksandr Dugin, *В поисках темного Логоса. Философско-богословские очерки* (Moscow: Akademicheskiy Proyekt, 2013).

2. René Guénon, *Introduction to the Study of the Hindu Doctrines* (London: Luzac & Co., 1945), p. 166.

3. Guénon, *Introduction*, p. 19.

4. Guénon, *Introduction*, p. 105.

5. René Guénon, *East and West* (Ghent, NY: Sophia Perennis, 2001), p. 30.
6. Guénon, *Introduction*, pp. 291–2.
7. Guénon, *Introduction*, p. 290.
8. Guénon, *Introduction*, p. 115.
9. Guénon, *Introduction*, p. 90.
10. Julius Evola, *Revolt against the Modern World* (Rochester, VT: Inner Traditions International, 1995), p. xxxiv.
11. Evola, *Revolt against the Modern World*, p. 151.
12. Friedrich Nietzsche, *Zur Genealogie der Moral: Eine Streitschrift* (Leipzig: C. G. Naumann, 1887).
13. Mircea Eliade, *Cosmos and History: The Myth of the Eternal Return* (New York: Harper and Brothers, 1959), p. viii.
14. Mircea Eliade, *The Sacred and the Profane: The Nature of Religion* (New York: Harcourt, Brace and Company, 1959), p. 16.
15. Eliade, *The Sacred and the Profane*, p. 16.
16. Eliade, *The Sacred and the Profane*, p. 16.
17. Eliade, *Cosmos and History*, p. 3.
18. Frithjof Schuon, *Gnosis: Divine Wisdom* (Bloomington, IN: World Wisdom, 2006), pp. 9–10.
19. Huston Smith, 'Is There a Perennial Philosophy?', *Journal of the American Academy of Religion* 55 (1987): 553–66.
20. Smith, 'Is There a Perennial Philosophy?', p. 558.
21. Smith, 'Is There a Perennial Philosophy?', p. 563.
22. Smith, 'Is There a Perennial Philosophy?', p. 561.
23. Smith, 'Is There a Perennial Philosophy?', p. 561, note 14.
24. Smith, 'Is There a Perennial Philosophy?', p. 563.

CHAPTER 4: TRADITIONALIST HISTORY

1. Marco Pallis, Foreword, *Introduction to the Study of the Hindu Doctrines* by René Guénon (London: Luzac, 1945), pp. 7–16, at p. 15.
2. Hesiod, *Works and Days*, in *Theogony and Works and Days* (Oxford: Oxford University Press, 1999).
3. Ovid, *Metamorphoses* (London: Penguin, 2004).
4. Jacques-Bénigne Bossuet, *Discours sur l'histoire universelle: Depuis le commencement du monde jusqu'à l'empire de Charlemagne* (Paris, 1784).
5. Voltaire, *Essai sur les mœurs et l'esprit des nations* (Paris, 1756).

6. Anne-Robert-Jacques Turgot, 'Plan de deux Discours sur l'Histoire Universelle', in *Oeuvres de Turgot*, ed. Gustave Schelle (Paris: Félix Alcan, 1913), vol. 1, pp. 274–323, at p. 276.
7. Arthur de Gobineau, *Essai sur l'inégalité des races humaines* (Paris: Firmin Didot Frères, 1855), vol. 4, p. 358.
8. René Guénon, *The Crisis of the Modern World* (Hillsdale, NY: Sophia Perennis, 2001), p. 9.
9. Guénon, *Introduction*, p. 41.
10. Guénon, *Introduction*, p. 84.
11. Frithjof Schuon, *Light on the Ancient Worlds* (Bloomington, IN: World Wisdom, 2006), pp. 32–3.
12. Schuon, *Light on the Ancient Worlds*, p. 37.
13. Frithjof Schuon, *The Transcendent Unity of Religions* (Wheaton, IL: Quest Books, 1993), p. 85.
14. Frithjof Schuon, *Sufism: Veil and Quintessence* (Bloomington, IN: World Wisdom, 2006), p. 20.
15. Schuon, *Sufism*, pp. 20–21.
16. Reprinted in Frithjof Schuon, *Language of the Self: Essays on the Perennial Philosophy* ([Belgrade]: Mikrotheos, 2012), pp. 105–24.
17. Seyyed Hossein Nasr, *Man and Nature: The Spiritual Crisis of Modern Man* (London: Unwin Paperbacks, 1990), p. 53.
18. Seyyed Hossein Nasr, *Nature Religion & the Order of* (New York: Oxford University Press, 1996), p. 101.

CHAPTER 5: THE TRADITIONALIST CRITIQUE OF MODERNITY

1. Jürgen Habermas, *The Philosophical Discourse of Modernity: Twelve Lectures* (Cambridge, MA: MIT Press, 1987), p. 4.
2. Habermas, *Philosophical Discourse of Modernity*, pp. 83–4.
3. Karl Marx and Friedrich Engels, *The Communist Manifesto: A Modern Edition* (London: Verso, 2012), p. 38.
4. Charles Baudelaire, 'The Painter of Modern Life', in Baudelaire, *Selected Writings on Art and Literature* (London: Penguin, 2006), pp. 390–435, at p. 403.
5. Marx and Engels, *The Communist Manifesto*, p. 41.
6. John Ruskin, *On the Nature of Gothic Architecture: And Herein of the True Functions of the Workman in Art* (London: Smith, Elder & Co., 1854), pp. 10, 8.
7. Søren Kierkegaard, *For Self-Examination Judge for Yourself!*, trans. Howard V. Hong and Edna H. Hong (Princeton: Princeton University Press, 1990), pp. 47–8.

8. Friedrich Nietzsche, *Thus Spake Zarathustra*, trans. Thomas Common (Ware, Hertfordshire: Wordsworth, 1997), p. 10. I have slightly modernized the language.

9. Jacques Maritain, *Antimoderne* (Paris: Éditions de la Revue des jeunes, 1922), pp. 18–19, 20, 199.

10. Julius Evola, *The Path of Cinnabar* (London: Integral Tradition Publishing, 2009), p. 97.

11. René Guénon, *Introduction to the Study of the Hindu Doctrines* (London: Luzac & Co., 1945), p. 113.

12. René Guénon, *The Crisis of the Modern World* (London: Luzac & Co., 1942; Hillsdale, NY: Sophia Perennis, 2001); René Guénon, *The Reign of Quantity and the Signs of the Times* (Ghent, NY: Sophia Perennis, 1995).

13. René Guénon, *East and West* (Ghent, NY: Sophia Perennis, 2001), p. 16.

14. Guénon, *Crisis of the Modern World*, p. 93.

15. Guénon, *East and West*, p. 67.

16. Guénon, *East and West*, p. 23.

17. Guénon, *Crisis of the Modern World*, p. 38.

18. Guénon, *East and West*, p. 41.

19. Guénon, *Reign of Quantity*, p. 60.

20. Guénon, *Reign of Quantity*, p. 60.

21. Guénon, *Reign of Quantity*, p. 66.

22. Guénon, *Reign of Quantity*, p. 52.

23. Guénon, *Introduction*, p. 125.

24. Guénon, *East and West*, p. 22.

25. Guénon, *Reign of Quantity*, p. 79.

26. Guénon, *Introduction*, p. 220.

27. Guénon, *Crisis of the Modern World*, p. 72.

28. Guénon, *Reign of Quantity*, pp. 4, 5.

29. Guénon, *East and West*, p. 24.

30. Guénon, *East and West*, p. 28.

31. Guénon, *East and West*, p. 62.

32. Julius Evola, *Revolt against the Modern World* (Rochester, VT: Inner Traditions International, 1995), p. 163. I have amended the translation slightly.

33. Julius Evola, 'Paths of the Western Spirit', in Julius Evola and the UR Group, *Realizations of the Absolute Individual*, vol. 3 of *Introduction to Magic*, trans. and ed. Joscelyn Godwin (Rochester, VT: Inner Traditions, 2021), pp. 4–7, at p. 5.

34. Evola, *Revolt against the Modern World*, p. 183.

35. Evola, *Revolt against the Modern World*, p. 165.

36. Julius Evola, *The Metaphysics of Sex* (New York: Inner Traditions International, 1983), p. 7.

37. Evola, *Metaphysics of Sex*, p. 64.

38. Evola, *Revolt against the Modern World*, p. 284.

39. Julius Evola, *Men among the Ruins: Postwar Reflections of a Radical Traditionalist* (Rochester, VT: Inner Traditions International, 2002), p. 166.

40. Julius Evola, *Ride the Tiger* (Rochester, VT: Inner Traditions International, 2003), p. 23.

41. Evola, *Ride the Tiger*, p. 31.

42. Evola, *Ride the Tiger*, p. 177.

43. Frithjof Schuon, *Understanding Islam* (Bloomington, IN: World Wisdom, 1998), p. 31.

44. Schuon, *Understanding Islam*, p. 29.

45. Schuon, *Understanding Islam*, p. 25.

46. Frithjof Schuon, *Light on the Ancient Worlds* (Bloomington, IN: World Wisdom, 2006), p. 12.

47. Schuon, *Light on the Ancient Worlds*, p. 32.

48. Jordan B. Peterson, *Maps of Meaning: The Architecture of Belief* (New York: Routledge, 1999), p. 3.

49. Peterson, *Maps of Meaning*, p. 265.

50. Jordan B. Peterson, *12 Rules for Life: An Antidote to Chaos* (Toronto: Random House Canada, 2018), p. xxxiii.

CHAPTER 6: TRADITIONALISM, THOUGHT, AND SOCIETY

1. Mark 16:15–16.

2. Hebrews 10:24–5.

3. Denis Diderot, 'Encyclopédie', in *Encyclopédie ou Dictionnaire raisonné des sciences, des arts et des métiers* (Paris: 1751–72), vol. 5 (1755), pp. 635–48, at p. 642. Translation adapted from *The Encyclopedia of Diderot & d'Alembert: Collaborative Translation Project*, University of Michigan, at https://quod.lib.umich.edu/d/did/index.html.

4. Diderot, 'Encyclopédie', p. 642.

5. René Guénon, *Introduction to the Study of the Hindu Doctrines* (London: Luzac & Co., 1945), p. 347.

6. René Guénon, *Introduction générale à l'étude des doctrines hindoues* (Paris: Guy Trédaniel, 1921) and *Orient et Occident* (Paris: Payot 1924).

7. René Guénon, *The Crisis of the Modern World* (Hillsdale, NY: Sophia Perennis, 2001), p. 35.

8. Guénon, *Introduction*, p. 340.

9. Guénon, *Introduction*, pp. 314–24.

10. Guénon, *Crisis of the Modern World*, pp. 8–9.

11. René Guénon, *East and West* (Ghent, NY: Sophia Perennis, 2001), p. 114.

12. Guénon, *East and West*, pp. 148–9.

13. Guénon, *East and West*, p. 126.

14. Julius Evola, *Pagan Imperialism* (NP: Gornahoor Press, 2017), p. 124.

15. Julius Evola, *Revolt against the Modern World* (Rochester, VT: Inner Traditions International, 1995), p. 359.

16. Evola, *Pagan Imperialism*, p. 94.

17. Evola, *Pagan Imperialism*, p. 94.

18. Evola, *Pagan Imperialism*, p. 51.

19. Frithjof Schuon, *Understanding Islam* (Bloomington, IN: World Wisdom, 1998), p. 26.

20. Schuon, *Understanding Islam*, p. 28.

21. Frithjof Schuon, *Language of the Self* (Madras: Ganesh & Co., 1959), p. 140.

22. Frithjof Schuon, *The Transcendent Unity of Religions* (Wheaton, IL: Quest Books, 1993), p. 82.

23. Schuon, *The Transcendent Unity of Religions*, pp. 82, 87.

24. Schuon, *The Transcendent Unity of Religions*, p. 107.

25. David Brooks, 'The Jordan Peterson Moment', *New York Times*, 25 January 2018, https://www.nytimes.com/2018/01/25/opinion/jordan-peterson-moment.html.

CHAPTER 7: SELF-REALIZATION

1. Plato, *Plato in Twelve Volumes*, translated by Harold N. Fowler (Cambridge, MA, Harvard University Press, 1925), vol. 9, p. 483.

2. René Guénon, *The Symbolism of the Cross* (Ghent, NY: Sophia Perennis et Universalis, 1996), p. x.

3. René Guénon, *Perspectives on Initiation* (Ghent, NY: Sophia Perennis, 2001).

4. René Guénon, *Man and His Becoming according to the Vedanta* (Hillsdale, NY: Sophia Perennis, 2001), p. 23.

5. Guénon, *Man and His Becoming*, p. 31.

6. René Guénon, *Introduction to the Study of the Hindu Doctrines* (London: Luzac & Co., 1945), p. 266.

7. René Guénon, *The Reign of Quantity and the Signs of the Times* (Hillsdale, NY: Sophia Perennis, 2004), p. 63.

8. Guénon, *Introduction*, p. 263.

9. Guénon, *Perspectives on Initiation*, p. 26.

10. Guénon, *Perspectives on Initiation*, p. 12.

11. Guénon, *Perspectives on Initiation*, p. 24.

12. Guénon, *Perspectives on Initiation*, p. 200.

13. Guénon, *Perspectives on Initiation*, p. 38.

14. Guénon, *Perspectives on Initiation*, p. 24.

15. Guénon, *Perspectives on Initiation*, p. 53.

16. Guénon, *The Reign of Quantity*, p. 56.

17. Julius Evola, 'On the Limits of Initiatic "Regularity"', in Julius Evola and the UR Group, *Realizations of the Absolute Individual*, vol. 3 of *Introduction to Magic*, trans. and ed. Joscelyn Godwin (Rochester, VT: Inner Traditions, 2021), pp. 173–86, at p. 178.

18. Evola, 'On the Limits of Initiatic "Regularity"', p. 180.

19. Evola, 'On the Limits of Initiatic "Regularity"', p. 176.

20. Julius Evola, 'Paths of the Western Spirit', in Julius Evola and the UR Group, *Realizations of the Absolute Individual*, vol. 3 of *Introduction to Magic*, trans. and ed. Joscelyn Godwin (Rochester, VT: Inner Traditions, 2021), pp. 4–7, at p. 5.

21. Evola, 'Paths of the Western Spirit', p. 6.

22. Julius Evola, *Revolt against the Modern World* (Rochester, VT: Inner Traditions International, 1995), p. 159.

23. Julius Evola, *Pagan Imperialism* (NP: Gornahoor Press, 2017), pp. 12, 17.

24. Evola, *Pagan Imperialism*, p. 151.

25. Evola, *Pagan Imperialism*, p. 54.

26. Evola, *Pagan Imperialism*, p. 100.

27. Evola, *Revolt against the Modern World*, p. 214.

28. Evola, *Revolt against the Modern World*, p. 13.

29. Evola, *Revolt against the Modern World*, p. 299.

30. Evola, *Pagan Imperialism*, pp. 81–2.

31. Evola, *Revolt against the Modern World*, pp. 37, 57.

32. Julius Evola, *Men among the Ruins: Postwar Reflections of a Radical Traditionalist* (Rochester, VT: Inner Traditions International, 2002), p. 125.

33. Evola, 'Paths of the Western Spirit', p. 6.

34. Evola, *Ride the Tiger*, p. 6.

35. Evola, *Ride the Tiger*, p. 57.

36. Friedrich Nietzsche, *The Gay Science*, trans. Walter Kaufmann (New York: Vintage, 1974), p. 270.

37. Evola, *Ride the Tiger*, p. 63.

38. Evola, *Ride the Tiger*, p. 60.

39. Julius Evola, *The Path of Cinnabar* (London: Integral Tradition Publishing, 2009), p. 16.

40. Julius Evola, 'First Ascent', in Julius Evola and the UR Group, *Realizations of the Absolute Individual*, vol. 3 of *Introduction to Magic*, trans. and ed. Joscelyn Godwin (Rochester, VT: Inner Traditions, 2021), pp. 256–66, at p. 258.

41. Evola, *Ride the Tiger*, pp. 110–11.

42. Evola, *Ride the Tiger*, p. 58. Emphasis in original.

43. Frithjof Schuon, *The Transcendent Unity of Religions* (Wheaton, IL: Quest Books, 1993), p. 38.

44. Frithjof Schuon, *Gnosis: Divine Wisdom* (Bloomington, IN: World Wisdom, 2006), p. 26.

45. Schuon, *The Transcendent Unity of Religions*, p. 12.

46. Schuon, *The Transcendent Unity of Religions*, p. 119.

47. Schuon, *Sufism: Veil and Quintessence* (Bloomington, IN: World Wisdom, 2006), p. 52.

48. Schuon, *The Transcendent Unity of Religions*, pp. 132–3.

49. Schuon, *The Transcendent Unity of Religions*, p. 136.

50. Frithjof Schuon, *Light on the Ancient Worlds* (Bloomington, IN: World Wisdom, 2006), p. 59.

51. Schuon, *Light on the Ancient Worlds*, p. 67.

52. Schuon, *Light on the Ancient Worlds*, p. 125.

53. Frithjof Schuon, *Language of the Self* (Madras: Ganesh & Co., 1959), p. 140.

54. Seyyed Hossein Nasr, *Man and Nature: The Spiritual Crisis of Modern Man* (London: Unwin Paperbacks, 1990), pp. 53–4.

55. Nasr, *Man and Nature*, p. 55.

56. Nasr, *Man and Nature*, p. 61.

57. Jordan B. Peterson, *12 Rules for Life: An Antidote to Chaos* (Toronto: Random House Canada, 2018), p. 86.

58. Peterson, *12 Rules for Life*, p. xxxiii.

59. Peterson, *12 Rules for Life*, p. 27.

60. Peterson, *12 Rules for Life*, p. 158.

CHAPTER 8: RELIGION

1. René Guénon, *The Reign of Quantity and the Signs of the Times* (Hillsdale, NY: Sophia Perennis, 2004), pp. 62–3.
2. René Guénon, *Perspectives on Initiation* (Ghent, NY: Sophia Perennis, 2001), p. 44.
3. René Guénon, 'The Necessity of Traditional Exoterism', in *Initiation and Spiritual Realization* (Ghent, NY: Sophia Perennis, 2001), pp. 41–4, at p. 43.
4. René Guénon, 'The Role of the *Guru*', in *Initiation and Spiritual Realization*, pp. 122–6, at p. 126.
5. Guénon, 'The Necessity of Traditional Exoterism', p. 43.
6. René Guénon, 'Conversions', in *Initiation and Spiritual Realization*, pp. 61–4, at pp. 61–3.
7. Evola, *The Mask and Face of Contemporary Spiritualism*, quoted in Julius Evola, *The Path of Cinnabar* (London: Integral Tradition Publishing, 2009), p. 131.
8. Frithjof Schuon, *The Transcendent Unity of Religions* (Wheaton, IL: Quest Books, 1993), p. xxxi.
9. Schuon, *The Transcendent Unity of Religions*, p. xxxiii.
10. Frithjof Schuon, *Gnosis: Divine Wisdom* (Bloomington, IN: World Wisdom, 2006), p. 64.
11. Frithjof Schuon, *Understanding Islam* (Bloomington, IN: World Wisdom, 1998), pp. 106–7.
12. Schuon, *Gnosis*, p. 5.
13. Schuon, *The Transcendent Unity of Religions*, p. 7.
14. Schuon, *The Transcendent Unity of Religions*, p. 23.
15. Schuon, *Understanding Islam*, p. 14.
16. Schuon, *The Transcendent Unity of Religions*, p. 26.
17. Schuon, *The Transcendent Unity of Religions*, p. 23.
18. Frithjof Schuon, *Light on the Ancient Worlds* (Bloomington, IN: World Wisdom, 2006), p. 121.
19. Schuon, *Light on the Ancient Worlds*, p. 4.
20. Schuon, *Light on the Ancient Worlds*, p. 27.
21. Schuon, *The Transcendent Unity of Religions*, p. 10.
22. Schuon, *The Transcendent Unity of Religions*, p. 9.
23. Schuon, *Understanding Islam*, pp. 97–8.
24. Schuon, *Understanding Islam*, p. 17.
25. Schuon, *Understanding Islam*, pp. 98–9.
26. Schuon, *The Transcendent Unity of Religions*, p. 83.

27. Schuon, *Gnosis*, p. 6.

28. Seyyed Hossein Nasr, *Religion & the Order of Nature* (New York: Oxford University Press, 1996), p. 16.

29. Nasr, *Religion & the Order of Nature*, p. 13.

30. Nasr, *Religion & the Order of Nature*, p. 12.

31. Huston Smith, with Jeffery Paine, *Tales of Wonder: Adventures Chasing the Divine* (New York: HarperOne, 2010), p. 113.

32. Jordan Peterson, 'Biblical Series I: Introduction to the Idea of God', YouTube, 20 May 2017, https://youtu.be/f-wWBG06a2w.

CHAPTER 9: POLITICS

1. John Ruskin, *On the Nature of Gothic Architecture: And Herein of the True Functions of the Workman in Art* (London: Smith, Elder & Co., 1854), p. 9.

2. René Guénon, *The Crisis of the Modern World* (Hillsdale, NY: Sophia Perennis, 2001); René Guénon, *Spiritual Authority and Temporal Power* (Ghent, NY: Sophia Perennis, 2001).

3. Guénon, *Spiritual Authority and Temporal Power*, p. 12.

4. René Guénon, *East and West* (Ghent, NY: Sophia Perennis, 2001), p. 107.

5. René Guénon, *Introduction to the Study of the Hindu Doctrines* (London: Luzac & Co., 1945), p. 82.

6. Guénon, *Spiritual Authority and Temporal Power*, p. 29.

7. Guénon, *Introduction*, p. 216.

8. René Guénon, *Lord of the World* (Moorcote, North Yorkshire: Coombe Springs Press, 1983), p. 7 note 6.

9. Guénon, *Spiritual Authority and Temporal Power*, p. 31.

10. Guénon, *Spiritual Authority and Temporal Power*, p. 30.

11. Guénon, *Crisis of the Modern World*, p. 71.

12. Guénon, *Crisis of the Modern World*, p. 88.

13. René Guénon, *The Reign of Quantity and the Signs of the Times* (Hillsdale, NY: Sophia Perennis, 2004), p. 176.

14. Julius Evola, *Revolt against the Modern World* (Rochester, VT: Inner Traditions International, 1995), p. 91.

15. Evola, *Revolt against the Modern World*, p. 98.

16. Evola, *Revolt against the Modern World*, pp. 330–31.

17. Julius Evola, *Pagan Imperialism* (NP: Gornahoor Press, 2017), p. 94.

18. Evola, *Pagan Imperialism*, p. 135.

19. Evola, *Pagan Imperialism,* pp. 140–41.

20. Evola, *Pagan Imperialism*, pp. 142–4.

21. Evola, *Pagan Imperialism*, pp. 14, 26.

22. Evola, *Pagan Imperialism*, p. 95.

23. Evola, *Pagan Imperialism*, p. 29.

24. Evola, *Pagan Imperialism*, p. 92.

25. Evola, *Revolt against the Modern World*, p. 163.

26. Julius Evola, *The Path of Cinnabar* (London: Integral Tradition Publishing, 2009), p. 165.

27. Evola, *Revolt against the Modern World*, p. 56.

28. Evola, *The Path of Cinnabar*, p. 167.

29. Evola, *The Path of Cinnabar*, p. 178.

30. Evola, *Revolt against the Modern World*, p. 242.

31. Julius Evola, *Fascism Viewed from the Right* ([United Kingdom]: Arktos Media, 2013), p. 25.

32. Julius Evola, *Men among the Ruins: Postwar Reflections of a Radical Traditionalist* (Rochester, VT: Inner Traditions International, 2002), pp. 144, 151.

33. Evola, *Men among the Ruins*, p. 175.

34. Evola, *Men among the Ruins*, p. 113.

35. Julius Evola, *Ride the Tiger* (Rochester, VT: Inner Traditions International, 2003), p. 175.

36. Evola, *Ride the Tiger*, p. 75.

37. Frithjof Schuon, *Language of the Self* (Madras: Ganesh & Co., 1959), p. 164.

38. Schuon, *Language of the Self*, p. 158.

39. Schuon, *Language of the Self*, p. 164.

40. Schuon, *Language of the Self*, p. 166.

41. Schuon, *Language of the Self*, p. 166.

42. Schuon, *Language of the Self*, p. 138.

43. Schuon, *Language of the Self*, p. 166.

44. Frithjof Schuon, *Understanding Islam* (Bloomington, IN: World Wisdom, 1998), pp. 27–8.

45. Frithjof Schuon, *Light on the Ancient Worlds* (Bloomington, IN: World Wisdom, 2006), pp. 7–8.

46. Jordan B. Peterson, *12 Rules for Life: An Antidote to Chaos* (Toronto: Random House Canada, 2018), p. 310.

47. Peterson, *12 Rules for Life*, p. 36.

48. Jordan Peterson, in John Stossel, 'Jordan Peterson: The Full Interview', YouTube, 9 November 2021, https://youtube.com/watch?v=p3368WAloqM.

49. Jordan Peterson, 'Professor against Political Correctness', part II, YouTube, 3 October 2016, https://youtu.be/f-7YGGCE9es.
50. Jordan Peterson, 'Identity Politics and the Marxist Lie of White Privilege', YouTube 13 November 2017, https://youtu.be/PfH8IG7Awk0.

CHAPTER 10: ART

1. Ernest Binfield Havell, *Indian Sculpture and Painting* (London: John Murray, 1908) and *The Ideals of Indian Art* (New York: E. P. Dutton and Co., 1911).
2. John Ruskin, *On the Nature of Gothic Architecture: And Herein of the True Functions of the Workman in Art* (London: Smith, Elder & Co., 1854), p. 12.
3. Julius Evola, *Revolt against the Modern World* (Rochester, VT: Inner Traditions International, 1995), p. 102.
4. Julius Evola, *Ride the Tiger* (Rochester, VT: Inner Traditions International, 2003), p. 155.
5. Evola, *Revolt against the Modern World*, p. 109.
6. Evola, *Ride the Tiger*, pp. 151–2.
7. Ananda Coomaraswamy, *The Village Community and Modern Progress* (Colombo: The Colombo Apothecaries Company, 1908), pp. 1–7.
8. Ananda Coomaraswamy, *Buddha and the Gospel of Buddhism* (London: George G. Harrap, 1916).
9. Ananda Coomaraswamy, *Christian and Oriental Philosophy of Art* (New York: Dover Publications, 1956), p. 19.
10. Coomaraswamy, *Christian and Oriental Philosophy of Art*, p. 46.
11. Coomaraswamy, *Christian and Oriental Philosophy of Art*, p. 39.
12. Coomaraswamy, *Christian and Oriental Philosophy of Art*, p. 21.
13. Ananda Coomaraswamy, *The Transformation of Nature in Art* (Cambridge, MA: Harvard University Press, 1934).
14. Coomaraswamy, *Christian and Oriental Philosophy of Art*, p. 45.
15. Coomaraswamy, *Christian and Oriental Philosophy of Art*, pp. 63–4.
16. Coomaraswamy, *Christian and Oriental Philosophy of Art*, p. 47.
17. Coomaraswamy, *Christian and Oriental Philosophy of Art*, p. 22.
18. Coomaraswamy, *Christian and Oriental Philosophy of Art*, p. 26.
19. Frithjof Schuon, *The Transcendent Unity of Religions* (Wheaton, IL: Quest Books, 1993), p. 62.
20. Schuon, *The Transcendent Unity of Religions*, p. 67.
21. Schuon, *The Transcendent Unity of Religions*, p. 77.

22. Schuon, *The Transcendent Unity of Religions*, p. 76.

23. Schuon, *The Transcendent Unity of Religions*, pp. 65–6.

24. Schuon, *The Transcendent Unity of Religions*, p. 74.

25. Schuon, *The Transcendent Unity of Religions*, pp. 72–3.

26. Schuon, *The Transcendent Unity of Religions*, pp. 72–3.

27. Titus Burckhardt, *Art of Islam: Language and Meaning* (Bloomington, IN: World Wisdom, 2009), p. xv.

28. Titus Burckhardt, *Principes et méthodes de l'art sacré* (*Sacred Art in East and West: Its Principles and Methods*, 1958; English translation London: Perennial Books, 1967).

29. Burckhardt, *Sacred Art*, pp. 7, 13.

30. Burckhardt, *Sacred Art*, pp. 8–9.

31. Burckhardt, *Sacred Art*, p. 106.

32. Burckhardt, *Sacred Art*, p. 104.

33. Burckhardt, *Sacred Art*, p. 106.

34. Burckhardt, *Sacred Art*, p. 8.

35. Burckhardt, *Sacred Art*, p. 150.

36. Burckhardt, *Sacred Art*, p. 151.

37. Burckhardt, *Sacred Art*, p. 144.

38. Burckhardt, *Art of Islam*, p. 125.

39. Burckhardt, *Art of Islam*, p. 220.

40. Burckhardt, *Art of Islam*, p. 222.

41. Nader Ardalan and Laleh Bakhtiar, *The Sense of Unity: The Sufi Tradition in Persian Architecture* (Chicago: Kazi, 2000), p. 79.

42. Ardalan and Bakhtiar, *The Sense of Unity*, p. 35.

43. Ardalan and Bakhtiar, *The Sense of Unity*, p. 79.

44. Keith Critchlow, *Islamic Patterns: An Analytical and Cosmological Approach* (London: Thames and Hudson, 1976), p. 8.

45. Keith Critchlow, *The Hidden Geometry of Flowers: Living Rhythms, Form and Number* (Edinburgh: Floris Books, 2011), p. 26.

46. John Tavener, 'Towards the *Musica Perennis*', in *Every Man an Artist: Readings in the Traditional Philosophy of Art*, edited by Brian Keeble (Bloomington, IN: World Wisdom, 2005), pp. 222–30, at p. 225.

47. Tavener, 'Towards the *Musica Perennis*', p. 223.

48. Tavener, 'Towards the *Musica Perennis*', p. 224.

49. John Tavener, 'The Veil of the Temple', in Live Recording Concert Booklet, *The Veil of the Temple*, RCA 2005, p. 15.

CHAPTER 11: GENDER

1. Aristotle, *Historia Animalium*, vol. 4 of the *Works of Aristotle*, ed. J. A. Smith and W. D. Ross (Oxford: Clarendon Press, 1910), 608b.

2. Aristotle, *Historia Animalium*, 608b.

3. Mary Wollstonecraft, *A Vindication of the Rights of Woman* (London: J. Johnson, 1796), p. 34.

4. Wollstonecraft, *A Vindication of the Rights of Woman*, pp. 33, 2.

5. Arthur Schopenhauer, 'On Women', in *Parerga and Paralipomena: Short Philosophical Essays*, vol. 2, ed. A. Del Caro and C. Janaway (Cambridge: Cambridge University Press, 2015), pp. 550–61, at p. 551.

6. Schopenhauer, 'On Women', p. 553.

7. Arthur Schopenhauer, 'The Metaphysics of the Love of the Sexes', ch. XLIV of *The World as Will and Idea* (London: Trübner, 1886), vol. III, pp. 336–75, at p. 339.

8. Schopenhauer, 'Metaphysics', pp. 374–5.

9. Otto Weininger, *Sex and Character. An Investigation of Fundamental Principles*, edited by Daniel Steuer, with Laura Marcus (Bloomington: Indiana University Press, 2005), p. 13.

10. Weininger, *Sex and Character*, p. 47.

11. Weininger, *Sex and Character*, p. 70.

12. Weininger, *Sex and Character*, p. 4.

13. Simone de Beauvoir, *The Second Sex* (New York: Vintage Books, 2011), p. 330.

14. Weininger, *Sex and Character*, p. 41.

15. Judith P. Butler, *Gender Trouble* (New York: Routledge, 1999), p. 164.

16. Kate Millett, *Sexual Politics* (Urbana: University of Illinois Press, 2000), p. 33.

17. Shulamith Firestone, *The Dialectic of Sex: The Case for Feminist Revolution* (New York: Bantam, 1970), pp. 8–11.

18. René Guénon, 'Feminine Initiation and Craft Initiations', in *Studies in Freemasonry and the Compagnonnage* (Hillsdale, NY: Sophia Perennis, 2004), p. 54.

19. Guénon, 'Feminine Initiation and Craft Initiations', p. 54.

20. Julius Evola, *The Path of Cinnabar* (London: Integral Tradition Publishing, 2009), p. 101.

21. Julius Evola, *The Metaphysics of Sex* (New York: Inner Traditions International, 1983), p. 33.

22. Evola, *The Metaphysics of Sex*, p. 30.

23. Evola, *The Metaphysics of Sex*, p. 32.
24. Evola, *The Metaphysics of Sex*, p. 63.
25. Julius Evola, *Revolt against the Modern World* (Rochester, VT: Inner Traditions International, 1995), p. 159.
26. Evola, *The Metaphysics of Sex*, p. 34.
27. Evola, *Revolt against the Modern World*, p. 165.
28. Evola, *Revolt against the Modern World*, p. 159.
29. Evola, *The Metaphysics of Sex*, p. 44.
30. Evola, *The Metaphysics of Sex*, p. 2.
31. Evola, *The Metaphysics of Sex*, p. 67.
32. Evola, *The Metaphysics of Sex*, p. 164.
33. Evola, *Revolt against the Modern World*, p. 158.
34. Frithjof Schuon, *Light on the Ancient Worlds* (Bloomington, IN: World Wisdom, 2006), p. 36.
35. Frithjof Schuon, *Language of the Self: Essays on the Perennial Philosophy* ([Belgrade]: Mikrotheos, 2012), p. 102.
36. Frithjof Schuon, *Gnosis: Divine Wisdom* (Bloomington, IN: World Wisdom, 2006), p. 36.
37. Schuon, *Gnosis*, p. 36.
38. Frithjof Schuon, *Understanding Islam* (Bloomington, IN: World Wisdom, 1998), p. 109.
39. Frithjof Schuon, *Christianity/Islam: Perspectives on Esoteric Ecumenism,* (Bloomington, IN: World Wisdom, 2008), p. 69.
40. Schuon, *Christianity/Islam*, p. 69.
41. Frithjof Schuon, *The Transcendent Unity of Religions* (Wheaton, IL: Quest Books, 1993), p. 123.
42. Schuon, *Understanding Islam*, p. 31.
43. Schuon, *Understanding Islam*, p. 31.
44. John Tavener, *The Music of Silence: A Composer's Testament* (London: Faber and Faber, 1999), p. 133.
45. Jordan B. Peterson, *12 Rules for Life: An Antidote to Chaos* (Toronto: Random House Canada, 2018), p. 301.
46. Peterson, *12 Rules for Life*, p. 298.
47. Peterson, *12 Rules for Life*, p. 318.
48. Jordan Peterson, 'Professor against Political Correctness', part I, YouTube, 27 September 2016, https://youtu.be/fvPgjg2o1wo.
49. Jordan Peterson, in John Stossel, 'Jordan Peterson: The Full Interview', YouTube, 9 November 2021, https://youtube.com/watch?v=p3368WAloqM.

50. Alice Lucy Trent, *The Feminine Universe: An Exposition of the Ancient Wisdom from the Primordial Feminine Perspective* (London: The Golden Order Press, [1997]), p. 125.

51. Trent, *The Feminine Universe*, p. 42.

52. Trent, *The Feminine Universe*, p. 44.

53. Trent, *The Feminine Universe*, p. 44.

54. Trent, *The Feminine Universe*, p. 112.

CHAPTER 12: NATURE

1. George Perkins Marsh, *Man and Nature; or, Physical Geography as Modified by Human Action* (London: Sampson Low, Son and Marston, 1864), p. iii.

2. Joseph Sittler, Jr, 'A Theology for Earth', *Christian Scholar* 37, no. 3 (1954): 367–74, at 372.

3. Rudolf Steiner, *Agriculture Course: The Birth of the Biodynamic Method* (Forest Row: Rudolf Steiner Press, 2004), pp. 73–4.

4. Lord Northbourne, *Look to the Land* (Hillsdale, NY: Sophia Perennis, 2003), p. 16.

5. E. F. Schumacher, 'Buddhist Economics', in *Asia: A Handbook*, ed. Guy Wint (New York: Frederick A. Praeger, 1966), pp. 695–701, at p. 696.

6. Schumacher, 'Buddhist Economcs', pp. 698–9.

7. René Guénon, *The Crisis of the Modern World* (Hillsdale, NY: Sophia Perennis, 2001), p. 89.

8. Julius Evola, 'Paths of the Western Spirit', in Julius Evola and the UR Group, *Realizations of the Absolute Individual*, vol. 3 of *Introduction to Magic*, trans. and ed. Joscelyn Godwin (Rochester, VT: Inner Traditions, 2021), pp. 4–7, at p. 7.

9. Julius Evola, *Men among the Ruins: Postwar Reflections of a Radical Traditionalist* (Rochester, VT: Inner Traditions International, 2002), p. 176.

10. Julius Evola, *Revolt against the Modern World* (Rochester, VT: Inner Traditions International, 1995), p. 284.

11. Julius Evola, *The Hermetic Tradition: In its Symbols. Doctrine, and 'Royal Art'* (Rochester, VT: Inner Traditions International, 1995), p. 15.

12. Evola, *Revolt against the Modern World*, p. 153.

13. Frithjof Schuon, *Language of the Self* (Madras: Ganesh & Co., 1959), p. 155.

14. Schuon, *Language of the Self*, p. 156.

15. Schuon, *Language of the Self*, p. 156.

16. Seyyed Hossein Nasr, *Man and Nature: The Spiritual Crisis of Modern Man* (London: Unwin Paperbacks, 1990), p. 18.

17. Seyyed Hossein Nasr, *Religion & the Order of Nature* (New York: Oxford University Press, 1996), p. 9.

18. Nasr, *Religion & the Order of Nature*, p. 18.

19. Nasr, *Religion & the Order of Nature*, p. 271.

20. Nasr, *Man and Nature*, p. 55.

21. Nasr, *Man and Nature*, p. 73.

22. Nasr, *Man and Nature*, p. 83.

23. Nasr, *Man and Nature*, p. 81.

24. Nasr, *Man and Nature*, p. 94.

25. Nasr, *Religion & the Order of Nature*, p. 21.

26. Nasr, *Religion & the Order of Nature*, p. 31.

27. Nasr, *Man and Nature*, p. 118.

28. Nasr, *Religion & the Order of Nature*, p. 271.

29. Nasr, *Religion & the Order of Nature*, p. 272.

30. Nasr, *Religion & the Order of Nature*, pp. 236–7.

31. Nasr, *Religion & the Order of Nature*, p. 238.

32. Nasr, *Religion & the Order of Nature*, p. 236.

33. Ghazi bin Muhammad, Reza Shah-Kazemi and Aftab Ahmed, *The Holy Qur'an and the Environment* (Amman: The Royal Aal Al-Bayt Institute for Islamic Thought, 2010).

34. Prince Charles, with Tony Juniper, and Ian Skelly, *Harmony: A New Way of Looking at Our World* (London: Blue Door, 2010). That the book has two co-authors, the environmental activist and writer Tony Juniper and the BBC journalist Ian Skelly, raises the possibility that the Traditionalist philosophy developed in *Harmony* comes from Juniper or Skelly, not from Prince Charles himself. However, there are many indications of an interest in Traditionalism on the part of the prince, and none in the case of his co-authors. Juniper's own books occasionally show sympathy with the prince's perspectives, but they are in general a long way from Traditionalism in their approach. There are no visible connections between Skelly and Traditionalism.

35. Prince Charles, *Harmony*, p. 3.

36. Prince Charles, *Harmony*, p. 8.

37. Prince Charles, *Harmony*, p. 118.

38. Prince Charles, *Harmony*, p. 136.

39. Prince Charles, *Harmony*, p. 183.
40. Prince Charles, *Harmony*, pp. 96–7.

CHAPTER 13: DIALOGUE

1. S. Mark Heim, *Is Christ the Only Way? Christian Faith in a Pluralistic World* (Valley Forge, PA: Judson Press, 1985), p. 150.
2. René Guénon, *Introduction to the Study of the Hindu Doctrines* (London: Luzac & Co., 1945), p. 334.
3. Seyyed Hossein Nasr, *Religion & the Order of Nature* (New York: Oxford University Press, 1996), p. 14.
4. Seyyed Hossein Nasr, 'Islamic-Christian Dialogue: Problems and Obstacles to be Pondered and Overcome', *The Muslim World* 88, no. 3–4 (October 1998): 218–37, at 000.
5. Nasr, 'Islamic-Christian Dialogue', 221.
6. Nasr, 'Islamic-Christian Dialogue', 235.
7. Rusmir Mahmutćehajić, *Sarajevo Essays: Politics, Ideology, and Tradition* (Albany: SUNY Press, 2003), pp. 45–6.
8. Rusmir Mahmutćehajić, *The Denial of Bosnia* (University Park: The Pennsylvania State University Press, 2000), p. 74.
9. Mahmutćehajić, *The Denial of Bosnia*, pp. 16–17.
10. Mahmutćehajić, *The Denial of Bosnia*, p. 21.
11. Mahmutćehajić, *The Denial of Bosnia*, p. 26.
12. Seyyed Hossein Nasr, '"A Common Word" Initiative: *Theoria* and *Praxis*', in *Muslim and Christian Understanding: Theory and Application of 'A Common Word'*, ed. Waleed El-Ansary and David K. Linnan (New York: Palgrave, 2010), pp. 21–8, at p. 23.
13. Ali Goma'a, '"A Common Word between Us and You": Motives and Applications', in *Muslim and Christian Understanding: Theory and Application of 'A Common Word'*, ed. Waleed El-Ansary and David K. Linnan (New York: Palgrave, 2010), pp. 15–19, at p. 17.
14. Reza Shah-Kazemi, *Common Ground between Islam and Buddhism* (Louisville, KY: Fons Vitae, 2010), p. 2.
15. Shah-Kazemi, *Common Ground*, p. 4.

CHAPTER 14: THE RADICAL RIGHT

1. Alain de Benoist and Charles Champetier, 'Manifeste pour une renaissance européenne', translated as 'The French New Right in the Year 2000', *Telos* 115 (Spring 1999): 117–44, at 118.

2. Benoist and Champetier, 'French New Right', 119.

3. Benoist and Champetier, 'French New Right', 119.

4. Benoist and Champetier, 'French New Right', 120.

5. Benoist and Champetier, 'French New Right', 120.

6. Benoist and Champetier, 'French New Right', 123.

7. Benoist and Champetier, 'French New Right', 132.

8. Benoist and Champetier, 'French New Right', 133.

9. Alain de Benoist, *On Being a Pagan* (Atlanta: Ultra, 2004), p. 16.

10. Benoist and Champetier, 'French New Right', 124.

11. Benoist and Champetier, 'French New Right', 131.

12. Benoist and Champetier, 'French New Right', 136.

13. Benoist and Champetier, 'French New Right', 135.

14. Benoist and Champetier, 'French New Right', 135.

15. Anton Barbashin and Hannah Thoburn, 'Putin's Brain: Alexander Dugin and the Philosophy behind Putin's Invasion of Crimea', *Foreign Affairs*, 31 March 2014, https://www.foreignaffairs.com/articles/russia-fsu/2014-03-31/putins-brain; James Heiser, 'Putin's Rasputin: The Mad Mystic Who Inspired Russia's Leader', *Breitbart*, 10 June 2014, https://www.breitbart.com/national-security/2014/06/10/putin-s-rasputin-the-mad-mystic-who-inspired-putin/.

16. Aleksandr Dugin, 'Рене Генон: Традиционализм как язык', ch. 1 of *Философия Традиционализма* (Moscow: Arktogeya, 2002), http://arcto.ru/article/113.

17. Dugin, 'Рене Генон'.

18. Aleksandr Dugin, *Метафизика Благой Вести: Православный эзотеризм* (Moscow: Arktogeya, 1996).

19. Aleksandr Dugin, 'Три теологии', part of *В поисках темного Логоса. Философско-богословские очерки* (Moscow: Akademicheskiy Proyekt, 2013), http://www.platonizm.ru/content/dugin-v-poiskah-temnogo-logosa.

20. Dugin, 'Три теологии'.

21. Dugin, 'Три теологии'.

22. Aleksandr Dugin, 'Traditionalism as a Theory: Sophia, Plato and the Event', ch. 8 of *В поисках темного Логоса. Философско-богословские очерки* (Moscow: Akademicheskiy Proyekt, 2013), translated at https://eurasianist-archive.com/2019/06/13/traditionalism-as-a-theory-sophia-plato-and-the-event-alexander-dugin/.

23. Aleksandr Dugin, *Основы геополитики: геополитическое будущее России* (Moscow: Arktogeya, 1997).

24. Dugin, 'Рене Генон'.

25. Dugin, 'Рене Генон'.

26. Aleksandr Dugin, 'Археомодерн: В поисках точки, где и модерн, и архаика ясны как парадигмы', http://arcto.ru/article/1472 & 1473

27. Dugin, 'Археомодерн'.

28. Dugin, 'Рене Генон'.

29. Dugin, 'Археомодерн'.

30. Aleksandr Dugin, *Четвертая политическая теория* (St Petersburg: Amfora, 2009), translated as *The Fourth Political Theory* (London: Arktos, 2012).

31. Gábor Vona, Foreword, *A Handbook for Right-Wing Youth* by Julius Evola (2012; London: Arktos, 2017).

32. Benjamin Teitelbaum, *War for Eternity: The Return of Traditionalism and the Rise of the Populist Right* (London: Penguin, 2021).

33. Teitelbaum, *War for Eternity*, p. 160.

34. Teitelbaum, *War for Eternity*, p. 159.

35. Markus Willinger, *Generation Identity: A Declaration of War against the '68ers* (London: Arktos, 2013).

36. Michael O'Meara, 'The Primordial and the Perennial: Tradition in the Thought of Martin Heidegger and Julius Evola', *Tyr* 3 (2007): 67–88, at 67.

37. O'Meara, 'The Primordial and the Perennial', 67.

38. O'Meara, 'The Primordial and the Perennial', 82.

39. O'Meara, 'The Primordial and the Perennial', 68.

40. Alexander Wolfheze, 'The Identitarian Revolution: Dutch Preliminaries', Geopolitika.ru, 7 August 2018, https://www.geopolitica.ru/en/article/identitarian-revolution-dutch-preliminaries.

41. Wolfheze, 'The Identitarian Revolution'.

42. Alexander Wolfheze, 'The Light of Traditionalism', *Arktos Journal* 4 (November 2019), https://arktos.com/2019/11/04/the-light-of-traditionalism/.

43. Wolfheze, 'The Light of Traditionalism'.

44. Martel Mosley, 'Alt-Right Essentials: A Handbook for Right-Wing Youth – Julius Evola'. AltRight.com, 28 March 2017, https://altright.com/2017/03/28/altright-essesntials-a-handbook-for-right-wing-youth-julius-evola/.

45. John Morgan, 'What Would Evola Do?', *Counter-Currents*, 19 May 2018, https://counter-currents.com/2018/05/what-would-evola-do-2/.

46. *Fedeltà è più forte del fuoco*
    Rialzarsi, risorgere
    Creare una forma e un ordine
    In piedi tra le rovine
    Scegliere la strada più dura
    Forgiare il nostro coraggio
    Rinati fino nel sangue
    Forti del nostro onore
    Kshatriya

    The album *Kshatriya* is available on Apple Music, https://music.apple.com/us/album/kshatriya/1538787701.

Index

Abdul-Hadi (Ivan Aguéli) 13, 51, 150, 314
Abraham (biblical character) 29, 73
Abrahamic religions 23, 301, 312, 325
academic perennialism 35–7, 39,
    57, 339
acroamatics 30
Adam (biblical character) 29, 73,
    74, 262
Adorno, Theodor 100
Advaita Vedanta 140–42, 147–9, 175,
    240, 340
AfD 9
Age of Aquarius 76, 91
Age of Pisces 76
Aguéli, Ivan (Abdul-Hadi) 13, 51, 150, 314
Ain Soph: *Kshatriya* 353
Alawiyya 17, 18
Albertus Magnus (Albert of Lauingen) 146
alienation 97–8, 101, 107, 112, 171,
    299, 307
al-Qaeda 315
alt-right 199, 222, 352
anima 147, 151
Anselm of Aosta 146
Anthroposophical Society 292–3
anti-Semitism 83–4, 86, 110, 208, 213, 215,
    226, 311, 312, 352
Aquinas, Thomas 143, 146
archetypes 26, 38, 57
Ardalan, Nader 250–53, 257
Arendt, Hannah 97, 100, 114,
    115, 361
Aristasia 283–6
aristocratic clite 128–9

Aristotle 30, 88, 142–3, 144, 172, 201, 259,
    261–2, 263–4, 265, 272, 276
Arktos 346
art 11, 229–57; Ancient Greek aesthetics
    230–31, 232; Ardalan's architecture
    250–51, 252, 257; Burckhardt's philosophy
    of 242, 245–50, 252, 253, 254, 257;
    Coomaraswamy's Traditionalist views
    of 230, 236–42, 243, 244, 245, 253, 256,
    257; Critchlow's Islamic patterns 252–3,
    257; Evola and 235–7, 238, 243, 244,
    256; Guénon and 229, 230, 235, 236,
    238, 239, 240, 244, 249, 256; Middle
    Ages 231; nineteenth century 233–5;
    post-Renaissance aesthetic theory 232;
    Renaissance 231–2; Schuon and 238,
    242, 243–5, 248, 253–4, 255, 256–7; taste,
    discussions of 232–3; Tavener's music
    250, 253–6, 257
Arts and Crafts movement 234
Aryamehr University, Tehran 89
Aryan race 77, 82, 83–4, 86–7, 88, 89,
    91, 172
asceticism 139, 161, 162
astral sphere 34
atheism 147, 368
Atlantis 34, 35, 76
atman 147–8, 153–4
authority 95, 97
autobiographical memory 67
avatar 187
Averroes (Ibn Rushd) 88
Avicenna (Ibn Sina) 88
axial precession 76

Bachofen, Johann Jakob: *Mother Right: An Investigation of the Religious and Juridical Character of Matriarchy in the Ancient World* 83, 85, 271–2, 284
Bakhtiar, Laleh: *The Sense of Unity: The Sufi Tradition in Persian Architecture* 250
Bannon, Steve 8, 9, 348–50, 355
barakah 279
Baranyi, Tibor 348
Baudelaire, Charles 96
Beatles 101, 253
Beauvoir, Simone de: *The Second Sex* 267–8, 272
Benoist, Alain de 332–7, 340, 346–9, 350, 351, 354–6, 367; 'Manifesto for a European Renaissance' 333–7
Berger, Peter 27
Berlin, Isaiah: 'The Counter-Enlightenment' 24, 97
Bible 28, 196–7, 261, 325
bisexuality 266
Blake, William 24, 255–6
Blood Axis 353, 354
Bosnia 132, 198, 309, 315, 319–23, 324, 326, 328, 367
Bossuet, Jacques-Bénigne: *Discourse on Universal History* 73
Boucher, François 233
Bourdieu, Pierre 101, 115
bourgeois epoch/bourgeois modernity 96, 120–22
bourgeois liberalism 212, 217, 345
brahman 147–9, 153–4, 155, 162, 165
Brahmins 202, 206, 209, 210
Breitbart 337
Buckley, Joshua 353–4
Buddhism 10, 32, 33–4, 36, 38, 43, 44, 86, 160, 192, 196, 237, 246, 294–5, 296, 298, 324, 325, 326; Buddhist economics 294–5
Burckhardt, Carl 242
Burckhardt, Titus 242, 245–50, 252, 253, 254, 257, 305, 306, 365; *Art of Islam: Language and Meaning* 245, 248–50; *Principles and Methods of Sacred Art* 245–8
Bussi, Giovanni Andrea 71

Butler, Judith 268
Byzantine Empire. *See* Eastern Roman Empire

capitalism 75, 95, 96, 97, 98, 101, 112, 113, 115, 117, 122, 124, 203, 269
Carson, Rachel: *Silent Spring* 291
caste 203, 206–11, 213–14, 219, 220, 222, 223, 225–6, 270, 271, 336, 348–9, 363
Catholic Church 180, 262, 355; *Nostra aetate* (Declaration on the Relation of the Church with Non-Christian Religions) (1965) 312; Secretariat for Non-Christians 312, 314; Secretariat for Promoting Christian Unity 311
Catholicism 5, 10, 14, 22, 27, 28, 43, 48, 64, 85, 95, 100, 120, 126, 140, 146, 151, 170, 180, 184, 190, 191, 207, 243, 262, 263, 315–16, 348
Ceylon Reform Society 237
Champetier, Charles 333
charismatic authority 95
Charlemagne 73, 74
Charles, Prince (King Charles III) 253, 289, 304–8, 366; *Harmony: A New Way of Looking at Our World* 304
Chicago Parliament of Religions (1893) 310
China 47, 73, 74, 78, 126–7, 200, 205, 224, 233, 240, 301, 342, 346, 349
chinoiserie 233
Christianity: art and 231, 237, 240, 246, 255–6; gender and 262–3, 278–9; historical perennialism and 23, 26–8, 30–33, 35, 36; interfaith dialogue and 309–15, 318–19, 321, 324–5, 326, 327–8, 366–7; modernity and 99, 108, 112; nature and 292, 294, 297, 298, 300, 301, 307; politics and 210, 213, 216; radical right and 333, 334, 340; religion, Traditionalist views on and 180, 183–4, 186–90, 196–7, 198, 363; self-realization in Traditionalism and 140–41, 143, 146, 149, 163, 167, 168, 169–70, 172, 176; society and 120, 123–4, 131; Traditionalist perennialism and 43, 44, 48, 50, 55, 59–60, 63–4, 68, 69, 70, 71–2, 73, 75, 76, 79, 84, 85, 86, 87, 88, 90–91. *See also* Catholicism, Orthodox churches, Protestantism
Co-Masonry 271

common mode of thinking 121, 123, 124, 134
Common Word Between You and Us, A
    324–7, 367
Compagnonnage 158, 159, 271
Confederation of the Iroquois 221
Confucianism 47, 200, 201, 202, 204
Constantine, Emperor 71, 72, 73
Coomaraswamy, Ananda 55, 230, 236–42,
    243, 244–5, 253, 256–7, 294, 295, 296–7,
    306, 364–5; *Art and Swadeshi* 294–5,
    296; *Buddha and the Gospel of Buddhism*
    237; *History of Indian and Indonesian Art*
    237; *Mediaeval Sinhalese Art* 237; *The
    Transformation of Nature in Art* 240; *Why
    Exhibit Works of Art* 240
counterculture 101
Counter-Enlightenment 24, 38, 97
counter-initiation 109–10
Cowen, Tyler 133
Cragg, Kenneth 312, 313, 317
Critchlow, Keith 250, 252–3, 257, 305, 306,
    365; *Islamic Patterns: An Analytical and
    Cosmological Approach* 252–3; *The Hidden
    Geometry of Flowers: Living Rhythms, Form
    and Number* 252
Cudworth, Ralph 30, 43

Dada movement 15, 235, 236
dark ages 68, 72, 73, 74–5. *See also*
    Middle Ages
Dayton Agreement (1995) 320, 321
de Beauvoir, Simone. *See* Beauvoir,
    Simone de
de Benoist, Alan. *See* Benoist, Alain de
Deism 31, 33, 44, 63, 65
democracy 4, 84, 106–8, 109, 110, 121,
    200–202, 203, 208, 212, 217, 363
'descent', concept of 186, 187
dialogue, interfaith 309–28; *A Common
    Word Between You and Us* 324–7;
    Christian initiatives 311–13; Evola and
    316–17, 327; Guénon and 314, 316–17, 327;
    inter-communal 310–12; Mahmutćehajić
    and International Forum Bosnia 319–23;
    Muslim initiatives 314–15; Nasr and
    interfaith theory 317–19; religious

conflict, return of 315–16; Royal Aal al-
    Bayt Institute and 324–7; theological
    310–12; Traditionalist views 316–23;
    universalist 310–12
Diderot, Denis 119–21, 122, 123, 124, 125, 134
disenchantment (*Entzauberung*) 95
Divine Principle 155
division of labour 98–9
Dominicans 120, 146
Dugin, Aleksandr 3, 6, 7–8, 19, 44, 199, 222,
    331, 332, 337–46, 349, 351, 354, 355, 356, 361,
    367, 368–9; *The Foundations of Geopolitics:
    The Geopolitical Future of Russia* 7, 341–6;
    The Fourth Political Theory 344–6, 355;
    The Metaphysics of the Gospel 339; *The
    Philosophy of Traditionalism* 338
Dugin, Darya 7
Durand, Gilbert 339–40

Eastern Roman Empire (Byzantine Empire)
    72, 239, 244, 341
Eckhardt, Meister 36, 37
Eclipse 283–5
Ein Sof 263
Eis und Licht 353
Elements 333
Eleusinian or Orphic Mysteries 144, 146
Eliade, Mircea 54, 55–9, 61, 64, 70, 170, 196,
    209, 280, 339, 360
Encyclopaedia of Diderot 120–21
Engels, Friedrich 75, 96
Enlightenment 23–4, 25, 26, 30, 38, 48, 62–3,
    65, 72, 74, 79, 81, 93, 94, 97, 101, 102, 115,
    119, 120–21, 134, 179–80, 232, 254, 305, 360
environmentalism 289–307, 309, 325, 366
esotericism 10, 13, 80, 89; art and 240,
    243–4, 245, 252, 256; gender and 278–9,
    287; historical perennialism and 30–39;
    interfaith dialogue and 313, 318–19, 323,
    324–5, 326, 327; modernity and 107–8;
    religion and 179, 180, 181–6, 190, 191, 192,
    193–4, 197–8; self-realization and 139,
    157, 159, 167, 168, 169–70, 176; society
    and 125, 128, 130, 135; Traditionalist
    perennialism and 43–5, 46–7, 51, 52, 59,
    60–61, 63, 64, 65

essentialist 78
Essex Press 237
ethnopluralism 336, 350, 354–5, 356
Études traditionnelles (Traditional Studies)
14, 127
Eurasianism 342, 344. *See also*
Neo-Eurasianism
Eurasian Youth Union 344
Eurasian Movement, International 344
Evola, Julius 7, 8, 9, 12–13, 15–17, 19, 360–61;
A Handbook for Right-Wing Youth 347,
352; anti-Semitism 83–4, 110–11, 215,
226; aristocratic elite 128–9, 134; art
and 235–6, 238, 243, 244, 256; *Fascism: A
Critical Analysis seen from the Right* 217;
gender and 259–60, 271–8, 284, 286–7,
365; historical narrative 82–5, 86, 87, 90,
91; interfaith dialogue and 316–17, 327;
Man as Potency, republished as *The Yoga
of Power* 160; *Men Among the Ruins*
216–17; modernity, critique of 102,
110–13, 115, 116–17, 362; nature and 296,
297, 298, 303, 306–7; *Pagan Imperialism*
16, 110, 128, 162, 212; perennialism 46,
54–5, 56, 57–8, 59, 60–61, 63, 64–5; politics
and 199, 209–22, 223, 224, 225–6, 363–4;
radical right and 331–2, 333, 334, 346–8,
350–51, 352–3, 354, 356; religion 179,
180, 184–5, 186, 190, 197, 362, 363; *Revolt
Against the Modern World* 82, 110, 162,
212, 226; *Ride the Tiger* 164, 235–6; self-
realization/metaphysics and 139, 159–66,
167, 169–70, 174, 175–6, 177, 368; *The
Doctrine of Awakening* 160; *The Hermetic
Tradition* 160
exoteric religion 30–31, 36, 38, 43–8, 51, 55,
56, 59, 60, 63, 65, 113, 126, 139, 157, 169,
170, 180–86, 192, 193, 194, 197, 278–9, 287,
318, 325, 327, 333, 335, 339, 360, 362–3, 366

Fall, myth of the 67, 68–71, 85
far right 10, 12, 199, 222, 352
fascism 3, 12, 13, 15–16, 17, 127, 128, 199,
212–13, 215, 216–17, 219, 225, 226, 331,
332–3, 345, 364
Faye, Guillaume 350

feminism 83, 259–60, 264–5, 267, 268–70,
273–4, 276, 279, 280, 283–8, 335, 365;
first-wave 264, 268; second-wave 259, 268
Ficino, Marsilio 27–9, 31, 34, 35, 38, 43
Finland 72
Firestone, Shulamith 269–70, 280
First Cause 144, 146
First World War (1914–18) 14, 15, 76, 77,
90, 104, 293
Fliess, Wilhelm 266
'forms', theory of 143–4
Foucault, Michel 101, 115, 344
Frankfurt School 100
Frazer, James: *The Golden Bough* 25, 26, 38,
39, 46, 56–9
Frederick I, Emperor 84–5
Freemasonry 131, 158–60, 179, 271
French Revolution (1789) 72, 201, 264
Freud, Sigmund 25–6, 65, 266

gender 11, 259–88; pre-Traditionalist
views of 260–70; Traditionalist views
270–88. *See also* feminism.
Ghazi bin Muhammad, Prince 303–4;
A Common Word Between You and Us and
324–7, 328, 367; 'The Holy Quran and the
Environment' 304
Gobineau, Count Arthur de: *Essay on the
Inequality of the Human Races* 77, 88, 90,
91, 214–15, 226
God 50, 140, 146–7, 148, 150–51, 152, 167–8,
170, 172, 187, 191, 194, 196–7, 202, 216, 220,
240, 253, 255, 260, 261, 262, 263, 279, 283,
289–90, 310, 313, 325, 334, 342; death of
99–100, 101, 102, 114, 115, 117
Goma'a, Ali 324, 325
'good minds' 121, 125, 134
Gramsci, Antonio 119, 123, 124, 134
GRECE ('Groupement de recherche et
d'études pour la civilisation européenne'
(Research and Study Group for European
Civilization) 332–3
Greece, ancient 23, 24–5, 27, 28, 29, 30,
69–70, 71, 72, 74, 80, 82, 84, 88, 141–2, 150,
172, 230–31, 232, 272, 277, 286, 300, 340–41
Grimm, Jacob and Wilhelm 24–5

Guénon, René 6, 7, 8, 9, 12–15, 17, 19, 43;
art and 229, 230, 235, 236, 238, 239,
240, 244, 249, 256; *East and West* 125;
Études traditionnelles (Traditional
Studies) 14, 127; 'Feminine Initiation
and Craft Initiations' 270; gender
and 270–71, 276–7, 285, 286, 287, 365;
General Introduction to Hindu Doctrines
125; historical narrative 68, 69, 70,
79–82, 83–4, 85, 86, 87, 88–9, 90–91;
'intellectual elite' and 125–7, 129, 194,
209; *Introduction to the Study of Hindu
Doctrines* 52; *Man and his Becoming
according to the Vedanta* 152; modernity,
critique of 102–14, 115–17; nature
and 296–7, 298, 303, 306, 314, 316–17,
327, 364; oral transmission and 50–51;
perennialism 43, 44, 45–55, 56, 57–8, 59,
60–61, 63, 64–5; *Perspectives on Initiation*
153; politics and 199–200, 203–9, 210,
215, 219–26; radical right and 331–2,
333, 334, 335–6, 337, 338–43, 350–51, 356;
religion and 179, 180–87, 190, 191, 192,
193, 194, 197, 360–64; self-realization
and 139, 140–41, 150, 152–70, 175–6,
362–3, 367–8; society and 124–7; *Spiritual
Authority and Temporal Power* 203; *The
Crisis of the Modern World* 103, 203; *The
Multiple States of the Being* 152; 'The
Necessity of Traditional Exoterism'
1 81–4; *The Reign of Quantity and the
Signs of the Times* 103; *The Symbolism of
the Cross* 152; Traditionalist model of
influence and 124–35
Guizot, François: *Lectures on the History of
Civilization in Europe* 74–5
Gurdjieff, George 165, 166

Habermas, Jürgen 94–5, 115
haqiqa 182, 279
Hartford Seminary: Center for the Study of
Islam and Christian-Muslim Relations
312, 314, 318
Havell, Ernest 233, 238, 240, 242
Hegel, Georg 73–4, 78, 81, 94–5, 97, 98, 101,
102, 106, 115, 341

Heim, S. Mark 313
Herder, Johann Gottfried 24
heretical imperative 27
Hermes 28, 29
Hesiod: *Works and Days* 70, 260–61, 262
Hick, John: *An Interpretation of
Religion: Human Responses to the
Transcendent* 313–14
Hinduism 14, 125, 126–7, 131, 341, 360, 363;
art and 237, 240, 246, 255; historical
perennialism and 32, 33–4, 36, 38–9;
nature and 301; politics and 206, 225;
religion in Traditionalism and 187, 189,
192, 196; self-realization, Traditionalist
and 147–9, 151, 155, 156, 160, 166, 169, 170,
171, 172, 176; Traditionalist history and
70–72, 79, 82, 86, 90–91; Traditionalist
perennialism and 45, 51, 52
history, Traditionalist 65, 67–91, 257, 283,
320, 361, 366, 367; autobiographical
memory 67; cyclical narrative of history
and 70–71; decline, history as 77–8;
Evola's historical narrative 82–5; Fall,
myth of the 67, 68–71, 85; Guénon's
historical narrative 79–82; historical
narrative, Traditionalist 65; Judaeo-
Christian narrative of history 69–73, 75,
79, 85, 86, 90; Nasr's historical narrative
87–9; progress, history as 74–6; Schuon's
historical narrative 85–7; Traditionalist
scheme 79–91; tripartite narrative of
ancient, medieval and modern 67–9,
71–4, 79, 80, 81, 82, 84, 85, 90, 93, 94,
360–61; Whig history 75
Homer 94
homo aeroporticus 351
homogenization 335–6
homosexuality 112, 265–8, 273
Horkheimer, Max 100
Hugh of St Victor 231, 235;
Didascalicon 231
Hume, David: 'The Rise and Progress of the
Arts and Sciences' 74
Hungary 7–8, 347, 348, 350, 355
Huntington, Samuel: 'The Clash of
Civilizations' 78, 90, 315–16, 341

Huxley, Aldous: *The Perennial Philosophy* 27, 34, 37, 39, 61, 195
hyperborean civilization 82

Iamblichus 28
Ibn Arabi, Muhyi-al-Din 13, 51, 149–51, 251
Identitarian movement 332, 347, 350–51, 355, 356, 367, 368, 369
Illuminati 34
immigration 8, 335–6, 346, 354
incarnation, doctrine of 186–7
individualism 93, 95, 97, 101, 102, 106, 109, 111, 116, 217, 246, 300, 345
industrial worker 8, 9, 98, 106–7, 115, 122, 234
'intellectual elite' 125–9, 194, 209
inter-communal/interfaith dialogue 11, 12, 309–28, 364, 365, 366, 368. *See also* dialogue, interfaith
International Eurasian Movement 344
International Forum Bosnia 319–23, 326
Introduction to the Study of Hindu Doctrines 52
Iran 87, 89, 154, 172, 193, 195, 250, 251, 289, 301, 315
iron cage of bureaucracy 98, 101
Islam 5, 6, 7, 13, 17, 18, 23, 32, 108, 127, 132, 303–4, 362, 365, 366, 367; art and 229–30, 245–53, 257; gender and 262–3, 277, 278–9; interfaith dialogue and 309, 310, 312–13, 314–15, 317, 318–19, 324–7; modernity and 108, 127, 132; nature and 289, 290, 301, 303–4; politics and 200, 201, 202, 209, 216, 220; religion, Traditionalist and 179, 181, 182, 183–4, 186–92, 194, 195, 196, 197–8; self-realization, Traditionalist and 139, 149, 150, 151, 154, 162–3, 168, 172–3, 175; Traditionalist history and 69, 72, 73–4, 87, 88; Traditionalist perennialism and 47, 51, 52
Izetbegović, Alija 319–20, 322

James, William: *The Varieties of Religious Experience* 35–6, 37, 39, 57, 61–2, 65
Jesus 31, 71, 73, 170, 186, 187, 189, 192, 262, 278, 287, 310, 326

Jobbik 7–8, 347–8, 350, 355
John Paul II, Pope 32–3
Jordan 132, 200, 303–4, 309, 324, 326–7, 328, 367
Journal of the American Academy of Religion 61
Judaism 23, 47, 87, 188, 262–3, 309–10
Jung, Carl Gustav 26, 38, 39, 46, 54–5, 57, 59, 65, 196–7, 339

Kabbalah 262–3, 276, 278
Kafka, Franz 98, 107, 115
kali-yuga (Age of Strife) 70–71, 79–80, 81, 90, 93, 102, 103, 106, 109, 114, 115–17, 124–6, 128, 134, 238, 255, 352, 361, 362, 363
Keats, John: 'Ode on a Grecian Urn' 24–5
Kelmscott Press 235, 237
Kierkegaard, Søren 99, 108, 115
King Attila Academy 348
Knights Templar 29
Krishnamurti, Jiddu 34

La Gnose (Gnosis) 13
language, Traditionalism as 331, 337, 338–41, 349–50, 356
Lasch, Christopher: *The Revolt of the Elites and the Betrayal of Democracy* 348–9
'last man' 99
Lévi, Sylvain 51, 53
liberalism 4, 9, 109, 212, 217, 220, 333, 345; bourgeois liberalism 212, 217, 345

Macaulay, Thomas Babington 75
Mahmutćehajić, Rusmir 319–23, 324, 326–7, 328, 366–7
Maritain, Jacques: *Antimodern* 100
Marsh, George Perkins: *Man and Nature: Physical Geography as Modified by Human Action* 290–91
Martindale, Miss 283–4
Marxism 6–7, 9, 12, 44, 75, 76, 79, 83, 85, 98, 112, 117, 123, 207, 209, 222–3, 269, 271, 293–4, 342, 352
Marx, Karl 6, 8, 75, 96, 97, 98, 105, 107, 115, 116, 338, 361
Maryamiyya 18. *See also* Alawiyya

Massignon, Louis 312

materialism 79, 95–7, 101, 103, 112, 116, 140, 214, 238, 300, 334, 345

matriarchy 75, 82–3, 271–2, 284–5

metaphysics 4, 19; art and 235, 238–40, 244, 245, 250, 252, 256, 257, 364–5; gender and 259–60, 265–6, 271, 272, 273, 274–80, 287–8, 365; 'metaphysical' term 4; modernity, Traditionalist critique of and 105, 106, 107, 109, 116; nature and 299, 300–301, 302, 303, 305, 307; religion and *see* religion; self-realization and *see* self-realization; Traditionalist History and 80–81, 86–7, 88; Traditionalist perennialism and 45, 46–50, 52, 53, 57, 60–61, 62, 64

metapolitics 123–4

Middle Ages 68, 72, 81, 100, 120, 121, 206–7, 213, 221, 231. *See also* dark ages

millet (denomination) system 321, 323

Millett, Kate 269, 270

modernity, Traditionalist critique of 93–117; Evola and 102, 110–13, 115, 116–17; Guénon and 102–14; ideal modernity 94–7; modernity critiqued 97–101; 'modernity' term 94; Peterson and 114, 116; Schuon and 113–14, 116–17

morality 46, 48, 55, 70, 84, 86, 100, 103, 104, 107–8, 116, 180, 191, 213, 219, 231, 291, 343, 351, 361

More, Henry 172

Morgan, John 352

Morris & Co. 234

Morris, William 234–5, 237

Moses (biblical character) 28, 29, 50, 73

Mosley, Martel 352

Movimento Sociale Italiano (Italian Social Movement) 217–18

Moynihan, Michael 354

Muhammad, Prophet 50, 149–50, 152, 187, 191, 279, 287, 310, 312, 313

Muslim World, The 318

Mussolini, Benito 7, 15–16, 214

mysticism 146, 155–6, 237, 340

myth: history, Traditionalist and 67, 68, 69–73, 79, 82–3, 85, 90–91; modernity,

Traditionalist critique of and 114, 116–17, 135; mystical union 146, 149, 151, 152, 156, 161; perennialism, historical and 21–3, 24–6, 28, 38; perennialism, Traditionalist and 46, 51, 52, 54–61, 64–5

Nasr, Seyyed Hossein: 'Certain Applications to the Contemporary Situation' 301–2; interfaith dialogue and 309, 317–20, 324–6, 327–8, 364, 366–7; 'Islamic-Christian Dialogue: Problems and Obstacles to be Pondered and Overcome' 318; historical narrative of 87–9, 91, 361; *Islamic Life and Thought* 132; metaphysics 172–3, 175, 176; nature, philosophy of 289, 290, 298–303, 304–6, 307, 364, 366, 368; religion and 193–5, 197–8, 363; 'Some Metaphysical Principles Pertaining to Nature' 300–301; 'The Intellectual and Historical Causes' 300; *The Need for a Sacred Science* 132; 'The Problem' 299

National Conference of Jews and Christians 310–11

Native Americans 18, 32, 33, 58, 170–71, 176, 221, 245, 301

nature 11, 289–307; 'Buddhist Economics' 294–5, 296, 298, 306294–5, 296–7, 298; early Traditionalist views 296–8; environmentalism, origins of 289–92, 295, 303–4, 306; Nasr's philosophy of 298–303; organic agriculture 289, 290–91, 292–5; pre-Traditionalist views 290–92; Prince Charles views on 304–6; 'The Holy Quran and the Environment' 303–4

Nazi Party 7, 9, 16, 17, 77, 83–4, 85, 122, 124, 133, 164, 199, 209, 212–14, 215, 216–17, 219, 226, 345, 364

Neoclassicism 232, 233

Neo-Eurasianism 341, 344–6, 355, 369. *See also* Eurasianism

neofolk 352–3, 356

Neopagans 33, 83

Neoplatonism 88, 141–51, 154, 155, 159, 161, 170, 172, 173, 175, 176, 194, 231, 232, 233, 240, 263, 340–41, 362, 363

New Age movement 34, 76
New Class 335, 336, 346, 348–9, 354–5
New Right 332–7, 352. *See also* radical right
New York Times 8, 9, 133
Niebuhr, H. Richard 292, 300
Nietzsche, Friedrich 55, 70–71, 83, 84,
    99–100, 102, 108–9, 110, 114, 115, 161, 165,
    166, 180, 196, 219, 333, 334, 361, 363
nihilism 99, 101, 114, 173
9/11 315, 367
Noah 29, 64
Noble, Margaret 238
Northbourne, Lord 289, 306; *Look to the
    Land* 293–4, 295
nous ('the intelligence') 144
numinous, the 36–7, 39, 152

occultism 13–14, 15–17, 34–5, 39, 43, 44, 63–4,
    109–10, 333
Oedipus, myth of 26
O'Meara, Michael 350, 354
One, the 144–5, 148, 150–51, 155, 194–5,
    263, 272
oral transmission 50–53, 58, 360
Ordine Nuovo (New Order) 218–19, 226
organic agriculture 289–95, 304, 305, 306, 366
Orientalism 12, 14, 45, 53
Orpheus 28
Orthodox churches 5, 170, 253, 255, 311, 315,
    321, 323, 339, 341, 355, 367
orthodoxy, Traditionalist concept of 181,
    188, 190, 362
Orphic or Eleusinian Mysteries 144, 146
Ottoman Empire 202–3, 321–2, 323, 328
Otto, Rudolf 39, 57, 61–2, 65, 339;
    Mysticism East and West 36; *The Idea of
    the Holy: An Inquiry into the Non-Rational
    Factor in the Idea of the Divine and its
    Relation to the Rational* 36
Ovid: *Metamorphoses* 70

Pallavicini, Abd al-Wahid 6
Pallis, Marco 68
Palmieri, Matteo 71
pantheism 146–7, 151, 162, 272
paradigmatic matrix 44, 45, 49, 51, 54, 63

patriarchy 83, 211, 268–70, 280–82, 284,
    285, 288, 339
Paul, Saint 120
perennialism 10, 21–65, 90, 93, 117, 134–5,
    141, 152, 175, 193, 195, 236, 256, 284, 303,
    313, 331, 332, 334, 336–7, 339, 340–41, 348,
    350, 359–61, 363, 367; academic 35–7, 39;
    definition 21–2; early modern 29–31,
    38; Eliade and 55–9; esoteric perennial
    philosophy 30–31, 38–9; Evola and
    54–5; Guénon and 46–54; historical/
    development of 19, 21–39; myth and
    24–6, 38; Peterson and 59; religion and
    26–7, 38; Renaissance and 27, 28–9, 38,
    43–4; Schuon and 59–61; Smith and
    61–3; Theosophical 33–5, 39; tradition
    and 22–4, 38; Traditionalist 43–65;
    universalist 31–3, 38
Perrault, Charles: *Parallel of the Ancients and
    the Moderns* 94
Peterson, Jordan B. 119; gender and 259,
    280–82, 286, 287–8; modernity, critique
    of 114, 116–17; perennialism and 59;
    politics and 199, 222–5, 226; 'Professor
    against Political Correctness' 132, 223–4,
    282; radical right and 332; religion and
    196–7, 198; self-realization/metaphysics
    and 173–5, 176–7; *12 Rules for Life:
    An Antidote to Chaos* 132–3, 174, 223;
    YouTube following 132–3
Petrarch 71, 73, 80, 94
Philip IV, King 207, 210
Pico della Mirandola, Giovanni 28–9
Plato 28, 50, 141–7, 153, 229, 231, 242, 272,
    340–41, 364–5
Platonism 89, 141–7, 148, 230, 232, 238, 243,
    252, 256, 261, 273, 277, 278
Plotinus 28, 142, 143, 144–5, 149, 153, 156,
    172, 263, 271–2
politics 11, 199–226; 'China model' 200;
    contemporary and pre-modern political
    theory 200–203; Evola and 209–19;
    Guénon and 203–9; 'New Confucianism'
    200; Peterson and 222–4; popular
    sovereignty 200, 203, 225–6; Schuon
    and 219–22

polytheists 29–30, 38, 140
postmodernism 101
post-Traditionalism 12, 329–56, 367
pre-Raphaelites 97
primitive communism 75, 76, 83
primordial images 26, 38
primordial tradition 125, 126, 135, 360, 361, 362, 367; art and 240, 246; gender and 278, 284, 287; modernity and 102; nature and 298, 307; politics and 209–10, 225; radical right and 333–4, 351, 354–5; religion and 181, 185, 187, 190; self-realization and 140, 154, 159, 170–71, 175; Traditionalist history and 80–82, 86; Traditionalist perennialism and 43–65
Protestantism 48, 107–8, 109, 180, 190, 342
Putin, Vladimir 3, 337–8, 344, 346

race 3, 7, 16, 17, 69, 77, 81–4, 86–7, 89, 91, 160, 214–15, 223, 224, 226, 331–2, 335, 336, 345, 346, 354, 355, 364
radical right 12, 17, 119, 123, 139, 226, 331–56, 367, 368; Dugin 337–46; French New Right 332–7; Identitarian movement 350–51; mainstream politics and 347–50; Traditionalism as symbol 352–4. See also alt-right, New Right
rational-bureaucratic authority 95, 97
rationalism 24, 26–7, 38, 46, 75, 88, 97, 98, 111, 115, 172, 248, 300, 302, 340, 343
religion 179–98; Evola and 179, 180, 184, 185, 186, 190, 197; Guénon and 179–87, 190–94, 197; interfaith dialogue 309–28; Nasr and 193–5, 197–8; Peterson and 196–7, 198; Schuon and transcendent unity 179, 180, 184–93, 195–6, 197–8; Smith and 193, 195–6, 197–8
Renaissance 21, 27, 28–9, 38, 43–4, 65, 69, 71–2, 80, 81, 84–5, 88–9, 135, 231–2, 238, 240, 241, 244, 247–8, 249, 300, 303, 305, 333, 340–41, 360
resacralization 350, 354, 356, 366
residual categories 34–5
'Rights of Man' 264
Roman Empire 30, 68, 70, 72, 73, 74, 78, 82, 84, 85, 90, 94, 163, 164, 210, 212, 221

Romantic movement 24, 25, 26, 38, 97, 233, 290, 300
Royal Aal al-Bayt Institute 324–7
Ruskin, John 98, 106–7, 113, 115, 203, 234–5, 237, 238, 242, 256, 295, 297, 361, 364

sacred order 3, 4, 7, 10, 11, 14, 19, 21, 46, 69, 90, 108, 198, 359
Said, Edward: Orientalism 53
Samkhya (school) 32, 172
satya-yuga (Age of Truth) 70, 72, 79, 204
Schiller, Friedrich 24
Scholasticism 47, 52, 140, 141, 142–7, 172, 175
Schopenhauer, Arthur 264–6, 267, 273, 274; 'Metaphysics of the Love of the Sexes' 265–6; 'On Women' 265
Schumacher, E. F. 289; 'Buddhist Economics' 294–5, 296, 298, 306; Small Is Beautiful: A Study of Economics as if People Mattered 295
Schuon, Frithjof 12–13, 17–19; art and 238, 242, 243, 244–5, 248, 253–4, 255, 256–7, 364, 365; gender and 259–60, 276–80, 286–7, 364, 365; Gnosis: Divine Wisdom 168; historical narrative 85–7, 89, 90, 91; interfaith dialogue and 317, 318, 327; metaphysics 167–71, 172, 176; modernity, critique of 113–14, 116–17; perennialism and 46, 48, 54, 59–61, 63, 64–5; politics and 199, 219–22, 226; 'Principle of Distinction in the Social Order' 219; religion and 59–61, 179, 180, 184–93, 195–6, 197–8, 303, 317, 318, 327, 360–61, 362–3, 366, 368; spiritual elite 129–32, 134; sustainable development and 297–8; 'The Meaning of Race' 87–8, 91; The Transcendent Unity of Religions 17, 59–60
science 23–4, 26–7, 34, 38, 62–3, 64, 100, 102, 103–6, 109, 113, 114, 116, 190, 211, 293, 295, 298, 299, 300–302
Second Vatican Council (1962–5) 22
Second World War (1939–45) 8, 17, 76, 100, 104, 112, 199, 210, 212, 267–8, 311
'Secret Way' 160
Sedgwick, Mark: Against the Modern World 6–7, 9

sefirot 263

self-realization 11, 12, 16, 139–77, 179,
185, 303, 362, 363, 364, 367–8; Advaita
Vedanta 147–9; art and 229; Evola
and 159–66; gender and 259–60, 271,
274, 275, 276–7, 284, 287, 365; Guénon
model 153–4; Guénon realization 155–9;
modernity and 95, 97–8, 115; Nasr's
metaphysics 172–3; Neoplatonism *see*
Neoplatonism; nontheistic paths to
140–42; Peterson's view of life 173–4;
radical right and 334, 353; Scholasticism
see Scholasticism; Schuon's metaphysics
167–71; Sufism and 149–52; Traditionalist
understandings 152–77

Semites 86–7

sentimentality 46–7, 48, 64, 102–3, 106,
107, 109, 180, 190, 197, 235, 238, 239, 240,
272, 317, 360

sexual rituals 160, 276, 287

Shah-Kazemi, Reza 304, 325, 326;
'The Holy Quran and the
Environment' 304

shamanism 58, 64, 83, 209, 239,
301, 360

Shankara 36, 37, 147–9, 153, 155, 156

Sharia 47, 182, 191, 192, 202, 263, 318

Shelley, Percy Bysshe: *Prometheus
Unbound* 24–5

Shiva, school of 32

Shudras 202, 206, 207, 220, 221, 336, 363

Silver Sisterhood 283

Sinnett, Alfred: *Esoteric Buddhism*
33–4, 43, 44

Sister Breca 283–4

Sittler, Joseph 292

Smith, Huston 37, 39, 363; *The Religions
of Man* (later, *The World's Religions*) 37,
61–3, 64, 65, 131–2, 135, 193, 195–8

social chaos 102–3, 108

society, Traditionalism and impact
of thought on 119–35; 'bourgeois'
modernity and indirect impact 120–21;
direct and indirect impact of thought
on society 120–23; Evola's aristocratic
elite 128–9; Guénon's 'intellectual elite'

125–7; mass modernity and direct impact
121–3; metapolitics and indirect impact
123; Peterson's YouTube following
132–3; Schuon's spiritual elite 129–32;
Traditionalist model 124–7

Soil Association 294

soul 86–7, 107, 111, 143–9, 150, 151, 154,
169, 172, 187, 231, 247, 273, 277–8,
297, 302

Soviet Union 6, 76, 337, 342–3, 344, 345

Spencer, Richard B. 352

Spengler, Oswald: *Decline of the West*
77–8, 90

Spinoza, Baruch 147

spiritism 109–10

spiritual elite 128, 129–32, 169, 244

spiritus 147, 151, 154

Steiner, Rudolf 292–4

Steuco, Agostino 29, 35, 43

Sufism 5–6, 7, 10, 11, 12–13, 14, 17–18,
19, 129–30, 131, 314, 355, 360, 362–3,
368; art and 249, 250, 251, 255; gender
and 262–3, 271; religion, Traditionalist
view of and 179, 181, 182, 191, 192; self-
realization and 139, 140–42, 147, 149–53,
154, 155, 156–9, 165, 166, 168–70, 172–3,
175, 176; Traditionalist perennialism and
47, 50, 51, 61

Supreme Council for Islamic Affairs,
Egypt 312

sustainable development 289, 295–6,
306–7

symbolism 11, 105, 157, 239, 240, 241,
244, 256

syncretism 153, 157, 159, 194, 254

Talbi, Mohamed 314

Tantra 160

Taoism 47, 51, 52, 140, 141, 152–3,
192, 246

Tao Te Ching 141, 301

taste 232–3

Tavener, Sir John 230, 250, 253–6, 257, 280,
303, 306, 365; 'Song for Athene' 255–6;
'The Lamb' 255–6; *The Veil of the Temple*
255–6; 'The Whale' 253

Teitelbaum, Benjamin 348, 349

terrorism 3, 17, 219, 368

'tragedy of the commons' 291

theological dialogue 310–12, 327–8

Theosophical perennialism 33–5, 38–9, 43, 44, 52, 64, 65

Theosophical Society 33–5, 38–9, 43, 292–3, 359–60

Tilak, Bal Gangadhar: *The Arctic Home in the Vedas* 82, 83, 85

Toland, John 30–31, 33, 38, 44

totalitarianism 100, 101, 114, 217, 335

tradition: definition of 22–4, 38; 'the' 10–11; traditional authority 95; word 23. *See also* primordial tradition

transcendent, the 36, 88, 104, 113, 139, 143, 154, 165, 166, 175, 179, 243, 248–9, 257, 274, 276–7, 286, 287, 289–90, 292–3, 298, 307, 313, 343, 348, 349, 351, 354; 'transcendent unity of religions' 179, 184 93, 194, 195–6, 238, 303, 317, 318, 321, 323, 327, 328, 363, 366, 368

transgenderism 260, 262

transvaluation 99

Trent, Alice Lucy 283–8; *The Feminine Universe: An Exposition of the Ancient Wisdom from the Primordial Feminine Perspective* 284

tripartite narrative, historical (ancient, medieval and modern) 67–9, 71–4, 79, 80, 81, 82, 84, 85, 90, 93, 94, 360–61

Trismegistus, Hermes 28

Trojan Wars 73, 74

Trump, Donald 3, 8–9, 348, 349

Truzzi, Marcello 34–5, 44, 360

Turgot, Anne-Robert-Jacques: *Plan for Two Discourses on Universal History* 74

Twitter 133, 282

Tyr 354

Übermensch 100

Ukraine, invasion of (2022) 3, 7, 338, 369

United Nations (UN): 'World Interfaith Harmony Week' 326

uniformity 106, 107, 109, 116, 220, 361

unity in diversity 248, 320–302

Unity of Being, doctrine of the (*wahdat al-wujud*) 151, 154

universal histories 73–4

Universalism 31–4, 38, 39, 61, 135, 195, 237–8, 310–12, 335, 336, 350, 359, 366

Universal Man 155

Universal Soul 145, 148, 150, 151

University of Chicago 55, 88–9, 298

University of Paris 142–3

University of Toronto 132, 196, 224

Upanishads 147, 194

USSR. *See* Soviet Union

Vaisheshika (school) 32

Vedanta 45–6, 50–52, 53–5, 57, 61, 64, 85, 135, 140–42, 147–9, 152–3, 157, 167, 175, 182, 186, 225, 240, 340, 360

Vedanta Society 34

Vedas 79, 82, 233

Virgin Mary 18, 19, 244, 245, 262–3, 278–9, 287

Vivekananda, Swami 32, 237–8

Voltaire: *Essay on Universal History* 73, 78, 81

Vona, Gábor 7–8, 347–8, 352

Wagner, Richard 25

Wahhabis of Saudi Arabia 173

Waldorf school system 293

Warburton, William 30–31, 33, 43, 44, 46

Washington Agreement (1994) 320

Weber, Max 95–6, 98, 107, 115

Weininger, Otto: *Sex and Character: An Investigation of Fundamental Principles* 266–8, 271–3, 286

Western Roman Empire 72, 73

Whig history 75

White, Lynn 292, 294, 297, 298, 307

white privilege 224–5

white supremacism 224, 331–2, 352

Willinger, Markus: *Generation Identity* 350

Wirth, Herman: *The Dawn of Humanity* 83

Wolfheze, Alexander 351, 356

Wollstonecraft, Mary: *A Vindication of the Rights of Woman* 264, 266, 268, 285
World Council of Churches 311–12
World of Islam Festival, London (1976) 230, 248, 249, 317, 327, 365
World's Parliament of Religions, Chicago (1893) 32, 34, 237

yoga 101, 149, 151, 160, 196
YouTube 132–3
yugas 70, 79–80, 86

Zeitgeist 94–5
Zeus 94
Zoroaster 28, 29